D0955888

The Psychology of
Left and Right

The Psychology of Left and Right

MICHAEL C. CORBALLIS
McGILL UNIVERSITY

IVAN L. BEALE
UNIVERSITY OF AUCKLAND

 LAWRENCE ERLBAUM ASSOCIATES, PUBLISHERS
1976   Hillsdale, New Jersey

DISTRIBUTED BY THE HALSTED PRESS DIVISION OF
JOHN WILEY & SONS
New York   Toronto   London   Sydney

Lawrence Erlbaum Associates, Inc., Publishers
62 Maria Drive
Hillsdale, New Jersey 07642

Distributed solely by Halsted Press Division
John Wiley & Sons, Inc., New York

Library of Congress Cataloging in Publication Data

Corballis, Michael C.
  The psychology of left and right.

  Includes bibliographical references and indexes.
  1. Left and right (Psychology) I. Beale,
Ivan L., joint author. II. Title.
BF311.C676   152.3'35   76-13233
ISBN 0-470-15104-8

Printed in the United States of America

Contents

Preface

This book just grew. We began working together at the University of Auckland in 1966, on mirror-image discrimination in pigeons. Gradually, it dawned on us that mirror-image discrimination was one aspect of the more general problem of telling left from right. We discovered that the literature was not very clear about what it means to tell left from right, but that the problem was nonetheless a pervasive one in many areas of psychology. We wrote a general article, which was published in the *Psychological Review* in September, 1970 in which we tried to establish criteria for what it means to tell left from right, and to relate the problem to the bilateral symmetry of the nervous system. We also reviewed some of the evidence on left–right confusion.

But still the problem grew. We found out that the left–right problem plays an important role in child development, that it has been linked to reading disability and other pathological conditions. We realized that we would have to pay closer attention to handedness and cerebral lateralization, and their relations to telling left from right. This raised the whole question of symmetries and asymmetries in organisms — how they are shaped by evolution, and how they are transmitted from one generation to the next. We learned that the difference between left and right was a source of speculation in other disciplines besides psychology, including philosophy, anthropology, biochemistry, and theoretical physics. We discovered that symmetry, especially left–right symmetry, seems to play a special role in visual perception, and more particularly in art and design. By this time we knew that we had to write a book. Here it is.

It has been a difficult book to write, for we have had to read widely in areas beyond our own specialties. In this, we have been greatly helped by the generous advice and criticism of many colleagues. We are most deeply grateful to Michael J. Morgan for his enthusiastic and creative contributions. We should like also to record our thanks to Dalbir Bindra, J. Christopher Clarke, Olga E. Favreau, Charles R. Hamilton, Lauren J. Harris, R. John Irwin,

Marcel Kinsbourne, Jerre Levy, Peter M. Milner, Peter J. Riddick, Carlos E. Roldan, and Robert J. Williams for their helpful suggestions and comments. In spite of the excellent advice of these and other individuals, however, we cannot be sure that we have represented everyone's views fairly and correctly. To those whose ideas have been trampled, we apologize; the fault is ours. As James Thurber said: "Don't get it right, just get it written."

We make no claim to have reviewed the literature exhaustively. Our approach was rather to develop our own ideas, documenting the evidence as we went. No doubt our selection is in some cases idiosyncratic. Thus we apologize not only to those we failed to get right, but also to those we left out. In general, we have thought it better to be wrong but interesting than right and dull. We suspect that, in places, we have succeeded in both.

Preparation of the book was made possible by a Canada Council Leave Fellowship to M.C.C., which enabled him to spend the 1974–75 academic year at the University of Auckland, where I.L.B. is usually to be found. Canada Council and the University of Auckland generously provided funds for typing, photography, and other expenses associated with preparation of the manuscript. Our own research, some of which is described in the book, has been supported by the Defence Research Board of Canada, the National Research Council of Canada, the Faculty of Graduate Studies and Research at McGill University, the New Zealand Universities Grants Committee, and the University of Auckland. We are grateful.

We are also grateful to our wives, who looked after the kids, and to Barbara E. Corballis in particular who performed doubly by typing the final version of the manuscript. Earlier drafts were typed by Lila Bordeleau, Frida Demaio, and Wanda Poulin.

Finally, we reluctantly confess that this book is not about politics. Maybe there is another book there, one that *will* make us rich.

The Psychology of
Left and Right

1

Introduction

We had been flying for three hours. A brightness that seemed to glare spurted on the starboard side. I stared. A streamer of light which I had hitherto not noticed was fluttering from a lamp at the tip of the wing. It was an intermittent glow, now brilliant, now dim. It told me that I had flown into a cloud, and it was on the cloud the lamp was reflected. I was nearing the landmarks upon which I had counted; a clear sky would have helped a lot. The wing shone bright under the halo. The light steadied itself, became fixed, and then began to radiate in the form of a bouquet of pink blossoms.

—*Wind, Sand and Stars*
ANTOINE DE SAINT-EXUPÉRY

Saint-Exupéry's vivid description is wrong in just one detail. The starboard light is green, not red. To have seen "a bouquet of pink blossoms" Saint Exupéry must have been looking at the *port* wing of the aircraft.

The print shown in Fig. 1.1 is from a woodcut made by an anonymous French master in about 1536. This early example of poster art was probably designed to announce the forthcoming marriage between Francis I and Eleonore of Austria, who are shown exchanging a heart and a rose. The charm of this bold print is somewhat marred by four errors in the orientation of letters; two N's and two S's have been reversed. Since mistakes in a woodcut can rarely be corrected, the artist makes each cut with care, so the reversals are probably best accounted for as resulting from confusion rather than from carelessness. The artist's uncertainty about the orientation of certain letters was no doubt

1

aggravated by the need for the block to be mirror-reversed relative to the print to be struck from it, requiring the letters to be cut in reversed form.[1]

As these examples illustrate, people are often confused about left and right. The problem is so severe in some that the German psychologist Kurt Elze (1924) coined the phrase "right–left blindness," suggesting an analogy with color blindness. He tells, for example, of army recruits in Czarist Russia who were so bad at telling left from right that, to teach them the difference, they were drilled with a bundle of straw tied to the right leg and a bundle of hay to the left. Elze maintained, though, that right–left blindness was not simply a matter of low intelligence, claiming that such distinguished men as Sigmund Freud, Hermann von Helmholtz, and the poet Schiller were among those afflicted. Indeed, he even suggested that the problem of left and right might be especially common among the highly intelligent, remarking that subhuman animals appear to have no difficulty.

Elze was actually wrong in claiming that animals can easily tell left from right. In Chapter 4 of this book we shall examine the experimental evidence and find that many species may have considerable difficulty. A real-life example has been documented recently by David F. DeSante (1973). On September 17, 1971 he spent the day on southeast Farallon Island, which lies about 28 miles west of the Golden Gate Bridge in San Francisco, California. There, he captured one Tennessee Warbler, on Black-throated Blue Warbler, one Blackburnian Warbler, five Blackpoll Warblers, and two American Redstarts. These birds are generally regarded as typical Eastern Warblers, usually to be found at that time of year in Northeastern United States, some 2500 miles east of the Farallons. Yet so-called "vagrant warblers" have frequently been observed on the West Coast. For his doctoral dissertation at Stanford University, DeSante carefully documented the proposition that these birds are victims of a left–right confusion. Migrating from Central Canada, the birds apparently calculate the direction of flight with respect to a north–south line. The successful migrants head southeast to the Atlantic coast, where they accumulate a large quantity of subcutaneous fat before proceeding on the long overwater flight to the Lesser Antilles or the northern coast of South America. But the vagrant birds fly south*west,* in the mirror-opposite direction with respect to the north–south line, and so fly to the West Coast. It is presumed that most will persist with their confusion and fly out from the coast of California, to perish in the Pacific.

In humans, it is primarily during childhood, and perhaps especially up to the age of five or six years that the confusion of left and right is most acute. Although Elze cites Helmholtz as an example of a person who was right–left blind, we know of no evidence that he had any problem as an adult. However,

---

[1]The artist may also have been confused about the direction of twist in the horn of the unicorn. The myth of the unicorn is said to be based on the single-tusked cetacean, the narwhal, whose tusk twists not clockwise like that of the unicorn shown in the figure, but counterclockwise (Burton & Burton, 1969, p. 1554).

FIGURE 1.1 Woodcut, *Francis I offers his heart to Eleonore of Austria*, by anonymous French master (c. 1536), showing left–right reversals of letters.

in a famous lecture which he gave in 1903 on his seventieth birthday, he recalled his inability as a child to tell left from right. With Freud, too, it seems to have been mainly a childhood problem. In a letter to Fliess, he wrote

> I do not know whether it is obvious to other people which is their own or others' right and left. In my case in my early years I had to think which was my right; no organic feeling told me. To make sure which was my right hand I used quickly to make a few writing movements [Freud, 1954, p. 243].

The examples we have considered illustrate something of the nature and range of the problem of telling left from right, which we shall more thoroughly explore in the following chapters. But before we outline the plan of the book and introduce our major themes, we shall digress to consider the nature of *mirror images*, and what it is that mirrors do. This will enable us to clarify some matters of terminology, and at the same time, we hope, to furnish the reader with some preliminary insight into the left–right problem.

MIRROR IMAGES—AND MIRRORS

First, let us consider what is meant by the term "mirror images." In two-dimensional space, a pattern can be converted to its mirror-image by reflecting it about a line. For example, the lower-case letters b and d are mirror images because each can be obtained from the other by reflection about the vertical. They may be termed left–right mirror images because they differ only with respect to the left–right orientation, and one can tell them apart only if one can tell left from right. As we shall see, animals and human children find it more difficult to discriminate left–right mirror images, such as b and d, than to discriminate up–down mirror images, such as b and p.

Three-dimensional mirror images are obtained by reflection about a plane. Examples include a left and right shoe, a left and right glove, or the two box-like shapes depicted in Fig. 1.2. Such mirror-image pairs are sometimes called *enantiomorphs*. The person you see in the looking glass, if real, would be your own enantiomorph. Enantiomorphs may be said to have the same basic shape, at least in the sense that the distance between any two surface points on one is matched by an identical distance on the other. Yet they are also different, in the sense that it is in general impossible to replace one by the other and have it occupy the same space. This "paradox" was discussed by Kant in 1768, and has been a source of fascination to philosophers ever since (see, e.g., Bennett, 1970).

In principle, enantiomorphs can be rotated to identity through a higher dimension. For example, a two-dimensional shape can be converted to its mirror image by rotating it 180° through a third dimension. If you write a b on cellophane and turn it over, it becomes a d. Similarly, three-dimensional

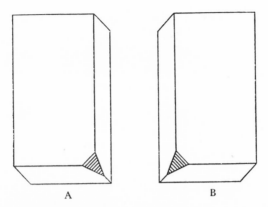

FIGURE 1.2 Enantiomorphs. (From Bennett, 1970.)

enantiomorphs can in principle be made identical by rotating one of them 180° through a *fourth* dimension. Imagine that, if you will! In "The Plattner Story," by H.G. Wells, the hero is blown into four-dimensional space by an exploding powder, stays there for a while, and is then blown back into three-dimensional space. When he returns, however, he has been turned around, so that his heart is on the right and he writes backward with his left hand.[2]

Optically, but not physically, mirror images can be created by mirrors. We can certainly see what the enantiomorphic world would look like and imagine what it would be like to be there by simply looking into a mirror. This of course provides much of the fun of Lewis Carroll's *Through the Looking Glass*. But there is a common confusion about mirrors, which again concerns the left–right dimension. Many people are puzzled by the apparent fact that mirrors reverse left and right, but not up and down or back and front. We look into the mirror and see ourselves, upright, but with the hair-parting on the wrong side, or a mole on the left cheek instead of the right; we hold script up to a mirror, and it is then seen to be virtually illegible, running from right to left instead of from left to right. This, then, is the so-called "mirror problem" (Bennett, 1970): Why should the left–right dimension be singled out for special treatment?

The answer, as Martin Gardner (1967) makes admirably clear, is that it is not! In the direct optical sense, mirrors do not reflect left and right, they reflect about their own planes. If you look into a mirror, what you see is not really a left–right reflection of yourself, but a *back–front* reflection. To obtain a left–right reversal, you should stand beside the mirror, and for an up–down reversal stand under it or on top of it. Yet, in terms of internal structure, all of these mirror images are the same and constitute your enantiomorph. If you could

[2]From *Selected Stories*, by H. G. Wells (Hammondsworth: Penguin, 1958).

stand them all upright and make them face in the same direction, they would be seen to be identical to one another.

Reflection about any one plane is equivalent to reflection about any other, plus a rotation and translation. Of the "person" who peers back at you out of the mirror, one could say that he or she is a back–front reflection of yourself; it is as though your nose, mouth, eyes, and so on have all been pushed through to the back of the head, and the back of the head pushed through to the front. One could also say the person is an up–down reflection of yourself, rotated back about a horizontal axis to the upright position. But generally we prefer to say that he or she is a left–right reflection, and we may omit to mention that there has also been a rotation through 180° about a vertical axis.

Why should we prefer this last description, given that alternatives are available? According to Pears (1952), one reason is that we take it tacitly for granted that we normally turn about a vertical axis. We say the confronting mirror image is left–right reversed since we scarcely even notice, or consider it important, that this description also requires a 180° turn about the vertical. We do not say it is up–down reversed because this would require an additional 180° turn about the *horizontal*, and it is unusual for anyone but an acrobat to rotate about the horizontal. However, this is not the whole story because it does not explain why we do not prefer the optically simpler description that back and front have been reversed, a description which requires no additional rotation at all.

A further and perhaps more important reason for preferring to speak of left–right reversal is that our own bodies are very nearly left–right symmetrical and are therefore largely unaltered by left–right reflection. The *physical* (as distinct from the optical) description is therefore simpler than in the case of up–down or back–front reflection. The left and right hands might exchange places, but they are both still *hands*. The only descriptive differences between a man and his left–right reflection concern trivialities; the parting of his hair, the mole on his cheek, the ring on his finger. As Pears (1952) puts it, the two might wear the same clothes. A back–front reflection, by contrast, involves considerable descriptive complexity. The back of the head must gain a nose, mouth, eyes, and so on, while the front must lose these features; there is no simple mapping of one feature into another. The ruptures created by an up–down reflection are if anything even more complex.

Martin Gardner summarizes this way:

A mirror, as you face it, shows absolutely no preference for left and right as against up and down. It *does* reverse the structure of a figure, point for point, along the axis perpendicular to the mirror. Such a reversal automatically changes an asymmetric figure to its enantiomorph. Because we ourselves are bilaterally symmetrical, we find it convenient to call this a left–right reversal. It is just a manner of speaking, a convention in the use of words [Gardner, 1967, p.35].

It is not only the bodies of humans and animals which are largely unaltered by left – right reflection, however. From the vantage point of an upright observer, the left–right reflection of the world he sees in front of him would still look much like the real world. This is true of the generalities rather than the particulars; an actual scene, if reversed, would not look like the original, but it would still probably look like a real-world scene. A reversed tree still looks like a tree, albeit a different one; the same is true of hills, clouds, houses, and so on. In general, like Alice, we would not feel too disrupted in a world where the left and right were reversed, although particular, familiar objects and scenes might look strange. We may say, then, that there is a considerable degree of left–right equivalence in the way the world impinges on us; an object to the right of us might equally well have been to the left of us, in mirror-image form.

The fact that there is left–right equivalence in the world about us is therefore probably another reason why we prefer to interpret the mirror world as left–right reversed rather than back–front reversed. Indeed, it is left–right equivalence which is probably responsible for the evolution of bilateral symmetry, and for the tendency to confuse left and right. In the natural world, there is generally more to be gained by treating left and right as equivalent than by distinguishing them. We shall develop this theme in more detail in later chapters.

However, left and right are not always equivalent, especially in the man-made as distinct from the natural world. This is illustrated in Fig. 1.3. If you look into a mirror and see reversed script, its bizarre appearance stands in marked contrast to the apparent normality of the rest of the scene. On closer inspection, other objects may also look somewhat strange; automobiles have changed from left-hand to right-hand drive (or vice versa) and proceed along the wrong side of the road, people shake hands with their left hands, and so on. For the most part, the impression of strangeness applies to the symbols, conventions, and inventions of man.

This means that man's world has a consistent, built-in, left–right bias. This bias derives no doubt from man's evolved laterality, originating in his preference for the right hand. But the interaction is probably reciprocal and cumulative; the more man fashions an asymmetrical environment, the more asymmetrical he himself becomes, and the more important it is to be able to tell left from right. This is a second major theme of this book.

Before we outline in more detail the plan of the book, we have one more demonstration for the reader who remains convinced that mirrors reverse left and right. Write your name on a piece of transparent cellophane or glass and hold it *facing you* in front of a mirror. The script will remain perfectly legible. Mirrors do not always do what they are commonly supposed to do, which is to reverse left and right.

8

FIGURE 1.3 Mirrored scenes illustrate that the man-made world looks strange and wrong when left–right reversed, whereas the natural world looks normal in either orientation.

THE PLAN OF THE BOOK

We begin in the following chapter by defining what it means to be able to tell left from right. This leads to a specification of the kinds of tests which require the ability to tell left from right. We shall see that this ability does not necessarily involve any understanding or knowledge of the verbal labels "left" and "right," and can therefore be tested nonverbally as well as verbally. This means that it is possible to test animals as well as humans.

In Chapter 3 we establish an important principle: an organism that is perfectly bilaterally symmetrical could not tell left from right, and conversely, the ability to tell left from right requires some structural asymmetry. This principle is based on physical laws, not on empirical evidence. It was at least partly anticipated by the nineteenth-century Austrian scientist, Ernst Mach, who is indeed one of the heroes of this book. He argued that we tend to confuse visual patterns that are left–right mirror images because of the bilateral symmetry of the visual system:

> It is extremely probable that sensations of space are produced by the motor apparatus of the eye. Without entering into particulars, we may observe, first, that the whole apparatus of the eye, and especially the motor apparatus, is symmetrical with respect to the median plane of the head. Hence symmetrical movements of looking will determine like or approximately like space-sensations. Children constantly confound the letters b and d, as also p and q. Adults, too, do not readily notice a change from left to right unless some special points of apprehension or intellect render it perceptible. The symmetry of the motor apparatus of the eye is very perfect [Mach, 1897, pp. 49–50].

We shall enlarge on Mach's theory by considering left–right confusion (or left–right equivalence) as a general problem, not confined to vision, and by relating it in a more general and yet more precise way to the structural symmetry of the bodies and nervous systems of animals.

In Chapter 4 we examine the empirical evidence for left–right confusion among subhuman animals. We shall see that animals have difficulty with precisely those tasks which a perfectly symmetrical organism would find impossible; that is, with those tasks which require the ability to tell left from right. In many cases, however, animals do manage to solve these left–right problems, given enough trials, and we make some observations on the kinds of asymmetrical strategies they may use to accomplish this.

Although left–right confusion can be attributed fundamentally to bilateral symmetry, there have been several attempts to postulate more specific mechanisms for the psychological equivalence of left and right. In Chapter 5 we review some theories of shape recognition in which left–right equivalence is considered just one of the phenomena to be explained. Then, in Chapter 6, we examine three theories which bear uniquely on left–right equivalence and which share the common idea that there may be, at some level of processing, a left–right reversal in the encoding of spatial information between the two cerebral hemispheres of the brain. All three theories emphasize the structural symmetry of the brain.

Chapter 7 returns us to the speculations of Ernst Mach. He was interested, not only in the confusion of left–right mirror images, but also in the perceptual salience of patterns that are symmetrical about a vertical axis. People notice vertical symmetry much more readily than they notice horizontal symmetry or other comparable regularities. Once again, Mach thought that this was due to the bilateral symmetry of the nervous system:

> It is a fact, then, that the two halves of a vertically symmetrical figure are easily confounded and that they therefore probably produce very nearly the same sensations. The question, accordingly, arises, *why* do the two halves of a vertically symmetrical figure produce the same or similar sensations? The answer is: Because our apparatus of vision, which consists of our eyes and of the accompanying muscular apparatus is itself vertically symmetrical [Mach, 1898, p. 96].

Mach evidently regarded the salience of vertical symmetry simply as a manifestation of left–right confusion. We do not find this particularly convincing, since the perception of symmetry does not require the ability to tell left from right as we shall define it in Chapter 2. Moreover, we do not think a person would normally confuse a vertically symmetrical pattern with one that consists of the same elements repeated across a vertical axis, as Mach's interpretation seems to imply. Nevertheless there is some evidence that similar principles may underlie both the perception of symmetry and the confusion of left and right. In particular, both may depend on the symmetry of some projection area in the brain.

Up to Chapter 7, the book is mainly concerned with the psychological consequences of structural symmetry. In the remaining chapters we place more emphasis on the role of asymmetry, particularly in relation to human culture. Chapters 8 and 9 constitute a sort of bridge where we discuss the symmetry and asymmetry of organisms, first in Chapter 8 from an evolutionary perspective, then in Chapter 9 in terms of biological inheritance. These chapters allow us the opportunity to review the current state of knowledge on handedness and cerebral lateralization and to place these phenomena in their biological context. In Chapter 9, for example, we advance the view that human laterality, like the many other asymmetries to be found throughout the animal kingdom, is an expression of a fundamental cytoplasmic asymmetry and is little influenced by genetic variations. Our conclusions about human laterality set the stage for the subsequent chapters where the emphasis is on man's ability to tell left from right.

In Chapter 10 we consider how the human child develops the so-called "left–right sense," or the ability to tell left from right. We have said that this ability requires some structural asymmetry, and once again it is Ernst Mach who provides us with a theme:

> ... the whole human body, especially the brain, is affected with a slight asymmetry, — which leads for example, to the preference of one (generally the

right) hand, in motor functions. And this leads, again, to a further and better development of the motor functions of the right side, and to a modification of the attendant sensations. After the space-sensations of the eye have become associated, through writing, with the right hand, a confusion of those vertically symmetrical figures with which the art and habit of writing are concerned no longer ensues. This association may, indeed, become so strong that rememberance follows only the accustomed tracks, and we read, for example, the reflexion of written or printed words in a mirror only with the greatest of difficulty. The confusion of right and left still occurs, however, with regard to figures which have no motor, but only a purely optical (for example, ornamental) interest [Mach, 1897, p. 50].

This extract encapsulates much of the evidence we shall review. In particular, there is considerable evidence that asymmetries develop first in response systems and in response strategies for coping with left–right discriminations. These asymmetries later invade perceptual and sensory systems to give some validation to the term "left–right sense."

To read or write languages such as English in which the script maintains a consistent left–right orientation and direction requires the ability to tell left from right. It has been suggested, therefore, that reading disability, or in more extreme cases dyslexia, may be due to a poor left–right sense, which in turn may be the result of incomplete or weak cerebral lateralization. This view was advanced by Samuel T. Orton (e.g., 1937) in the 1920s and 1930s. Unfortunately, Orton buttressed the proposition with a neurological theory that is illogical and wrong, as we shall see in Chapter 6, and his ideas have not always been taken seriously. Nevertheless, the link between reading disability, poor left–right sense, and weak lateralization can be logically sustained quite apart from Orton's eccentric neurological ideas, and in Chapter 11 we discuss the empirical evidence for it.

In Chapter 12 we review the clinical evidence on left–right confusion and left–right reversal as symptoms of pathological disorders. Cases of left–right reversal following unilateral brain lesions, such as mirror-writing following left-hemisphere damage and reversed map drawing following right-hemisphere damage, can be interpreted as evidence for a theory of interhemispheric mirror-image reversal, discussed in Chapter 6. Evidence for left – right *confusion* following unilateral lesions, as in Gerstmann's syndrome, is more puzzling, and we suggest that it is often due to an aphasic disturbance (i.e., failure to understand the *terms* "left" and "right") rather than an inability to tell left from right. It is sometimes said that left – right confusion is also a symptom of Turner's syndrome, a chromosomal abnormality, but we suggest that this is really a more general spatial deficit which has little to do with the left–right sense per se.

In the final chapter we present an overview of the major themes of the book and enlarge on the role of the left–right distinction in the physical and cultural environments.

2

Telling Left from Right: Definitions and Procedures

I do not not like these "left" and "right" classifications; they are conditional concepts, they are loosely bandied about, and they do not convey the essence.

—*The Gulag Archipelago*
ALEXANDER SOLZHENITSYN

BASIC DEFINITIONS

The Oxford English Dictionary[1] defines "left" and "right" as follows:

> *Left.* The distinctive epithet of the hand which is normally the weaker of the two, and of the other parts on the same side of the human body (occasionally of their clothing, as in *left boot, glove, sleeve*); hence also of what pertains to the corresponding side of any other body or object. Opposed to *right*.

> *Right.* The distinctive epithet of the hand normally the stronger; by extension also of that side of the body, its limbs, their clothing, etc.; hence in a transferred sense of corresponding parts of other objects. *Right bank* (of a river), that on the right of a person facing down the stream.

One might perhaps quibble with the choice of physical strength as the defining criterion to distinguish the left from the right hand, since the hands also differ with respect to other, perhaps more obvious attributes, such as preference or skill (hence "dexterity"); nevertheless it is true that in most people the right hand is capable of the stronger grip (Woo & Pearson, 1927). One might even question whether left and right are best distinguished in terms of handedness; for example, we shall see in Chapters 8 and 9 that definitions couched in terms of cerebral asymmetries would probably apply to a larger proportion of the popu-

---

[1] 1933 Edition. London: Oxford University Press.

lation, although they would be less useful in an everyday setting. But what the definitions make clear is that in its most basic sense the left–right distinction refers to the sides of the body.

To be able to tell left from right, then, is to be able to label each side of the body distinctly and consistently. The labels could be the words "left" and "right" themselves, although we shall often prefer labels that are nonverbal. One reason for this is that we shall be concerned with the ability of animals as well as of men to tell left from right. Another is that correct use of the labels "left" and "right" may require skills that go beyond the basic ability to tell left from right. We shall return to this point toward the end of the chapter.

Any arbitrary stimuli or responses could serve as appropriate labels, with one important restriction: the labels must not themselves be left–right mirror images. Just as the ability to copy script does not prove that one can read, so the ability to give mirror-image responses to mirror-image stimuli does not prove that one can tell left from right. It is merely tautologous; the answer just repeats the question. In the natural world, at least, most asymmetrical behavior is of this type, and reveals nothing of the ability to tell left from right: a cow swishes its tail to one or other side to brush off a fly, a sheep turns left or right to follow a track, a falcon swoops left or right to seize a prey. Indeed, one is hard pressed to think of natural examples in which the information governing the choice of a left or right response is not directly available in the stimulus configuration. This is not true of the man-made world, however, where there are many consistent asymmetries which provide cues as to which is left and which is right.

There are two ways in which we can test an organism's ability to tell left from right. First, we can set up alternative stimulus events which are left–right mirror images with respect to the organism and test its ability to give different responses that are not themselves left–right mirror images to each stimulus. Let us call this *mirror-image stimulus discrimination*, or simply *mirror-image discrimination*.[2] Here, the stimuli can be said to represent the left–right difference, and the responses are the labels. The subject's task might be considered one of encoding the left–right difference into some other (response) dimension. Examples which illustrate mirror-image discrimination include the following: a dog which salivates when touched on the left flank but not when touched on the right flank, a pigeon which pecks a circular key when the key displays a left-pointing arrowhead but not when it displays a right-pointing arrowhead, a rat which approaches a goal box when parallel 45° lines are visible on the door but does not approach it when 135° lines are visible. These examples all obey the rule that the stimuli are left–right mirror images while the reponses to them are not.

---

[2]Unless we specify otherwise, we shall for convenience take it that the term "mirror image" refers to *left–right* mirror images with respect to the animal being tested.

The second way to test the ability to tell left from right is to set up two stimulus events which differ only in respects other than left–right orientation (such as a red and a green light), and require a left response to one and a right response to the other. We shall refer to this as *left–right response differentiation,* or simply *left–right differentiation.* In this case the stimuli serve as labels which the subject must decode into a left or right response. Examples include a rat turning left in a T maze when a symmetrically placed light is on and right when the light is off or a dog lifting its left paw when a bell rings and its right paw when a buzzer sounds. In these examples, the stimuli convey no left–right information, but the responses do.

One might also consider a simpler kind of left–right differentiation in which there is a single stimulus event which conveys no extrinsic left–right information and the subject must give a consistent left or right response. Left–right response differentiation is implied in that when the subject chooses a left response, say, it implicitly rejects a right response. Examples include a rat which consistently turns left in a symmetrical T maze, a mouse which always reaches with its right paw to obtain food from a projecting tube, or a dog which consistently holds out its right paw to shake hands.

THE AMBIGUITY OF SIMULTANEOUS MIRROR-IMAGE DISCRIMINATION

It is important to note that, according to our definition, mirror-image discrimination requires that the stimuli to be discriminated be presented one at a time. In the experimental literature, however, the term "mirror-image discrimination" is often applied to tasks in which the stimuli are presented simultaneously, and the subject must choose between them. Commonly, the stimuli are displayed side by side and are interchanged between some trials according to a random schedule. Strictly, however, this is a test of left–right differentiation, not of mirror-image discrimination, because the two possible configurations comprising each *pair* of stimuli are bilaterally symmetrical and the subject must choose a left or a right response. This is illustrated in Fig. 2.1, where the stimuli are mirror-image oblique arrows rotated anticlockwise through 45° and 135° from the horizontal. The subject's task is ostensibly to touch the 135° arrow ("correct") and not the 45° one ("incorrect"). On half of the trials, however, the stimuli form a V-shaped configuration (left panel), while on the other half the configuration is like an inverted V (right panel). In the first case the correct response is to touch the left-hand stimulus, while in the second case the subject must touch the right-hand stimulus.

But, of course, the presence of configurational cues does not guarantee that the subject will use them, and even if he does he may also attend to the individual stimuli. The evidence suggests that simultaneous discrimination

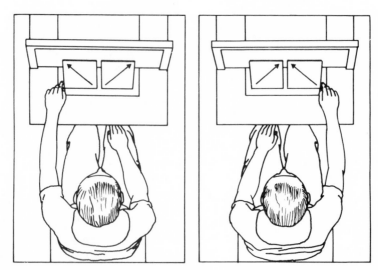

FIGURE 2.1   Subject making mirror-image responses to bilaterally symmetrical stimulus configurations.

problems are usually solved on the basis of the individual stimuli rather than the total configuration. Solutions based on configurational cues are usually observed only when the individual stimuli do not provide a simpler basis for solution (Trabasso & Bower, 1968). This could well be the case when the stimuli are mirror images, however. We must therefore recognize that a task such as that illustrated in Fig. 2.1 might be treated either as a problem of mirror-image discrimination or as one of left–right differentiation, or both. The argument might seem unimportant, since both strategies require the ability to tell left from right. As we shall see in later chapters, however, there is evidence that mirror-image discrimination and left–right differentiation may not be equally difficult, and different mechanisms may be involved.

Ideally, the simultaneous discrimination paradigm should either be avoided or subjected to a careful analysis to determine the cues which actually control the choice of response. One way to do this is follow training on simultaneous discrimination with test trials in which the stimuli are presented one at a time, thus eliminating configurational cues.

EXTRANEOUS CUES

Even in relatively straightforward paradigms of mirror-image discrimination or left–right differentiation, there may be extraneous cues which enable the subject to solve the problem without reference to knowledge about left and right. For example, if the experimenter always views the experiment from one side, the subject could conceivably code the difference between mirror-image stimuli or left and right responses in terms of their orientation with respect to the experimenter. Consistent asymmetrical cues might also be present in the apparatus itself, or in the testing room. Suppose, for example, that the apparatus depicted in Fig. 2.1 were set up in a room with a window to the left of the subject. The subject need only note that the correct arrow is the one pointing toward the window, and thus solve the problem without reference to left–right orientation per se.

Sometimes extraneous cues are associated with the stimuli themselves. In mirror-image discrimination, some minor blemish or irregularity on one stimulus but not on the other might give the game away. But more fundamentally, it is in practice very difficult to arrange stimuli that are *precisely* left–right mirror images with respect to the subject's midsagittal plane. The solution to this difficulty is not to rely on single examples of each stimulus but to present many different examples. What is important is that there should not be any *systematic* basis for distinguishing the stimuli other than their left–right orientation. Variations of other features of the stimuli such as size, brightness, or orientation should be equivalent for both stimuli. Consider again the experiment illustrated in Fig. 2.1. Were the experiment to rely on only two stimulus cards, it would be difficult to ensure that the two arrows were identical except for left–right orientation. The problem is overcome by using new cards on successive trials, relying on chance to balance out the distribution of irregularities between the correct and incorrect stimuli.

It also follows that one requires the ability to tell left from right in order to be able to distinctly label *any* two enantiomorphs such as a left and a right shoe or the A and B boxes depicted in Fig. 1.2, provided that they are presented to the subject in unsystematic orientations. For example, if A boxes are always presented with the flattened corner on the top corner on the top surface and B boxes with the flattened corner on the bottom, a subject could label them correctly by simply knowing the difference between top and bottom. But if one orientation is as likely as another, the subject must know the difference between left and right in order to label the boxes. One cannot describe the difference between a left and a right shoe, or a left and a right screw, without directly or indirectly making use of the terms "left" and "right."

In tests of left–right differentiation, too, it is important that there be no systematic left–right asymmetries, either in the stimuli or in the environment. Ideally, the stimuli should be symmetrical with respect to the midsagittal plane of the subject, but this may be impossible to arrange in practice. In repeated testing, it is sufficient that there be no *consistent* asymmetry. If the instruction "left turn" always came from the left and "right turn" from the right, a soldier need not know which is left and which is right in order to comply with the command; all he need do is turn toward the sound source. But if each instruction is as likely to come from one side as from the other, he must be able to tell left from right if he is to function in a proper military manner.

In everyday life, the environment sometimes does provide cues to help us make left–right decisions. In driving an automobile, for example, there are many rules referring to left and right. In the United Kingdom and Australasia, one must drive on the left-hand side of the road, overtake on the right, and give way to traffic on the right. Confusingly enough, these rules are reversed in Europe or North America. However, there are internal asymmetries in the automobile itself which provide appropriate cues. Most conspicuously, the steering wheel is to one side so that the driver can easily distinguish his side of the car from the passenger's. He need therefore only remember to drive so that the passenger's side is the one nearest the curb, to give way to traffic approaching from his own side, and so on; the same rules apply both to left-hand drive and to right-hand drive countries. Perhaps this is why Americans driving in Britain for the first time often have less difficulty than they anticipate. Nevertheless we suspect that most drivers do tend to rely at least partly on their own "left–right sense," so that the switch from left-hand drive to right-hand drive usually creates some initial disturbance.

RESPONSE-GENERATED CUES

Asymmetrical cues may be generated by the subject himself, particularly with the discrimination of so-called "distal" stimuli. For example, an animal is usually free to look at whatever part of a visual pattern it chooses, or to otherwise orient itself so that any two patterns which are lateral mirror images of each other in space are not longer mirror images with respect to its own midsagittal plane. This may not be crucial with repeated testing provided there is no systematic bias. To a freely watching animal, any given visual pattern can be considered a potentially infinite set of possible stimuli, depending on the animal's position or orientation relative to it. A visual mirror-image discrimination is therefore, in effect, a discrimination between two *sets* of stimuli, and we need only require that the sets be mirror images on the average. The test can be considered valid if the exact mirror image of any particular stimulus in one set can be considered at least potentially a member of the other set.

However, there is some evidence, which will be discussed in more detail in Chapters 4 and 10, that subjects may sometimes orient asymmetrically with the apparently deliberate intent of destroying the mirror-image relation. For example, a pigeon may learn to discriminate between mirror-image oblique lines by cocking its head consistently to one side, so that, with respect to the axes of its head, one line is seen as vertical and the other as horizontal (see Chapter 4, and especially Fig. 4.2). Notice, however, that in such cases the animal must still be able to tell left from right because asymmetrical orientation implies left–

right differentiation, albeit of the most elementary kind. By adopting this strategy, the animal may transform a difficult left–right problem, mirror-image discrimination, into a simpler one.

Ideally, then, the subject should be observed during the course of an experiment for any signs of asymmetrical response strategies. Better still, there should be some attempt to determine experimentally the cues which actually govern the subject's behavior. We shall encounter some examples of both procedures in Chapters 4 and 10.

COMPLEXITIES ASSOCIATED WITH THE LABELS "LEFT" AND "RIGHT"

We have noted that the actual words "left" and "right," as spoken or heard, are appropriate labels for testing the ability to tell left from right. They are neutral, in a physical sense, with respect to left–right orientation. One might test mirror-image discrimination in a child by touching one or other of his hands and asking him to say "left" or "right," as appropriate; or one might test left–right differentiation by asking him to hold out his left or his right hand. The words "left" and "right" are of course arbitrary; so is their assignment to the two sides. A child can be said to tell left from right according to our criteria even if he systematically reverses the instruction and consistently holds out his left hand when asked for the right and his right when asked for his left. This point has been recognized by Benton (1958), but other investigators have misleadingly classified systematic reversals as a failure to tell left from right. True failure to tell left from right would imply random responding.

Further complexities arise when we consider the way in which the labels "left" and "right" are applied to objects or to bodies other than our own. As the dictionary definitions suggest, these labels are essentially defined for an individual in terms of his own body. In order to determine the "left" or "right" of another person, then, the individual must effectively map his own body coordinates onto that person's. For instance, a child may systematically reverse the labels in discriminating which is the left or right of a confronting person, not because he is confused about left and right per se, but because he does not perform the mental operation of imagining his own coordinates rotated through 180°. In determining the left or right sides of other persons or of animals, the mapping rules are fairly clear, if implicit; if one speaks of a monkey's left ear, for example, it is understood that one is referring to a coordinate system within the monkey that is homotopic with that within one's own body (as well as the listener's). In specifying the left and right sides of objects or of geographic features, we may need to know additional conventions. For instance, the dictionary definition of the "right bank" of a river specifies that left and right are to be understood in relation to a person proceeding downstream. To speak intelligibly of landmarks on the left or right bank of a river, we may perhaps imagine ourselves sailing down the river—a complex mental operation, particularly if we are comfortably entertaining (or boring) our friends in the drawing room. It should be clear, then, that general competence in using the labels "left" and "right" requires more than just the ability to tell left from right; it requires knowledge of the conventions which specify how left and right must be mapped from our own bodies onto other bodies, objects, or places, and it requires the spatial ability to perform the mapping operations.

These complexities do not generally apply to other spatial dimensions. The words "top," "bottom," "back," and "front" usually refer to properties intrinsic to the object or body in question and do not require reference to the coordinates of the observer. The front of a house is where the main entrance is, the top of a mountain is the highest point above sea level. This distinction between the left–right dimension and other spatial dimensions is a consequence of the lack of any consistent asymmetry in the natural environment itself. Up and down are specified by gravity and back and front by movement or by access; but once these poles are established there is usually no consistent feature to distinguish the poles of the third (left–right) dimension. It is true that there are consistent asymmetries in the man-made world, but these are not very useful as *general* definitions of left and right. There are also consistent asymmetries in organic molecules and in those weak subatomic interactions thought to disobey the law of conservation of parity (these are discussed further in the final chapter), but definitions of left and right couched in terms of these asymmetries would scarcely be useful for everyday purposes. Inevitably, "left" and "right" remain largely egocentric concepts which we must first understand in relation to our own bodies.

The important point, then, is that confusion about "left" and " right" need not imply confusion about left and right! One should exercise care in drawing conclusions from experiments or tests in which the subject is required to use the actual labels "left" and "right," particularly with reference to other bodies or objects. This is most strikingly illustrated by our discussions in Chapter 12 of Gerstmann's and Turner's syndromes; in both cases there is evidence that an apparent left – right confusion can be attributed in fact to a deficit that is unrelated to the ability to tell left from right per se. In general, it is probably safest to avoid the labels "left" and "right" in testing the ability of human subjects to tell left from right.

CONCLUSION

In this chapter, we have tried to make it clear what it means to be able to tell left from right. We defined two tests, *mirror-image stimulus discrimination* and *left – right response differentiation*. We urge the reader to take careful note of the precise definitions of these tests because they will serve, explicitly or implicitly, as the objective criteria for what we mean by the ability to tell left from right. We shall also see that a number of authors have made misleading claims about left–right confusion on the basis of tests which do not meet these criteria.

We shall discuss actual experimental paradigms again in Chapter 4, where we shall review the evidence that most animals find it difficult, sometimes impossible, to perform tasks requiring them to tell left from right. Before we do so, however, we have an important theoretical point to make: any hypothetical creature or machine that is perfectly bilaterally symmetrical must be quite unable, by either of our test criteria, to tell left from right. This is the topic of the next chapter.

3

Implications of Bilateral Symmetry

God, Thou great symmetry
Who put a biting lust in me
From whence my sorrows spring,
For all the frittered days
That I have spent in shapeless ways
Give me one perfect thing.

—*Envoi*
ANNA WICKHAM

It will perhaps be clear already that the question of whether an organism can tell left from right is intimately related to bilateral symmetry. Indeed, the question would become trivial if animals and men were not at least approximately bilaterally symmetrical. To illustrate this, consider what it means to be able to tell back from front. From considerations analogous to those of the previous chapter, we might test ability to tell back from front by requiring different responses, but not responses that are back–front mirror images, to stimuli that *are* back–front mirror images—this would be a test of back–front mirror image discrimination. However, it is scarcely even possible to have stimuli that are back–front mirror images simply because the bodies of higher organisms are not symmetrical with respect to back and front. A punch on the nose is not the mirror-image of a punch on the back of the head, and one can readily tell them apart by virtue of the fact that the nose is involved in one case and not the other.

Therefore it is only when an organism is bilaterally symmetrical, or nearly so, that the problem of telling left from right becomes an interesting and nontrivial one. But we can go further than that. It is easy to show that any device or mechanism that is *perfectly* bilaterally symmetrical could not tell left from right, where left and right are defined relative to its plane of symmetry.

To understand this, observe first that a symmetrical mechanism would be quite unaltered by mirror reflection. It would be essentially the same mechanism. Now imagine such a mechanism responding to some stimulus. Mirror reflection would reveal the *same* mechanism giving the mirror-image response to the mirror-image stimulus. In other words, a perfectly bilaterally symmetrical mechanism *must* give mirror-image responses to mirror-image stimuli. This is sufficient to guarantee that it could accomplish neither mirror-image discrimination nor left–right differentiation: responses to mirror-image stimuli could not differ in other than a left–right sense, and the possibility of an asymmetrical response to a symmetrical stimulus is contradicted by its mirror reflection.

The reader who doubts our reasoning may like to amuse himself by attempting to construct a symmetrical device which *can* tell left from right by either of our test criteria. However, we must disallow him one option, that of using those weak subatomic forces thought to disobey the law of conservation of parity. Nonconservation of parity implies that certain dynamic laws do not survive mirror reflection (see Chapter 13), so that in principle it might be possible to construct a symmetrical device whose behavior *would* be altered by mirror reflection. But we seriously doubt that this has any relevance to our topic, since the domain in which nonconservation of parity applies is presumably far removed from that of the neural events involved in discrimination and choice.

We can illustrate the plight of the symmetrical organism slightly differently. Imagine Alice through the looking glass in a world where everything except Alice herself is mirror-reversed. (We must also imagine that she has some way of averting the annihilation that would presumably result from the contact of matter with antimatter—a point understandably overlooked by Lewis Carroll.) Let us suppose that Alice is perfectly bilaterally symmetrical. There is then no way in which she could detect that the world she is in is not the real one. If it were the world that remained the same while Alice were reflected nothing would be different because Alice, being symmetrical, would be quite unaltered by reflection. In terms of her relation to the world—and therefore her ability to recognize and respond to it—the situation is exactly as it would be if the world were reflected and Alice were not. In either case, then, the world would appear quite unaltered.

The fact that Alice did observe some odd things about the looking-glass world can therefore be said to prove that Alice must have been asymmetrical—or more realistically, perhaps, that her creator was. This is happily confirmed for us by Martin Gardner in his Introduction to *The Annotated Alice* (1960):

> In appearance Carroll was handsome and asymmetric—two facts that may have contributed to his interest in mirror-reflections. One shoulder was higher than the other, his smile was slightly askew, and the level of his blue eyes was not quite the same [p. 10].

We are asserting, then, that an organism with perfect bilateral symmetry could not tell left from right on the implicit assumption that the processes involved are mechanical ones. We assume, in effect, that an organism, even a man, is just a complex mechanism. This is a step which few present-day psychologists will be unwilling to take, although there may those who insist on retaining a nonphysical element in choice behavior. Perhaps it is such a consideration which prompts Jonathan Bennett, discussing the left–right problem in philosophy, to remark:

> I have heard it insisted that if our bodies were spherical we could not remember the difference between A and B ⌊two mirror-image box shapes—see Fig. 1.2⌋, or between A-like boxes and B-like boxes, or between A-turns and B-turns; but I know of no principles in the epistemology of spherical rational animals which could justify this claim [Bennett, 1970, p. 181].

Certainly there are *mechanical* principles, if not epistemological ones, to justify the claim.

A symmetrical organism need have no difficulty discriminating up–down mirror images, but it would be unable to tell apart mirror images that can appear in *any* arbitrary orientation. For example, it would be unable to apply nonmirror-image labels to a left-handed and a right-handed glove. It could tell them apart if they were always presented as up–down mirror images. They might be presented with palms facing the organism and fingers pointing left, in which case they could be separately labeled according to whether the thumb points up ("right") or down ("left"). But if you toss a glove to a symmetrical organism such that it can land in any orientation, there is nothing the organism can do with it to label it as distinct from its mirror image (unless there is an environmental cue as to which is left and which is right).

These restrictions on the behavior of a bilaterally symmetrical organism are of some practical importance because although no organism is perfectly symmetrical, most nearly are. Further, many of the asymmetries that exist are probably irrelevant to cognitive decisions about left and right. In most humans, for example, the heart and stomach are displaced slightly to the left, and the liver and appendix to the right, but it is unlikely that these asymmetries provide cues to the behavioral distinction between left and right. Thus, on a priori grounds, it is reasonable to suppose that the difficulty that men and animals often have in telling left from right is related to the bilaterally symmetrical organization of the brain, nervous system, and external body parts.

PERCEPTION VERSUS PATTERN RECOGNITION

It is important to understand that a bilaterally symmetrical organism need have no difficulty *perceiving* the left–right orientation of an event. If a fly settles on the ear of a symmetrical horse, the horse need have no difficulty deciding which ear to flick to get rid of it. The act of flicking the ear does not require the horse to be able to tell left from right (as defined in Chapter 2) since both stimulus and response are asymmetrical, but it does require at least a perceptual distinction between the two ears. There are many other essentially perceptual tasks involving the left–right distinction which need not create difficulties for a bilaterally symmetrical organism. For instance, there need be no difficulty deciding whether two patterns are identical or whether they are mirror images, or in selecting from three patterns that which is the mirror image of the other two, or in matching one of a pair of mirror images to some template or standard. The point is that none of these tasks requires the ability to tell left from right; all require accurate perception of the left–right orientations of the stimuli, but they do not require the subject to attach different, nonmirror-image labels to them.

The problem of labeling is better conceived as one of *pattern recognition* rather than one of perception. Pattern recognition is the process by which we identify patterns — shapes, objects, tunes, and so on — regardless of such circumstantial attributes as size, distance, direction, intensity, and the like. When we see a table we recognize it as a table, no matter where it is located or, within limits, what size or specific shape it is. On the other hand, we are generally able to *perceive* these attributes well enough. The deer must recognize that it is a tiger which is prowling nearby, but it must also perceive how far away it is, and in which direction, and how fast it is approaching, in order to plan an effective escape.

It is not always possible to draw an absolute distinction between those attributes which are necessary for the recognition of patterns and those which are circumstantial; for example, angular orientation is important if one is to distinguish a square from a diamond, but unimportant if one is to recognize an apple as an apple. However, the left–right orientation of an object or an event is in general merely circumstantial, at least in the natural world where left–right orientation is arbitrary. Animals may appear in mirror-opposite profiles, danger may lurk on either side, and so on. Consequently, it would not be surprising if the mechanisms of pattern recognition might have evolved in such a way that patterns are recognized and labeled independently of the specific left–right orientation of the particular stimulus input. We shall consider theories of pattern recognition with just this property in Chapter 5.

There are of course some important exceptions to our claim that left–right orientation is merely circumstantial and irrelevant to the recognition of patterns. These occur primarily in the man-made world. For example, left – right orientation is clearly important if one is to recognize a b as distinct from a d. Nevertheless, it appears that even man may have to overcome a natural inclination to treat left–right mirror images as equivalent, for, as we shall see, children have a great deal of difficulty learning to discriminate mirror images. Most children eventually learn, of course, and how they do is a matter for discussion in Chapter 10.

MEMORY FOR LEFT AND RIGHT

Strictly, we can "recognize" only what we have encountered before, although some investigators have apparently used the term "pattern recognition" to include mechanisms that may be wholly innate. Even so, pattern recognition usually implies memory. It is useful to note, therefore, that a perfectly bilaterally symmetrical organism could have no memory for the left – right orientation of any event. This conclusion follows from the fact that to test for memory of left–right orientation is effectively to test the ability to tell left from right. For example, recognizing that a particular profile is familiar but that its mirror image is not is a demonstration of mirror-image discrimination, since the labels "familiar" and "unfamiliar" themselves convey no left–right information. Similarly, to recall left–right information and indicate it spatially, say by pointing or drawing, implies left – right response differentiation. Therefore a symmetrical organism could neither recognize nor recall the specific left–right orientation of any event or stimulus, although it may remember other spatial details. Conversely, storage of specific left – right information requires some structural asymmetry.

People, at least, usually *can* remember the left–right orientations of events, although we are often enough confused. (Can the reader state, for example, whether Whistler's famous painting, *Arrangement in Black and Gray: The Artist's Mother*, is in left or right profile?) Perhaps our ability to store left–right orientation depends on some preexisting structural asymmetry, or perhaps the very process of storing asymmetrical information creates the necessary asymmetry. But whatever the case, we shall review evidence in the next chapter which suggests that left – right confusion may often persist despite considerable asymmetrical experience. In Chapter 6, moreover, we shall entertain the hypothesis that there may be a tendency for the brain to record the mirror images of events along with the original events, and thus remain structurally symmetrical. As we have already intimated, mirror-image duplication of memories could serve an adaptive function; for example, if we have seen a particular face in only one profile, it could be important to be able to recognize it again in the opposite profile; or if an animal is attacked from the right and survives, it could be useful for it to generalize the experience so that it is equally alert to possible future attacks from the left.

Indeed, the advantages of *mirror-image generalization* generally outweigh the disadvantages of mirror-image confusion. It is difficult to think of situations outside of the laboratory where animals must tell left from right, but there are many potential situations in which it would be useful for them to generalize from specific events to their mirror images. Again, of course, man is the exception. Tasks that do require the ability to tell left from right include reading, writing, and giving and responding to verbal directional instructions, and these seem to be uniquely human accomplishments.

SUMMARY

This chapter has been mainly concerned with questions of logic. Using basically mechanical arguments, we have attempted to specify the psychological consequences of bilateral symmetry. We have suggested that left – right confusion is a problem of labeling and of memory, but not one of perception. Our hope is that this analysis will help clarify the kinds of questions we should be asking in experiments on left – right confusion in animals. It is time, therefore, to turn to the empirical evidence.

4

Left–Right Confusion:
Experimental Evidence

> Pooh looked at his two paws. He knew
> that one of them was the right, and he
> knew that when you had decided which
> one of them was the right, then the other
> one was the left, but he never could re-
> member how to begin.
> "Well," he said slowly . . .
>
> —*House at Pooh Corner*
> A. A. MILNE

In this chapter, we shall examine the experimental evidence on the confusion of left and right. As we explained in Chapter 2, the relevant experiments are those which test *mirror-image stimulus discrimination* and *left–right response differentiation*. We remind the reader of our definitions and discussions of these tests, for we shall encounter some experiments in fact which purport to test mirror-image discrimination, in particular, but which fail to meet our criteria. We also noted in Chapter 2 that experiments are easily contaminated by extraneous cues which might enable an animal to solve the problem without reference to left and right. Indeed, some of the experiments we shall review were not explicitly concerned with the left–right problem at all, and there was no reason to expect the experimenter to eliminate extraneous left–right cues except in the general interests of experimental control. We do not doubt that there were such cues in at least some of the experiments we shall review. In this respect, then, we can expect the evidence to overestimate the ability of animals to tell left from right.

On the other hand, there are also respects in which the evidence might underestimate the ability to tell left from right. A particular test of mirror-image discrimination or left–right differentiation might prove difficult for some reason which has nothing to do with left and right per se; the stimuli may be too complex, the animal may be insufficiently motivated, the training proce-dures may be ineffective. Indeed, it would be virtually impossible to *prove* an animal could not tell left from right, and we shall not in fact attempt to do so.

Our aim will be the more modest one of showing that left – right tasks are difficult, not that they are impossible. In any case, we shall see that most animals do seem to be able to solve left–right tasks if they are given enough time or enough trials. Moreover, in spite of instances of "right–left blindness" (Elze, 1924), most adult humans can cope without serious difficulty at all. It is well known that children usually have considerable difficulty, but we shall save the experimental evidence on left–right confusion in children until Chapter 10, where we consider the development of the left–right sense.

We shall review the evidence first on mirror-image discrimination, then on left–right response differentiation.

MIRROR-IMAGE DISCRIMINATION

Mirror-image stimulus discrimination, it will be recalled, requires an animal to make different, nonmirror-image responses to stimuli that are left–right mirror images. The reader may also recall from Chapter 2 that this test strictly requires that the stimuli be presented one at a time. If the stimuli are presented simultaneously, side by side, and are interchanged randomly, the test is then really one of left – right differentiation, although the animal may effectively treat it as one of mirror-image discrimination by attending to the stimuli one at a time. However, we shall yield to convention (and perhaps common sense) and include experiments on simultaneous discrimination in this section rather than under the heading of left – right differentiation, making it clear when simultaneous presentation was used.

In order to establish that animals find it difficult to discriminate left–right mirror images because of a difficulty of telling left from right, there should be some control task. In many cases, it is natural and appropriate to compare the discrimination of left–right mirror images such as C and Ɔ, with discrimination of corresponding up–down mirror images, such as ∩ and ∪. However, there is one special but frequently encountered case in which there is no such control. This is the case of mirror-image obliques—lines, rectangles, or grids oriented at, say, 45° versus 135°, or 60° versus 120°. Any pair of mirror-image obliques can be considered to be either left – right mirror images or up – down mirror images. The usual procedure has been to compare the discrimination of mirror-image obliques with that of horizontal versus vertical. We shall see in a moment, however, that this may not provide an altogether appropriate control.

In Chapter 3, we noted that the inability to tell left from right need not imply any perceptual deficit. An animal may be perfectly well able to perceive correctly the left–right orientation of each of two mirror-image stimuli, yet be unable to tell which is which in a discrimination paradigm. Ideally, then, experiments should also be designed to distinguish perceptual factors from those which have to do with telling left from right. As we shall see, few experiments are so designed.

This issue has special relevance to the discrimination of mirror-image obliques.

Appelle (1972) has documented what he calls the "oblique effect" in man and animals, suggesting that detection or perception of lines or bars is worse if they are oriented obliquely than if they are horizontal or vertical. However, Appelle includes in his review evidence that the discrimination of mirror-image obliques is poorer than that of horizontal versus vertical — evidence that is also reviewed below. But the question then arises as to whether mirror-image obliques are difficult to discriminate because they are obliques and are therefore perhaps difficult to perceive, or because they are mirror-images and are therefore difficult to label differently. We shall return to this issue at the end of the chapter.

We shall proceed species by species.

Octopus

Sutherland (1957) tried to teach octopuses to discriminate various simultaneously presented stimulus pairs, including mirror-image oblique rectangles, horizontal versus vertical rectangles, and T shapes presented either as left–right mirror images or as up–down mirror images. The octopuses failed to learn to discriminate the oblique rectangles, but had relatively little difficulty with the horizontal and vertical ones. The T shapes also proved extremely difficult, the left–right mirror images rather more so than the up–down ones. In another study, Sutherland (1960b) trained the discrimination of U shapes, presented either as left–right or up –down mirror images. Presentation of each pair was simultaneous. The octopuses were able to learn the up–down problem, but they were still performing at a chance level on the left–right problem after 400 training trials.

In the octopus, then, the problem of mirror image discrimination seems to be particularly severe.

Goldfish

Mackintosh and Sutherland (1963) trained goldfish to discriminate between simultaneously presented pairs of rectangles that were either mirror-image obliques (45° versus 135°) or horizontal versus vertical. The obliques proved much the more difficult to discriminate. Half of the fish failed to reach the criterion for mastery of the mirror-image discrimination, whereas all but one of the 16 fish mastered the discrimination of horizontal and vertical. The discrimination, once mastered, remained above chance level if the stimuli were presented successively rather than simultaneously.

Pigeon

Zeigler and Schmerler (1965) trained pigeons on both simultaneous and successive discrimination of rectangles in vertical, horizontal, 60°, and 120° orientations.

Discrimination of the mirror image pair, 60° versus 120°, seemed to be no more difficult than that of horizontal versus vertical, or that of either horizontal or vertical versus an oblique.

Williams (1971) found somewhat more evidence for mirror-image confusion. He trained pigeons to discriminate mirror-image pairs of circles that were half green, half red. These were presented successively, either as left–right mirror images or as up–down mirror images, on a circular translucent key. Under a so-called "center-key condition," the birds had to peck this same key when the appropriate stimulus was displayed in order to obtain food reinforcement. Under a "side-key condition," they had to peck a key to one or other side (varied randomly) of the display key to obtain food. When the birds viewed binocularly, the left–right problem appeared to be no more difficult than the up–down one under the center-key condition, but it was somewhat more difficult under the side-key condition. Curiously enough, the left–right problem was much the more difficult when the birds viewed monocularly, especially under the side-key condition, even though monocular viewing creates a consistent asymmetry. Nevertheless, these results suggest that although mirror-image discrimination does not normally present much of a problem to a pigeon, it may do so if the task is made more difficult in other ways.

Mirror-image confusion—or, more accurately, mirror-image generalization— is more readily demonstrated with a different procedure. If a pigeon is taught to peck a key displaying an oblique line and is then tested with the line in various different orientations, it typically displays a bimodal generalization gradient; that is, it pecks almost as much to the mirror image of the original line as to the original itself, and less to other orientations (Thomas, Klipec, & Lyons, 1966). Note that there is no attempt to "force" the mirror-image discrimination under this procedure; the bird apparently generalizes naturally from the original stimulus to its mirror image. Beale, Williams, Webster, and Corballis (1972) have confirmed this result and shown that the mirror image peak is abolished if the anterior, posterior, and tectal commissures of the brain are sectioned (see Fig. 4.1). We shall discuss the possible significance of this result in Chapter 6.

It is perhaps surprising that pigeons should generalize readily and naturally from a particular stimulus to its mirror image, yet have relatively little difficulty learning a mirror-image discrimination. There is some evidence that they may learn mirror-image discriminations by developing consistent response or postural asymmetries. For example, we have observed that a pigeon learning to discriminate mirror-image obliques apparently solved the problem by cocking its head to one side so that the 45° and 135° lines were then, respectively, vertical and horizontal with respect to the axes of the bird's head (Corballis & Beale, 1970a; and see Fig. 4.2). Clarke and Beale (1972) taught two pigeons to discriminate a circular disc that was red on the left and blue on the right from one that was blue on the left and red on the right, and observed that the birds solved the discrimination by standing to one side of the key that displayed the stimuli, and apparently attending only to that side. Subsequent tests revealed that the birds had effectively

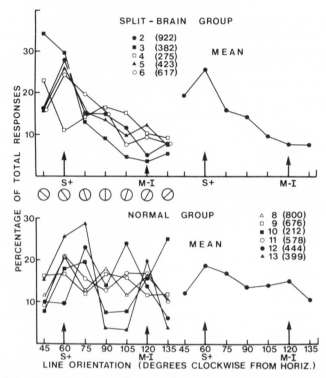

FIGURE 4.1   Generalization gradients to lines of varying angular orientation, for split-brain and normal pigeons previously trained to peck only to 60° line (S+). Normal group (lower) shows bimodal gradient with secondary peak at 120°; split-brain group (upper) shows unimodal gradient. (From Beale *et al.*, 1972.)

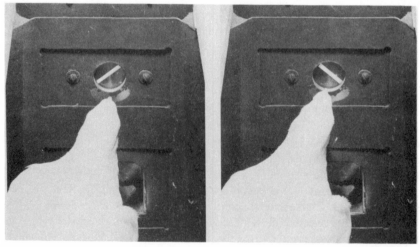

FIGURE 4.2   Pigeon tilting its head to one side to sole discrimination of mirror-image obliques. (From Corballis & Beale, 1970a.)

learned a simple color discrimination. Of course, the ability of the birds to maintain a postural or response asymmetry can be taken as evidence in its own right that the birds could tell left from right; in effect, the birds solved a mirror-image discrimination by making a left–right response differentiation. We shall suggest, however, that simple response asymmetries are fairly easily acquired by most species.

Rat

Lashley (1938) trained rats on simultaneous discrimination of both left–right and up–down mirror image pairs of stimuli, consisting of triangles and U shapes. The left–right mirror-image triangles seemed to be no more difficult to discriminate than the up–down mirror-image triangles, but the left–right U shapes proved much harder than the up–down ones. In another experiment, Lashley trained 20 rats on the simultaneous discrimination of mirror-image pairs of N and S shapes. They all failed to reach the criterion for mastery in 150 trials. Note, however, that each pair represents up–down as well as left–right mirror images. Another two rats failed to advance beyond chance performance in the discrimination of a clockwise from a counterclockwise involute of a circle.

Kinsbourne (1971) gave rats simultaneous discrimination training on various pairs of P-shaped stimuli. Nonmirror-image pairs were the easiest to discriminate. Only one out of six rats achieved mastery in 200 trials when the stimuli were up–down mirror images, but not one of seven rats could master the discrimination when the stimuli were left–right mirror images.

Earlier, Kinsbourne (1967) had claimed that discrimination of mirror-image obliques need cause no particular difficulty in the rat, provided the displays are conspicuous enough. However, he based this claim on a task which failed to meet our definition of mirror-image discrimination. The oblique lines were arranged (conspicuously) along the far walls of a Y maze and were oriented in the same way in *both* arms of the maze. The rats had to choose one arm when the lines were oriented one way, and the other when they were oriented the other way. This is not a mirror-image discrimination by our criteria because it requires mirror-image responses to mirror-image stimuli. In fact, all but one of the nine rats solved the discrimination within 300 trials, in a mean of 102.5 trials. This task was somewhat easier than one requiring judgments of sameness or difference. Oblique lines covered both walls of both arms, and the rats had to choose either that arm in which the orientations were the same, or that in which the orientations along the two walls were opposite. Nine of 12 rats reached criterion, in a mean of 143 trials; curiously enough, this task proved slightly easier than a comparable task in which sameness and difference were judged on the basis of whether the walls were black or white. Although these results suggest that rats have no particular difficulty perceiving the orientation of oblique lines, they provide no information about their ability to tell left from right.

An experiment by Tee and Riesen (1974) is more to the point. They compared performance on simultaneous discrimination with that on an oddity task. The stimuli, each consisting of parallel black and white lines, were displayed on two doors hinged at the top and placed somewhat apart. The two doors either displayed mirror-image obliques, or else one displayed horizontal and the other vertical lines. In discrimination training, the rats were taught to choose one stimulus and not the other in order to avoid shock. In oddity training, another stimulus was placed between the doors and the rat had to choose which of the three stimuli was unlike the other two; the correct choice was always one of the side stimuli, never the middle one. The two oddity tasks and the horizontal–vertical discrimination were all of comparable difficulty, and all rats reached criterion within 130 trials. However, the discrimination of the mirror-image obliques was significantly more difficult, and 6 of the 12 rats failed to reach criterion. Since the rats had no particular difficulty with the oddity task involving obliques, the poor performance on the discrimination cannot be attributed to an inability to *perceive* the orientation of oblique lines. For rats, at least, mirror-image obliques seem to be hard to discriminate because they are mirror images, not because they are obliques. This experiment is one of the very few which allow this crucial distinction to be drawn.

Rabbit

Van Hof (1966) has shown that rabbits can discriminate mirror-image diagonal striations. He used a simultaneous discrimination procedure, but performance dropped only slightly when he tested for successive discrimination. He was not primarily concerned with how long it took the rabbits to learn, but it does appear that they took slightly longer to discriminate the obliques than they took to discriminate horizontal from vertical striations. In a later study (Van Hof, 1970), he reported that rabbits could discriminate mirror-image oblique lines and dotted lines. These discriminations were not noticeably more difficult than the discrimination of horizontal from vertical. Moreover, Van Hof reported that there was no evidence for any "special head and eye movements" which may have facilitated discrimination of the obliques.

Cat

Sutherland (1963) trained four cats to discriminate mirror-image oblique rectangles and four others to discriminate horizontal from vertical rectangles using a simultaneous discrimination procedure. The tasks proved to be of approximately equal difficulty. When the cats were switched to successive discrimination, performance level dropped, but remained above chance and at about the same level on both tasks. Successive discrimination training was then continued for four days. The cats showed slight improvement on the horizontal–vertical task, but none on the discrimination of the obliques. This was the only evidence, albeit weak, that the obliques were any more difficult to discriminate than the horizontal and vertical.

However, Parriss (1964) reported that obliques were much more difficult to discriminate than horizontal and vertical when he used a successive discrimination procedure. His four cats learned both discriminations, but the discrimination between the obliques was the harder regardless of which discrimination they learned first. Parriss suggested that Sutherland's cats may have learned the simultaneous discrimination on the basis of the overall configurations formed by each pair and that configurational cues may have remained even when the task was switched to a successive one. This may be so, although it does not explain why the simultaneous discrimination of obliques was no more difficult than that of horizontal and vertical. No matter how one interprets the simultaneous discrimination paradigm, it still requires the ability to tell left from right (see Chapter 2).

In any event, Warren (1969) has confirmed that cats find it no more difficult to discriminate mirror-image obliques than to discriminate horizontal from vertical if the simultaneous discrimination procedure is used. However he found that U shapes were more difficult to discriminate if they were left–right mirror images than if they were up–down mirror images. He tested 35 cats on all four problems.

Tschirgi (1958) noted that it was impossible to teach cats to choose a circle when touched on one side of the body and a square when touched on the mirror-image point on the other side. He suggested that this was evidence of failure to discriminate the mirror-image touches, although the cats may also have had difficulty discriminating the circle from the square. Further, the procedure itself is a complex one which does not produce rapid learning with any stimuli (Sutherland, 1961). Unfortunately, Tschirgi provided neither experimental details nor any information which would identify the left and right touches as the source of the difficulty.

Dog

Pavlov (1927) cites experiments by Bikov and Grigorovich in which it was found virtually impossible to teach a dog to salivate in response to a touch on one side of the body, but not to salivate when touched on the symmetrically opposite place on the other side of the body. Pavlov does not record control experiments involving non-mirror-image touches, but he does note that the difficulty of discriminating the mirror-image touches disappeared when the principal fibers linking the two hemispheres of the brain were severed.

Monkey

Riopelle, Rahm, Itoigawa, and Draper (1964) taught 12 rhesus monkeys 48 different discriminations, involving stimuli ranging in complexity from V shapes to E- and K-like shapes. The discriminations were divided equally between up–down mirror images, left–right mirror images, rotations (each stimulus versus the same stimulus rotated 90° in its own plane), and various non-mirror-image pairs. Each pair was presented simultaneously, either side by side or one above the other. The latter arrangement always resulted in the slower learning. More to the point, the up–down mirror-image discriminations were the easiest, and the left–right ones the most difficult, regardless of the stimulus arrangement.

Chimpanzee

Nissen and McCulloch (1937) trained four chimpanzees on a variety of problems, including the simultaneous discrimination of mirror-image oblique lines and of horizontal and vertical lines. Because of procedural variations, it is difficult to compare performance on the two tasks accurately. Nevertheless, twice as many trials on the average were required to learn the mirror-image problem as to learn the horizontal–vertical problem. One animal failed to learn to master the discrimination of the obliques after 400 trials.

Humans

There is a good deal of evidence that children, especially up to the age of about seven years, find it very difficult to discriminate left–right mirror images. We shall review this evidence in detail in Chapter 10.

In contrast, most adults are not normally susceptible to left–right confusion. As we have seen, there is anecdotal evidence that there are a few individuals who may be described as "right–left blind" (Elze, 1924), and in Chapter 11 we shall review the evidence that specific reading disability, or dyslexia, may sometimes be the result of a poorly developed ability to tell left from right. But in the main, most normal, literate adults have little difficulty with the mirror-image discriminations required in reading, or in applying the labels "left" and "right" correctly to parts of the body or to external stimuli such as profiles, maps, or mazes.

It has been claimed that people may take longer to discriminate left–right mirror images than to discriminate up–down mirror images, but the evidence is not very compelling. For example, Sekuler and Houlihan (1968) recorded the time it took subjects to judge pairs of U shapes same or different, and reported that "different" judgments took longer when the shapes were left–right than when they were up–down mirror images. However, this task fails to meet our definition of mirror-image discrimination, and does not require the ability to tell left from right. In any case, the difference was statistically significant only when the stimuli were arrayed side by side, and was in fact reversed, although not statistically significant, when they were placed one above the other. It is difficult to accept the authors' conclusion that the left–right mirror-image pairs were the more difficult overall. In a very similar experiment, Wolff (1971) observed the same reversal; decision times were longer for the up–down pairs when they were aligned vertically, and longer for the left–right pairs when they were aligned horizontally, but overall it was the up–down pairs which yielded the longer times. Quite apart from the fact that these experiments fail to test true mirror-image discrimination, they do not convincingly demonstrate any difficulty associated with left–right mirror images.

An experiment by Butler (1964) is perhaps more pertinent. He had undergraduates make judgments of sameness or difference about various pairs of shapes, including left–right and up–down mirror-image T shapes. The stimuli were presented successively, with an interval of 3 seconds between each pair. The judgments took about 180 msec longer when the T shapes were left–right mirror images than when they were up–down mirror images. In a strict sense, this *was* a mirror-image discrimination; the subject pressed a "same" key for one stimulus and a "different" key for its mirror image, depending of course on what the first stimulus was. However, it is questionable whether the 3-second interval was really long enough for the judgment to be classed as nonperceptual. Clearly, the task does require memory for the first stimulus, but this memory is presumably short term and may resemble a percept rather than a long-term memory trace. Our arguments of the previous chapter suggested that mirror-image generalization, if such a process exists, would be represented in a structural trace, but not in the active percept itself.

Finally, we may note two experiments which suggest that there is indeed a process of mirror-image generalization influencing medium- or long-term memory. Standing, Conezio, and Haber (1970) showed people 2500 pictures, mostly of everyday scenes, and then tested for recognition. What was chiefly remarkable about this experiment was the high level of recognition that the subjects were able to achieve. However, they were just as likely to recognize a picture as familiar if it was the left–right mirror image of the original as if it was the original itself. Moreover, they were often unable to say whether a test picture had been mirror reversed, indicating a failure of mirror-image discrimination. Rock (1973) describes a previously unpublished experiment by Olshansky in which subjects were shown novel shapes, then tested two minutes later for recognition. Recognition was almost as accurate when the shapes were left–right reversed as when they were in their original orientations, and was significantly less accurate when they were up–down reversed. Accuracy was also impaired by rotation of the shapes through 45°, 90°, or 180° in their own planes, even though the subjects' heads were correspondingly rotated to preserve the same *retinal* orientations. These two experiments demonstrate the near equivalence of left – right mirror images in memory, at least under conditions under which the left – right orientation of an event is relatively unimportant.

LEFT–RIGHT RESPONSE DIFFERENTIATION

Left–right response differentiation requires an animal to give consistently asymmetrical responses in the absence of consistently asymmetrical stimulus cues. The simplest case is that in which the animal persists in giving a single asymmetrical response, such as turning right in a T maze, or lifting the left paw. The more interesting and complex case is that in which the animal gives a left response to one stimulus and a right response to another, where the stimuli themselves convey no extrinsic left–right information.

As we shall see, the evidence is scant compared with that on mirror-image stimulus discrimination.

Pigeon

Over (1969) trained two birds on what he described as the discrimination of mirror-image obliques, and another two on what he called the discrimination of horizontal from vertical. The stimuli were displayed on a center key and the birds had to peck a key to one side when one stimulus was displayed and a key to the other side when the other was displayed. Note that in the case of the mirror-image obliques, this was not a strict test of mirror-image discrimination according to our definition (see Chapter 2), because the birds were required to make mirror-image responses to mirror-image stimuli. On the other hand, the horizontal–vertical problem can be regarded as a test of left–right differentiation, since the stimuli themselves carried no left–right information which might have indicated to the birds which side key to peck. In any event, Over found no differences in performance on the two tasks in terms of either accuracy of choice or latency to respond.

Rat

It is well known that rats can fairly readily learn the simple left–right response differentiation of always turning into the same arm of a symmetrical T maze. However, they have considerable difficulty with more complex mazes involving several left–right choices unless there are external left–right cues, and they also learn the simple T maze more easily if such cues are available (Restle, 1957).

Rats often exhibit spontaneous alternation in a T maze, choosing alternate left and right turns on successive runs. This implies an ability to differentiate left and right responses, at least insofar as there are no left–right cues. Subtle cues may exist, however. Douglas (1966) reports that spontaneous alternation may depend partly on an odor trail left over in one arm of the maze from the previous run. However, he concludes that rats also show a tendency simply to turn in opposite directions independently of external cues. Rats can also learn quite readily to alternate turns in a T maze in order to obtain rewards in alternate arms, although their ability to do so declines as the interval between successive trials increases; even so, Petrinovitch and Bolles (1957) reported that a few rats were able to maintain above chance performance when the delays between successive runs lasted several hours.

Lawrence (1948) taught rats to turn left in a white T maze and right in a black T maze. He termed this "successive discrimination," although it also meets our definition of left–right response differentiation. He contrasted it with "simultaneous discrimination," in which the rats had to choose one or other alley of a symmetrical maze depending on which of two cues was associated with which alley — a task which does not require the ability to tell left from right. The successive-discrimination task was much the more difficult. Rats taught the simultaneous discrimination of black versus white alleys reached a group criterion of 90% correct in about 12 trials, but the same rats then took about 53 trials to reach the same criterion on the successive discrimination task. Rats that were first taught irrelevant simultaneous discriminations took even longer; they needed over 80 trials to reach the 90% criterion. However, it is not clear to what extent the difficulty was due simply to the fact that the cues were presented successively rather than simultaneously, or to the fact that the successive discrimination required the ability to tell left from right while the simultaneous discrimination did not.

In none of these studies was there any explicit concern with the left–right problem per se. We cannot be sure, therefore, how careful the investigators were to eliminate all possible left–right cues. In no case, moreover, was there any attempt to devise any control task to isolate the left–right component as the critical one.

Guinea Pig

Grindley (1932) found that guinea pigs could be taught quite readily to turn their heads consistently to one side when a buzzer sounded beneath them. This is a task of the same order as that in which a rat learns to turn into one arm of a T maze. We suspect that this, the simplest kind of left–right response differentiation, seldom causes serious difficulty in any species.

Dog

Dogs appear to have considerable difficulty with left–right response differentiation where opposite responses are required depending on which of two stimuli occur. Konorski (1964) cites a study in which it proved impossible to teach dogs to lift the right foreleg in response to a metronome and the left foreleg in response to a buzzer, but only so long as the sounds emanated from the same location. In another study, attributed to Lawicka, dogs were unable to learn to approach a food tray on the left or right, depending on which of two tones was sounded from a speaker. The difficulty with these tasks clearly did not lie in discriminating the stimuli because the dogs easily learned to discriminate them in classical conditioning or "go – no go" paradigms. The problem therefore seemed to have been one of differentiating the left and right responses.

Both of the above tasks proved quite easy when the sounds emanated from different spatial locations. It was clear, indeed, that spatial location, rather than differences in the sounds themselves, provided the necessary cue. We may surmise that the critical information that was available from the spatial separation was the left–right cue.

Human Adult

As we observed in Chapter 3, recall of the specific left–right orientation of an event can be regarded, technically, as a test of left–right response differentiation. It is therefore pertinent to note an observation by Bartlett (1932) on the recall of faces. Bartlett showed people pictures of faces in various profiles and tested verbal recall half an hour later. There was a marked tendency to recall particular pictures as having been in the opposite profile to the originals, even though other details were correct. This might be considered not very rigorous evidence of a process of mirror-image generalization, and adds to the evidence of Standing, Conezio, and Haber (1970) and of Olshansky (Rock, 1973), discussed earlier.

SUMMARY AND CONCLUSIONS

We found considerable evidence that animals find it difficult, sometimes apparently impossible, to discriminate left–right mirror-image stimuli. We also cited one study by Konorski (1964) which suggests that dogs, at least, find it virtually impossible to choose a left or a right response according to stimuli which convey no left–right cues. However, we found no evidence that animals find it particularly difficult to learn the simplest kind of left–right response differentiation in which all that is required is a consistent response asymmetry.

Very few investigators have addressed themselves to the issue of whether the confusion of mirror-image stimuli is basically a problem of perception or one of labeling and memory. We reviewed the experiments of Kinsbourne (1967) and Tee and Riesen (1974) in which the subjects, rats, were required to *perceive* the orientations of mirror-image stimuli but were not required to perform mirror-image discrimination as we defined it in Chapter 2. These tasks appeared to cause little difficulty compared with those which did test mirror-image discrimination. From the limited available evidence, therefore, we conclude that animals have no particular trouble in perceiving which way round things are—a point also made by Over (1967). The problem is to label mirror-image stimuli as distinct, using labels that are not themselves mirror images, and to remember which is which. It is a problem of pattern recognition, rather than one of perception per se.

This conclusion has implications concerning the so-called "oblique effect" (Appelle, 1972), since the stimuli presented by Kinsbourne and by Tee and Riesen were oblique lines. Apart from the evidence on the discrimination of mirror-image obliques, the evidence reviewed by Appelle had to do mainly with sensory or perceptual deficits associated with obliquely oriented lines or grids. For example, Appelle cites evidence that both acuity (e.g., Ogilvie & Taylor, 1958) and fine judgments of orientation (e.g., Jastrow, 1893; Smith, 1962) are poorer, at least in humans, for lines oriented obliquely than for horizontal or vertical lines. But such factors are probably of little consequence in experiments on the discrimination of mirror-image obliques where the stimuli are typically displayed continuously and conspicuously and where the angle separating the orientations to be discriminated is usually too great for errors in the judgment of orientation to influence the discrimination. Appelle did recognize the possibility that difficulties of memory as well as of perception might have contributed to some of the effects he reviewed, including experiments on the discrimination of mirror-image obliques. What he did not sufficiently emphasize was that the discrimination of mirror-image obliques confounds the problem of obliqueness with that of telling left from right.

We shall have more to say on this issue in Chapter 10 when we consider some of the problems that children experience with oblique orientations. We shall again conclude that the problem of telling left from right is at least one major source of difficulty in discriminating mirror-image obliques.

If mirror-image discrimination is not basically a perceptual problem, then one might argue analogously that left–right response differentiation is not primarily a motor one. Animals presumably have no difficulty deciding in which direction to move in order to escape predators or to hunt prey or which paw to lift to lick a wound or reach for food. The problem only arises when an animal must choose which response to make on the basis of a cue which conveys no left – right information; again, this is a problem of coding or of remembering which response goes with which stimulus. Hebb makes this very point, albeit anecdotally, when he writes of

. . . . the notorious difficulty of choosing between *left* and *right,* to be observed by anyone who tries to teach twelve-year-old children to "right turn" promptly on command. . . . The child can very readily learn at the age of three that "left" and "right" each refers to a side of the body—but ah me, which one? [Hebb, 1949, p. 118]

Let us now turn briefly to the possible role of response asymmetries in mirror-image discrimination. We described evidence that pigeons may solve visual mirror-image discriminations by adopting asymmetrical postures or response strategies. Since most species appear to have little difficulty acquiring simple response asymmetries, it would not be surprising if these were to play a rather general role in helping animals solve more complex problems of telling left from right.

We suggested that pigeons may learn to discriminate mirror-image obliques by cocking their heads to one side so that 45° and 135° lines, for example, might be seen as though horizontal and vertical. Oblique lines may naturally induce a head-tilting strategy. Indeed, there was some suggestion throughout our review of mirror-image discrimination that mirror-image obliques may be the easiest of mirror-image stimuli to discriminate despite the confounding influence of the "oblique effect." Thus, pigeons and cats appear to have no particular difficulty with mirror-image obliques while cats, at least, do have trouble with other mirror-image pairs. The octopus, on the other hand, apparently finds the discrimination of obliques to be as impossibly difficult as that of any other mirror-image pair. A head-tilting strategy would be of little avail to the octopus, however, since its eyes are automatically maintained in a horizontal position regardless of the orientation of the head or body (Young, 1962). We should also recall, though, that the rabbit can apparently discriminate mirror-image obliques without resort to obvious response asymmetries.

Postural asymmetries would be less effective in the case of tactile than in the case of visual stimuli. An animal is usually free to move relative to a stationary visual source and so translate the stimulus with respect to its own axes. By contrast, one can touch an animal at mirror-image points with respect to its midsagittal plane more or less regardless of the posture the animal chooses to adopt. Perhaps this explains why both cats and dogs are apparently unable to discriminate mirror-image touches while cats, at least, can usually solve visual mirror-image discriminations without serious difficulty.

We may summarize this chapter by observing that the experimental evidence is for the most part consistent with our proposition that left – right confusion is a fundamental consequence of bilateral symmetry. Animals are generally confused on precisely those tasks which a perfectly symmetrical organism would find impossible; namely, those which meet our criteria of telling left from right. They are not confused on tasks which simply require differential perception of mirror-image stimuli. We have suggested therefore that the confusion of mirror-image stimuli has to do with the processes of pattern recognition rather than of perception per se. In the next chapter, we shall examine some theories of pattern recognition which make explicit predictions about mirror-image confusion.

5

Mirror-Image Equivalence and Theories of Pattern

"Now, if you'll only attend, Kitty, and
not talk so much, I'll tell you all my ideas
about Looking-glass House."

—*Through the Looking-Glass*
LEWIS CARROLL

In the two previous chapters we suggested, on both logical and empirical grounds, that the confusion of left–right mirror images is not primarily a problem of perception, but is better characterized as a problem of pattern recognition. In this chapter we shall review a number of theories of visual pattern recognition which include among their properties some mechanism which causes left–right mirror images to be coded as indistinguishable. We may say that such a mechanism achieves *mirror-image equivalence*. However, the theories reviewed in this chapter are general in the sense that they are designed to account for other classes of stimulus equivalence as well, including equivalence with respect to size, location, and angular orientation.

We shall distinguish two different, though not mutually exclusive, approaches to the problem, one emphasizing the extraction of features from the input, the other emphasizing higher-order mental processes which may be loosely described as "cognitive."

FEATURE EXTRACTION MODELS

Feature extraction models of pattern recognition have been popular since the 1950s, although in recent years there has been a growing awareness of their limitations. The basic idea is that the brain extracts certain features from the pattern that impinges on the receptor surface and codes information about the pattern in terms of these features. This implies that the input is transformed in some way so that some information about it is retained and some discarded. We have referred to the discarded features or attributes as "circumstantial," necessary perhaps for the accurate perception of a pattern, but irrelevant to its recognition.

The models we shall review grew out of work carried out initially at Oxford University, principally by J. A. Deutsch, P. C. Dodwell, and N. S. Sutherland. Not only did these authors devote special attention to the problem of mirror-image equivalence, but their approach also represented the new trend in general theories of pattern recognition. Unlike earlier theorists of a more associationistic persuasion such as Hebb (1949), they emphasized "built-in" principles of classification rather than learned ones. This is not to say that learning was ignored, but at the very least it was implied that the innately determined structure of the brain imposed limitations on the classifications and discriminations an animal could make. The Gestalt psychologists (e.g., Koffka, 1935) had also emphasized innate principles, but the theoretical models they proposed were either physiologically naive or too vague to be useful. During the 1950s, however, there were developments in neurophysiology and computer science which opened up the possibility of more explicit structural models. Neurophysiologists began to discover how cells in the visual areas of the brain, especially in the frog and cat, were programmed to respond to specific features of the visual environment. These discoveries naturally encouraged a feature-extraction approach to pattern recognition. At about the same time, computer-oriented scientists began to develop an interest in the simulation of pattern recognition, with practical applications in diverse disciplines such as communications, engineering, meteorology, medical diagnosis, as well as psychology. The demands of the digital computer forced theorists to be explicit in the models they developed.

Although the Oxford trio were obviously influenced by these developments, they still attached primary importance to the explanation and prediction of empirical findings on discrimination learning in animals. Most of the early data came from the octopus and the rat. Perhaps we owe a debt of gratitude to these two species, in fact, because both suffer considerable difficulty with mirror-image discrimination, as we saw in the previous chapter. Mirror-image equivalence was therefore considered one of the basic facts to be explained.

By and large, theorists of pattern recognition have tended to equate pattern recognition with perception, although Uhr (1966), for one, points out that "perception" is the broader term. In so doing they have largely ignored the problem of how some attributes can be represented in the percept but not in the code on which recognition is based. Deutsch (1955) at least acknowledged this problem, observing that we *can* perceive such circumstantial attributes as size, location, and brightness, even though his model was designed explicitly to discard them. He simply sidestepped the issue by assuming there must be separate mechanisms devoted to them.

Milner (1974) discusses a limited aspect of the problem as follows:

> If the position of a feature is of no account in determining the meaning of a stimulus, how does an organism locate the object it is recognizing? This is an important problem

because the whole point of recognition is that it allows responses to be based on past experience, and there is little use in being able to choose the best response if it cannot be directed to the appropriate object. The paradox is that one part of the brain knows *what* the stimulus is but not *where* it is; the earlier stages of the visual system know *where* it is but not *what* it is [p. 523; Milner's italics].

Schneider (1969) has maintained that there are in fact two distinct systems in the mammalian brain for localizing and identifying visual patterns, the one involving the superior colliculus and the other the lateral geniculate body and visual cortex. However, localization is not the only attribute which may be considered circumstantial. What, for example, of size? If the visual cortex is designed to extract information about a pattern regardless of its size, how do we in fact perceive what its size is? The same question may be asked of left–right orientation. This problem is perhaps particularly critical for feature extraction theories which work on the principle that some features are extracted while others are discarded.

All of the models we shall describe are restricted to the recognition of two-dimensional shapes, presented visually. There has been little attempt to deal with the recognition of solid objects. In this respect the models are at least consistent with the experiments on which they are largely based; in nearly all experiments on visual discrimination, the shapes to be discriminated have been confined to flat surfaces.

Deutsch's Model

Deutsch (1955) was the first to make explicit the basic requirements of a model of shape recognition and to suggest some simple transformations which might meet these requirements. He proposed first that shapes are reduced to their contours. Thus a filled-in square is seen as equivalent to an outline drawing of a square. It is well known, in fact, that lateral inhibitory mechanisms in the early stages of visual processing serve to select and enhance information about contours or discontinuities in intensity gradients (see Dodwell, 1970, for a review), although we might also note that we can certainly *perceive* the difference between a filled-in shape and its outline.

Deutsch's second and main proposal was that shapes are then coded in terms of the distances between points on their contours. His earliest model accomplished this by transforming the distances into time intervals between successive pulses of a signal, which was thus patterned over time. Later, however, Deutsch (1962) proposed two alternative network systems which would accomplish essentially the same transformation with a spatially rather than a temporally distributed output. The details need not concern us. The main point is that if one reduces a shape to a frequency distribution of distances between pairs of points on its contours, the description is then invariant with respect to translation, rotation, and mirror reflection. (It was the mirror-image invariance which so intrigued Kant, as we remarked in Chapter 1.) In each of his various proposals,

Deutsch added a further transformation to express the distances as ratios rather than as absolute values, producing invariance with respect to size.

Deutsch's basic concept of intercontour distance coding thus models several important properties of shape discrimination with elegance and economy. The main difficulty is that it generalizes too much. The model achieves mirror-image equivalence, but this applies to mirror images about *any* axis (or plane) and not just to left–right mirror images. We saw in the previous chapter, however, that left–right mirror images are nearly always more difficult to discriminate than are up–down mirror images. Dodwell (1957) has also criticized Deutsch's model on the grounds that the recognition of shape is not generally independent of angular orientation (that is, of rotations of a shape in its own plane), at least in primitive visual systems. Later in this chapter we shall discuss evidence that even in humans the angular orientation of a figure is an important clue to its recognition.

Dodwell's Model

Dodwell (1957) argued that shapes were coded in terms of properties of the contours themselves rather than the distances between them. For example, he noted that rats can discriminate shapes according to whether or not there is a horizontal baseline. According to Deutsch's model there would be no way for a rat to focus on the base of a shape independently of the shape as a whole. Dodwell therefore proposed a model that emphasized properties of contours and which would also allow discrimination between the same shapes in different orientations.

We present here a somewhat simplified account. Essentially, the model involves both a horizontal and a vertical "sweep" of excitation across a two-dimensional representation of the contours of a shape. At the end of a sweep, the excitation is summed at right angles to the direction of the sweep and fed along a "final common cable." However, if any part of the sweep encounters a contour, it is delayed by a constant interval, so that the final signal is then patterned in time. The amplitude of the pulses and the intervals between them thus code spatial properties of the contours. For example, if the horizontal sweep encounters a horizontal line, a small component of the sweep is delayed by an interval proportional to the length of the line. The final signal would then consist of one large pulse followed after a delay by a small one. A vertical line would delay a larger porportion of the excitation by a smaller interval. The horizontal sweep would be maximally sensitive to small angular variations of a contour about the horizontal, but virtually insensitive to small variations about the vertical. Conversely, the vertical sweep would be most sensitive to variations about the vertical and least sensitive to variations about the horizontal.

This model effectively codes a shape in terms of the number and lengths of its contours, regardless of their locations in the visual field. It is sensitive to angular rotations of a shape. Horizontal and vertical contours are emphasized; oblique lines of different orientations would be barely distinguishable.

However, there are difficulties with this model too. Left–right mirror images would be indistinguishable, but so would up–down mirror images, which is of course counter to the evidence. Muntz (1970) selected two other shapes which should have been indistinguishable according to the model and found that even the octopus could discriminate between them. Because the model signals information about individual contours regardless of their locations in the visual field, it loses information about the *relations* among contours and thus seems to lose something of what we normally understand by "shape." In a more recent version of the model, Dodwell (1964) adds a component to account for perceptual learning. However, this does not overcome the deficiencies we have noted because the learning component is assumed to operate on the output of the contour analyzer; information that is lost at that stage cannot be recovered.

In his recent book on pattern recognition, Dodwell (1970) reviews the work of Hubel and Wiesel (e.g., 1963, 1965, 1968), who recorded from single cells in the visual cortex of cats and monkeys which respond selectively to straight lines or edges with particular orientations in the visual field. As one proceeds to higher levels in the visual system, these cells also become increasingly insensitive to the exact locations of the lines or edges in the field. Dodwell points out that these findings lend support to his basic contention that shapes are coded in terms of the orientations of their contours. Yet the point is elusive. For instance, Pollen, Lee, and Taylor (1971) have suggested that the mammalian visual cortex might undertake a spatial analog of a Fourier analysis over the entire visual field, and that the so-called "edge detectors" discovered by Hubel and Wiesel might actually be contributing to this more global process. But even if we accept that the visual cortex does indeed extract information about, say, the orientations and lengths of contours, it is still questionable whether this is sufficient for the recognition of shapes. We shall later have cause to question whether it is even necessary.

Sutherland's Theories

Yet another model for the recognition of shapes appeared in the 1950s, this one due to Sutherland (1957). This model was initially devised to account for shape discrimination in the octopus. Unlike Deutsch or Dodwell, Sutherland did recognize that left–right mirror images are more difficult to discriminate than up–down ones. His basic proposal was that two-dimensional shapes are coded in terms of their vertical or horizontal projections, as illustrated in Fig. 5.1. In the octopus, however, the horizontal projections were of primary importance, with the vertical projections contributing little or nothing to the discrimination process. Sutherland, Carr, and Mackintosh (1962) later suggested that the same might be true of the rat. This would explain why both rats and octopuses have extreme difficulty discriminating left–right mirror images but relatively little difficulty with up–down ones. As Fig. 5.1 illustrates, left–right mirror images

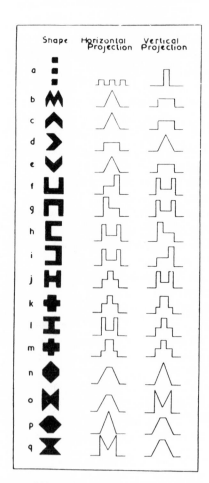

FIGURE 5.1 Horizontal and vertical projections of various shapes used in discrimination experiments. Shapes *h* and *i* illustrate that left – right mirror images have identical horizontal projections. (From Sutherland, 1960a.)

do not differ with respect to their horizontal projections, but up–down mirror images do.

This model has not been wholly successful in explaining the results of experiments on shape discrimination, even in the octopus. For instance, Sutherland (1960c) showed that octopuses could discriminate some shapes which, according to the model, should have been indiscriminable. He suggested that they might make use of an additional transformation representing the "openness–closedness" of a figure, which might be computed by dividing the total length of contour by the area of the figure. However, Muntz (1970) has shown that octopuses can discriminate figures which differ neither on this index nor on their horizontal projections. Of course, this does not necessarily mean that the transformations proposed by Sutherland are wrong; it could simply mean that they are insufficient, and should be supplemented by still further processes.

We suspect, though, that Sutherland's theory reveals a misunderstanding of the problem of mirror-image confusion. Sutherland's proposal that discrimination depends on the horizontal projections of a pattern implies that the left–right dimension is effectively lost. A two-dimensional pattern is therefore reduced to a single dimension, as on a television screen with the horizontal sweep disconnected. However, the confusion of left–right mirror images need not imply this. An animal may perceive and remember the spatial characteristics of a two-dimensional pattern, but simply forget which way round it was. We have made this point before in Chapter 3. For example, the reader who has difficulty remembering which profile Whistler painted of his mother may still recall something of the spatial characteristics of the portrait — the facial expression, the angle of the head, the way the subject is seated, and so on. We cannot speak for the octopus, but we suspect its problem is of the same kind. Muntz's (1970) experiment showed the octopus to be perfectly capable of discriminating non-mirror-image patterns with identical horizontal projections. This suggests that it is capable of encoding information represented in the left–right extent of a pattern, but may be unable to remember the sense or polarity of this information.

Sutherland does not appear to have been entirely oblivious to this point. Here is a passage, for example, which expresses views somewhat similar to our own:

> The reason why up–down mirror images are more readily discriminated by the Octopus than left–right mirror images may be that the equivalence of left and right has been learned, since a left–right inversion of a shape can occur through the Octopus swimming round to the other side of it, whereas this is not the case with up–down mirror images. In addition the vertical axis is more clearly differentiated by stable cues from both within and without the organism than is the left–right axis. . . . The fact that learning may play a part in producing greater ease of discrimination for shapes differing in their horizontal projections than for shapes differing in their vertical projections does not mean that the system is not that sketched above; it would simply mean that learning played some part in the setting up of the system [Sutherland, 1960b, p. 15].

Here, Sutherland has clearly recognized that there is a basis for the equivalence of left and right in external reality or in the way that an organism interacts with the environment. His theory is too strong, however, for it implies other equivalences which do not occur in the real world.

There is another issue here. Sutherland was clearly alert to the functional significance of mirror-image generalization in a world where the same patterns and stimuli can occur in mirror-opposite guises. However, we doubt that the process of mirror-image generalization is learned. Left–right equivalence is so ubiquitous a characteristic of the natural world that we suspect mirror-image generalization would be a product of evolution rather than of learning. We suggest, therefore, that learning may play the converse of the role proposed by Sutherland; that is, an animal must learn to discriminate mirror images rather than to generalize between them, and the discrimination is difficult precisely because of the innate tendency to generalize. It is consistent with this interpretation that human children find it much more difficult to discriminate mirror images than adults do, as we shall see in Chapter 10.

More recently, Sutherland (1969) has expressed dissatisfaction with all theories of visual pattern recognition, including his own. He suggests that the processes of discrimination and generalization are far too subtle and complex for any existing model to cope with, and presents an outline for the kinds of properties an adequate model might be expected to have. In Sutherland's opinion, such a model would have three components: a processor for extracting local spatial features, a mechanism for inducing an abstract description of information represented in the processor, and a store in which these descriptions are held. The abstract descriptions form the basis of recognition and generalization. Sutherland outlines a language, based on the work of Clowes (1967), which might specify shapes in such a way that basic equivalences are respected. For example, he suggests a particular description which does not distinguish a shape from its left–right mirror image, but does distinguish it from its up–down mirror image. We shall not go into details because at the present stage of development the descriptive language does little more than accommodate some of the known facts; it does not really explain them.

At best, Sutherland's new outline simply recognizes that the coding of patterns is more hierarchical and more abstract than that specified by the models we have considered thus far. In these respects, he seems to be advocating a more ''cognitive'' approach to the problem.

Milner's Model

The most recent attempt to develop a model for shape recognition, in the tradition particularly of Deutsch and Dodwell, is that of Milner (1974). Like Deutsch, Milner suggests that shapes might be coded in terms of the distances between pairs of points on their contours. For reasons of economy, he proposes that emphasis would be given to salient points, such as corners, intersections, or the end points of lines. As in Deutsch's model, size constancy is achieved by expressing the distances as ratios. Milner evidently considers distance ratios to be insufficient, however, and suggests that there may be additional mechanisms for counting the straight contours in a figure and for tabulating angles according to their sizes. Angles are particularly useful because they are invariant with respect to the overall size of a figure so that no further transformation is needed to achieve size or distance constancy. On the basis of known physiological principles, Milner speculates as to how these various features might be extracted and tabulated, and how line and angle features might be coded independently of their locations and orientations in the visual field.

Milner's model is capable of a more sophisticated representation of shapes than either Deutsch's or Dodwell's, although somewhat at the expense of parsimony. At the same time, it shares some of the defects of the earlier models. Milner assumes that shapes are equally recognizable in different angular orientations, which is generally untrue even for humans, as we shall see. This might be fairly easily rectified, however, by supposing that lines or angles are tabulated according to their angular orientations and not independently of them. The model also predicts mirror-image equivalence, but again this applies to mirror images about *any* axis. There seems no simple way to modify the model so that the equivalence applies only to left–right mirror images.

COGNITIVE APPROACHES

The models we have discussed so far, although ingenious and admirably explicit, have failed to provide a totally adequate account of the recognition of shapes, even of two-dimensional ones. Each model seemed to fail in some or other particular respect. We suspect also that feature extraction models suffer a more general limitation in that they imply that pattern recognition is simply a matter of extracting information from the input and feeding it into some store. What is lacking is an active cognitive component, which does not merely receive information passively from the analyzing mechanisms but seeks actively to impose structure.

We shall only briefly discuss the evidence that pattern recognition is an active, constructive process rather than a passive, analytic one; the evidence is well presented by Neisser (1967). The idea of an active cognitive component also lies at the heart of the so-called "analysis by synthesis" theory of pattern recognition (e.g., Halle & Stevens, 1959). This theory has it that the brain, from its store of knowledge about different possible patterns, actively generates different representations for matching against the input. Recognition occurs when a match is found. It is easy to find examples in which structure or pattern is evidently imposed from within rather than from information directly available in the input. A two-dimensional outline representation of a cube, for example, is not seen as a flat crisscrossing pattern of straight lines, although that is what it is. The brain imposes the interpretation that the pattern is a cube, presumably because this interpretation is somehow more coherent, even though it means assuming an extra dimension. We do not yet know the precise cognitive rules which specify that this interpretation should be the preferred one; it is clear, however, that this phenomenon is well beyond the scope of any of the feature extraction models we described above.

We do not mean to imply that feature extraction models are totally wrong or that all of the theorists discussed earlier were oblivious to the role of cognitive influences. We saw that Sutherland (1969) seemed to recognize a cognitive element in his most recent outline for a theory of pattern recognition. More explicitly, Milner (1974) discussed how central influences on particular aspects of the feature extraction process might explain problems of attention—how one shape is singled out from others that are simultaneously present. However, we suspect that neither Sutherland nor Milner go nearly far enough. Although information about contours, straight-line segments, angles between contours, and the like, almost certainly *can* contribute to the recognition of shapes, it is also the case that simple shapes can be represented, at least to the human eye, without contours at all. A triangle can be represented by dotted lines, or even just by three dots. An ingenious example of how a triangular shape can be inferred from gaps in a patterned field is provided by Gregory (1972), who coins the term "cognitive contours" to describe the phenomenon (see also Rock, 1973, pp. 115–116). In cases like this the recognition of shape is a matter of cognitive inference, an act of the imagination, rather than a direct outcome of the analysis of features in the array. The extraction of contour information is therefore neither necessary nor sufficient for the recognition of shape.

In recent years, insight into the nature of at least some aspects of cognitive processes in pattern recognition has come not from neurophysiological evidence or from computer simulation, but from human experimental psychology. We shall focus primarily on the work, carried out more or less independently, of Irvin Rock and R. N. Shepard. Both were concerned primarily with the role of angular orientation in perception and recognition, but their work has broader implications for the general nature of pattern recognition. It also bears on the problem of mirror-image equivalence.

Before we discuss this work, we should remind the reader that the feature extraction theories described earlier were developed, initially at least, to explain pattern recognition in relatively primitive organisms, such as rat and octopus, whereas the emphasis on cognitive components in pattern recognition has come mainly from human evidence. We simply do not know whether the work of Rock and Shepard has any strong bearing on pattern recognition in animals.

Rock's Contribution

We have seen that both Deutsch and Milner assumed that shapes could be recognized independently of their angular orientations. In other words, they assumed that a familiar, two-dimensional pattern would still be recognized if rotated in its own plane. The evidence described by Rock (1973) in his recent monograph makes it clear that this is not always so. A random shape seen in one angular orientation is not often recognized if it is later seen in another orientation, although, as we saw in the previous chapter, recognition is little impaired by left–right reflection. Rock argues that patterns are identified not only in terms of their "internal geometry," but also in terms of an assigned directionality specifying which is the top and which is the bottom. A square is interpreted as a square if we perceive a straight edge to be on top, but as a diamond if we perceive a corner to be on top. As shapes, the two are quite distinct. The assignment of an up–down axis does not necessarily depend on the orientation of the pattern on the observer's *retina*. We usually interpret patterns according to their orientations with respect to gravity; a square is seen as a square even if the observer tilts his head through 45 °, so that the shape is projected on his retinas as a diamond. This implies that there must be a correction process that compensates for head tilt or for the rotation of the object itself in space. Sometimes the up–down axis is aligned neither with the retinal nor with the gravitational vertical. For example, we can usually recognize a disoriented letter, which means that we can assign an axis to it regardless of the degree of disorientation. By an act of the imagination, we can see a square as a tilted diamond if we so choose. Clearly then, the assignment of the up–down axis is a cognitive act rather than a simple matter of extracting a feature. Rock argues that patterns are initially, fleetingly, interpreted according to their retinal orientations, but that correction for angular disorientation occurs almost immediately.

If a shape or pattern is complex, we may be unable to make a correction for angular orientation, especially if the disorientation is extreme. For example, even a familiar face is usually unrecognizable upside down, although we can tell that it is an upside-down face. Cursive script is extremely difficult to read upside down. According to Rock, one reason why recognition is impaired in these cases is that it is difficult to make corrections for several aspects at once. Another reason may be that upside-down components of a face or of cursive script look like *different* right-side-up components. For instance, an upside-down mouth still looks like a mouth, but the expression is changed. This may distract the observer from correct recognition.

The idea that shapes might be partly characterized by the specification of a directional up–down axis helps overcome one of the deficiencies of the concept of intercontour-distance coding proposed by Deutsch and Milner. It will be recalled that intercontour distances provide a description that is independent of angular orientation and of mirror reflection, but that this description fails to specify that mirror-image equivalence applies particularly to *left–right* mirror images. If we add an up–down axis to the description, however, it is then only with respect to reflection about this axis that the description is invariant. Up–down mirror images would be discriminable, but left–right mirror images would not.

Shepard's Studies of Mental Rotation

R. N. Shepard and his colleagues have examined another aspect of the processing of patterns in different angular orientations. Their experiments suggest that people can *mentally rotate* a pattern in a more or less analog fashion such that the internal representation of a mentally rotated pattern is at some level of processing the same as the representation of the same pattern *actually* rotated. In one study, for example, Shepard and Metzler (1971) showed subjects perspective line drawings of pairs of three-dimensional shapes depicted in varying orientations in three-dimensional space. Aside from orientation, the shapes in each pair were either the same, or else they were enantiomorphs (mirror images). The time it took the subjects to decide that two identical shapes were the same was a linear function of the solid angle between the orientations in which they were portrayed. From this result and from the subjects' own introspective accounts, Shepard and Metzler inferred that the subjects performed the task by mentally rotating one of the shapes in three-dimensional space in order to match it to the other.

A further set of experiments by Cooper and Shepard (1973) suggest that one can also mentally rotate a shape for comparison with an internally generated image, or under certain circumstances rotate an image for comparison with a visually presented shape. They found that the time it took subjects to decide whether a disoriented letter or digit was mirror-reversed or not was an increasing function of its angular departure from the upright. This was so even if the subjects were told in advance what the symbol would be but not its orientation, or if they were told its orientation but not its identity. But if they were told both the orientation and the identity, decision time was not influenced by angular orientation (see Fig. 5. 2). Cooper and Shepard conclude that in the absence of prior information about identity and orientation, an observer must rotate a symbol to the upright before he can decide whether or not it is mirror reversed. But if he knows the identity and angular orientation of the symbol beforehand, he can rotate a generated image before the actual symbol is presented and so make his decision without rotating the symbol itself.

It is important to distinguish mental rotation from the process of assigning directionality to the pattern, which Rock inferred from his experiments. The assigning of directionality must *precede* mental rotation. In Shepard and Metzler's experiment, for example, the subjects must have made some preliminary analysis of the two shapes, including an analysis of their relative orientations, before they could rotate one into congruity with the other. More strikingly, the subjects in Cooper and Shepard's experiments must have known the *identity* of each symbol before rotating it, for otherwise they could not have known its upright position. It is a remarkable fact that we can immediately recognize an upside-down R as an R, but we cannot at the same time be sure whether it is forward or backward. In this case, recognition of identity seems to be independent of both angular and left–right orientation—just as Deutsch's or

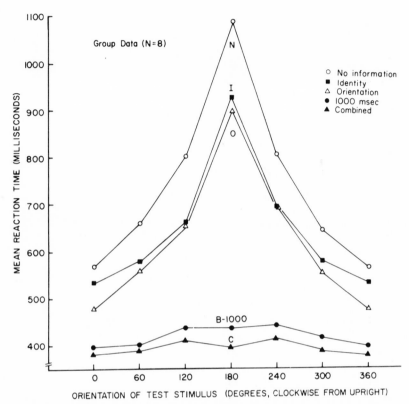

FIGURE 5.2   Mean reaction time to decide whether a rotated letter or digit was normal or mirror-reversed, as a function of angular orientation and of advance information. N = no advance information; I = advance information as to identity but not orientation; O = advance information as to orientation but not identity; B-1000 = advance information as to identity followed by advance information as to orientation; C = combined advance information as to identity and orientation. (From Cooper & Shepard, 1973.)

Milner's models would predict, in fact. However, a directionality must be assigned to the letter before it can be mentally rotated and then distinguished from its mirror image.

Cooper and Shepard (1973) write:

> . . . although mental rotation may not play any role in most ordinary processes of *recognition*, it may nevertheless play an indispensible role in certain other kinds of mental processes that are prominent in many familiar and sometimes very significant human activities. Consider, for example, such activities as the following: assembling the pieces of a jigsaw puzzle; rearranging furniture in a room; finding and fitting together the variously shaped parts of a complicated mechanical device; and (at a much more abstract, theoretical level) working out a creative solution to a problem in geometry, electrical engineering, stereochemistry, or theoretical physics. It seems doubtful that a person incapable of mental rotation would excel in these particular activities [p. 171; their italics].

From our own viewpoint, however, what is significant about Cooper and Shepard's results is that mental rotation should have been necessary to distinguish symbols from their mirror images. Mirror images are most easily understood as *left–right* mirror images. In Chapter 7 we shall present evidence that the symmetry of a pattern is most rapidly detected when it is symmetry about a vertical axis; that is, when it is left – right symmetry. Moreover, patterns that are symmetrical about other axes may be mentally rotated to the vertical before the symmetry is detected. If nothing else, these results remind us that the left–right dimension is fundamentally egocentric, and that to make judgments involving left and right requires mental transformations to align the axes of the pattern with those of the body. But we also suspect that the very concepts of reflection and symmetry are essentially left–right concepts based on the left – right symmetry of the nervous system itself. These themes are elaborated in the following two chapters.

CONCLUSIONS

Based on the evidence and theory we have reviewed, an integrated theory of shape recognition might perhaps run something like this: First, the brain induces a description of a shape that is independent of such circumstantial features as retinal position, size, angular orientation, and mirror reflection — although all of these features are still perceptually available. Such a description might well depend on a tabulation of intercontour distances, as both Deutsch and Milner proposed, although the extraction of contours may be a more cognitive act than either author supposed. In some cases, this description might be sufficient for recognition, especially of objects or shapes that are not normally confined to any particular orientation, such as a triangle, a cube, a knife, an apple, a tennis racquet. Recognition need not be automatic, however, but may require some active synthesis of descriptions from stored knowledge to match against the incoming description.

In other cases, however, recognition requires the specification of an up–down axis presumably because many objects are constrained by gravity or for reasons connected with gravity have a natural "top" and "bottom." There must be some flexibility, however, since we often tilt our heads or view objects from distorting angles. Sometimes, too, an object may be rotated away from its normal orientation; thus a bottle, for example, has a top and bottom, but is easily recognized on its side or upside down. In such cases we may suppose that recognition requires the assignment of an up–down axis to the description of the shape. This is a cognitive act because the axis seldom corresponds to the retinal vertical. The axis may have to be discovered by inference from other features, by information from environmental cues, or by the active synthesis of different possibilities.

We may suppose that the recognition of three-dimensional objects often requires the specification of a front–back axis as well as an up–down one. This would apply particularly in cases where movement is involved, as in the recognition of animals, airplanes, automobiles. However, we know little of the cues which enable us to specify front and back, since most investigators have restricted themselves to the analysis of two-dimensional shapes.

Finally, it is sometimes the case, especially in the man-made world, that recognition requires the correct labeling of the left–right orientation of a shape. This is so when we must distinguish b from d or p from q, or any other letter of the alphabet from its mirror image; or when we must distinguish a left from a right hand or a left from a right shoe. Such tasks evidently require rotation, mental or physical, so that the object or shape is aligned with the observer's own body coordinates. Correct identification must then rest on some asymmetry within the observer himself.

This theoretical summary carries the assumption that mirror-image equivalence is achieved by *reduction coding* — an assumption shared by all of the models reviewed earlier in this chapter; that is, it is assumed that the brain induces and stores a description of a shape that is independent of its left–right orientation. In cases where left–right orientation is important for some aspect of recognition, this orientation is stored with reference to some generalized gradient or asymmetry in the brain or nervous system itself. The left–right orientation of a particular shape can then be recovered only by performing certain cognitive operations, including mental rotation, to bring it into alignment with the observer's own coordinates.

In the following chapter we consider an alternate approach, which is that mirror-image equivalence is achieved by what we may call *duplication coding*; that is, the brain stores information about shapes in alternate forms, one the left–right mirror image of the other. This approach gains its main support from considerations about the structure of the brain. The mammalian brain is in many respects a double organ, with much duplication of function between its two halves. Moreover, to a high degree of approximation, each half is the left–right mirror image of the other, and there do appear to be mechanisms which would accomplish a mirror reflection in the transfer of information between them.

Before we proceed, however, we should make it clear that we do not wish to claim that reduction and duplication coding are mutually contradictory. We suspect in fact that the brain makes use of both principles in the storage of information. Moreover, duplication in mirror-image forms can be seen as a kind of reduction in the sense that information about left–right orientation is thereby lost. We offer the labels more as descriptions of different areas of research and theory than as representing a fundamental theoretical issue.

6

Interhemispheric Mirror-Image Reversal

Professor Jones had been working on time theory for many years.

"And I have found the key equation," he told his daughter one day. "Time is a field. This machine I have made can manipulate, even reverse, that field."

Pushing a button as he spoke, he said, "This should make time run backward run time make should this," said he, spoke he as button a pushing.

"Field that, reverse even, manipulate can made have I machine this. Field a is time." Day one daughter his told he, "Equation key the found have I and."

Years many for theory time on working been had Jones Professor.

—*Nightmares and Geezenstacks*
FREDRIC BROWN

But it is of course with reversal in space, not time, that this chapter is concerned. It is a fairly old idea that the two halves of the brain might encode information in mirror-opposite ways. The idea has been suggested by different authors, apparently independently of one another, as a possible explanation for the confusion of left–right mirror images. It has seemed to follow naturally from the fact that the cerebral hemispheres are themselves mirror images, at least to a fair degree of approximation (and notwithstanding the evidence for cerebral asymmetries, discussed in Chapters 8 and 9). Interhemispheric mirror-image reversal is also compatible with our general theme that the confusion of left and right is a fundamental consequence of structural bilateral symmetry. It is an elusive idea, however. It has not always been stated with precision, or even with logic, and it has been formulated in slightly different ways. In this chapter, we shall consider its historical development, examine the relevant experimental evidence, and so attempt to arrive at a version that is at least plausible, if not proven.

An early statement suggesting interhemispheric mirror-image reversal is to be found in a report by Ireland (1881). He described a neurological patient suffering from aphasia and hemiplegia of the right side who showed a marked tendency to write backward. Mirror writing persisted even when the patient had recovered sufficiently to be able to write with the right hand. Ireland has this to say:

> It may be asked, is the image or impression, or change in the brain tissue from which the image is formed in the mind of the mirror writer, reversed like the negative of a photograph; or if a double image be formed in the visual centre, one in the right hemisphere of the brain and the other in the left, do the images lie to each other in opposite direction; e.g., C on the right side and Ɔ on the left side? We can thus conceive that the image on the left side of the brain being effaced through disease, the inverse image would remain in the right hemisphere which would render the patient apt to trace the letters from right to left, the execution of which would be rendered all the more natural from the greater facility of the left hand to work in a centrifugal direction. Moreover, when one used the left hand to write there would probably be a tendency to copy the inverse impression or image on the right side of the brain [Ireland, 1881, p. 367].

Some 40 years later, basically the same idea occurred to Samuel T. Orton, a psychiatrist and physician who worked with children suffering from difficulties with reading and writing. Like Ireland's patient, these children often exhibited mirror writing. When reading, they tended to confuse mirror-image letters or words like *was* and *saw*. Orton also observed that children with these difficulties often appeared to lack a consistent cerebral dominance or that they came from families in which there was some incidence or history of mixed dominance. The relation between cerebral lateralization, the development of the left –right sense, and reading disability is a topic we shall leave for Chapter 11. For the present, our concern is with the more basic proposition that left–right confusion depends on the mirror-image relation between the hemispheres. Let us begin by considering Orton's version of this proposition in detail.

ORTON'S THEORY

Because the brain is symmetrical, Orton thought, its two halves should record events with opposite left–right orientations. As he put it:

> The exact symmetrical relationship of the two hemispheres would lead us to believe that the group of cells irradiated by any visual stimulus in the right hemisphere are the exact mirrored counterpart of those in the left [Orton, 1925, p. 607].

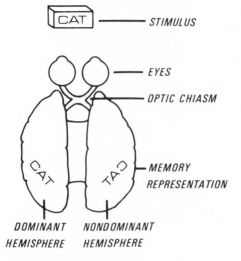

FIGURE 6.1 Schematic representation of Orton's theory in which it is assumed that a visual stimulus is represented in opposite orientations in the two cerebral hemispheres. (From Corballis, 1974; after Orton, 1925.)

He went on to argue that the dominant hemisphere normally recorded events in the correct orientation while the nondominant hemisphere recorded them in the reversed orientation. The stimulus C, for example, would be correctly recorded in the dominant hemisphere, but would be recorded as though it were the stimulus Ɔ in the nondominant hemisphere (see Fig. 6. 1). If a child failed to learn to suppress the activity of the nondominant hemisphere, the reversed record would intrude to create left–right confusion. Orton (1925) coined the term "strephosymbolia" to describe this condition.

Orton's argument is wrong. It simply does not follow that the two halves of a symmetrical brain would respond to any given stimulus pattern in mirror-opposite ways. This would only happen in general if the pattern were itself symmetrical with respect to the brain's plane of symmetry. To put it slightly differently, the two halves of the brain would respond in mirror-image fashion to stimuli that are *mirror images* of one another, but not to the *same* stimulus. It follows from simple geometry that the response of one half to the stimulus C would mirror that of the other half to the stimulus Ɔ; or that any neuron in one half which responds maximally to a 45° line, say, would be located symmetrically with respect to a neuron which responds maximally to a 135° line. But these facts tell us nothing about how the two halves of the brain would respond to the same C shape, or to the same oblique line. Ironically, Orton seems to have been the victim of a mirror-image confusion; he has confused the way a symmetrical brain would respond to the same stimulus with the way it would respond to mirror-image stimuli.

There is another aspect of Orton's theory which is not clear from the above quotation. He believed that the interhemispheric reversal was not a matter of *perceptual* registration, but had to do with the way in which *memory* traces, or engrams, were laid down. Here is a passage from a later article:

> This view that the confusions . . . do not rest on disturbances in the visual process but rather on the ambivalence or variability in the engrams with which visual experience is to be compared forms the basis of the explanation. . . . I believe that children with these problems *see as others do* but fail to elide completely one of the two antitropic engrams registered as a pattern for later comparison which forms the basis of recognition [Orton, 1931, p. 166; our italics].

We believe that Orton was correct in asserting that the problem was one of memory rather than perception, although his neurological theorizing does not make any provision for the distinction. It is not at all clear how perceptual input to the nondominant hemisphere could be veridical, yet leave an engram that is reversed. Neither is it clear why the nondominant hemisphere should be the one to suffer this bizarre malfunction.

NOBLE'S THEORY

A different version of the hypothesis of interhemispheric mirror-image reversal was proposed by John Noble, a psychologist who worked on discrimination learning in the monkey. Whereas Orton had seemed to suggest that reversal would occur simply in the way the two halves of the brain directly record events, Noble argued that it might occur in the *transfer* of information from one cerebral hemisphere to the other.

Noble's argument was stated explicitly for the monkey, but is easily extended in principle to other species. It runs as follows: The visual system of the monkey is organized so that the retina is mapped topographically onto area 17 of the visual cortex, which in turn maps topographically onto the neighboring prestriate region. Noble speculated that the topography of the retina might be carried on to the visual area in the inferotemporal cortex, but he lacked the necessary evidence. These various mappings were assumed to be confined within each hemisphere. Noble then went on to discuss the commissures which link the two hemispheres. He cited evidence that many of them are homotopic, which is to say they join mirror-image points in the two hemispheres (see also Cumming, 1970; Sperry, 1962). Given topographic representation in each cerebral hemisphere and homotopic connections linking them, it follows geometrically that the spatial representation of any pattern in any visual half-field would be mirror reversed in transfer from one hemisphere to the other (Noble, 1968). The same argument applies to any species in which there is topographic mapping within hemispheres and homotopic connections between them.

The essence of the theory is shown schematically in Fig. 6.2. It is of interest to compare it with Orton's theory, shown schematically in Fig. 6.1. Noble's

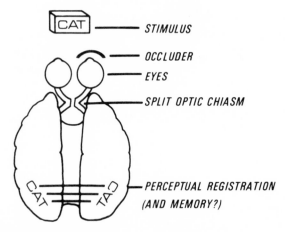

FIGURE 6.2   Schematic representation of Noble's theory, drawn for a split-chiasm preparation with the right eye occluded. The projection is reversed in transfer from the left to the right hemisphere. (From Corballis, 1974; after Noble, 1968.)

theory would not ordinarily imply, as Orton's does, that one hemisphere records one orientation and the other records its mirror image. We have illustrated the atypical case where input is restricted to one hemisphere, as in the experiments to be described below, which Noble carried out to test his theory. Normally, however, input would be transmitted veridically to both hemispheres and then each would send reversed projections to the other. *Both* hemispheres would therefore receive veridical as well as mirror-reversed representations.

Unlike Orton's version, Noble's is at least logically sound. Suppose the representation of some stimulus pattern is indeed left–right reversed in transfer from one hemisphere to the other, as Noble suggests. The representation in the receiving hemisphere would then be the same as that which would have been *directly* induced by the left–right mirror image of the original stimulus. In other words, the brain would have no way of telling which way round the actual stimulus is. Noble's theory therefore provides a consistent explanation for mirror-image confusion.

We think, however, that Noble's theory requires at least some modification. Before we discuss this, however, let us consider the experiments which Noble himself carried out as well as some comparable experiments carried out by others. We shall see that the data are somewhat equivocal.

EXPERIMENTAL STUDIES

It is appropriate to begin with Noble's own experiments on interhemispheric transfer of mirror-image discriminations in the monkey (Noble, 1966, 1968).

Noble sectioned the optic chiasms of his experimental animals so that information presented to only one eye would be projected directly to only one hemisphere (see Fig. 6. 2). He taught the animals various mirror-image discriminations with the stimuli presented simultaneously and vision restricted to one eye. Later, he tested for interhemispheric transfer by presenting the stimuli to the untrained eye. The animals tended to choose the negative stimulus, the mirror-image of the positive one, which Noble took to be evidence for interhemispheric mirror-image reversal.

Noble noticed, however, that the reversal usually took several trials to develop. On early testing, choice was random. In the first of his two reports, Noble (1966) suggested that the early test choices may have failed to show reversal because of a conflict between the two memory traces, the veridical one in the trained hemisphere and the transferred mirror-reversed one in the other hemisphere. The animals may have continued to "attend" to the trained hemisphere for some time after input had been switched to the untrained one. In his later report, Noble (1968) showed that the negative preference was more immediate when he took steps to enhance the attentional state of the untrained hemisphere prior to testing, either by teaching it a new unrelated discrimination or by simply allowing the monkey to view its surroundings with the untrained eye for a while between training and testing. He also found a more immediate negative preference if he cut the corpus callosum between training and testing so that the memory trace in the trained hemisphere could not have influenced the choice on test trials. In a somewhat different context, Butler (1968) has also produced evidence that attention may lag in the trained hemisphere while the untrained one is tested.

Yet Noble (1968) detected a flaw in his own logic. Suppose the veridical memory trace in the trained hemisphere *were* to continue to influence the choice of stimuli even when input was switched to the untrained hemisphere. Matching of the input to this veridical trace would still require interhemispheric projection, so the input should be mirror-reversed; that is, the choice should be mirror-reversed on test trials regardless of which hemisphere controls the discrimination. Yet there was conflict.

A more plausible explanation of this conflict comes from Hamilton and Tieman (1973), who question whether Noble's account of interhemispheric mirror-image reversal is correct. They also studied interocular transfer of mirror-image discrimination in split-chiasm monkeys. Unlike Noble, they found little direct evidence for reversal, but again there were signs of conflict; for example, transfer was more strongly veridical when the stimuli were up–down mirror images rather than left–right mirror images. Hamilton and Tieman argued, contrary to Noble, that spatial information is transferred veridically between the cerebral hemispheres, but that there is a competing reversal tendency created by the fact that a split-chiasm monkey typically attends to opposite sides of a pattern with each eye.

A monkey with a split optic chiasm is in fact blind in the temporal field of each eye. If it were to fixate the center of a pattern, therefore, it would see only the left half with the right eye, and only the right half with the left eye. To show that this could affect discrimination learning, Hamilton, Tieman, and Winter (1973) trained split-chiasm monkeys, viewing monocularly, on the successive discrimination of ㄊ from ㅈ and ✕ from ≺ . Note that the right halves of each pair are identical, but the left halves are different. Both discriminations proved quite easy when the monkeys viewed with their right eyes, but extremely difficult when they viewed with their left eyes. The reverse was the case when the patterns were rotated through 180°. These results seem to indicate that the monkeys, somewhat paradoxically, did fixate the center of each stimulus, even though this meant they could only see half of it. Lehman and Spencer (1973) have reported similar evidence when the stimuli to be discriminated were presented simultaneously rather than successively.

Since opposite sides of mirror-image stimuli are alike, a tendency to see opposite halves of a stimulus with each eye would favor interocular mirror-image reversal. But if Hamilton and Tieman (1973) are correct, this reversal tendency would compete with the effects of veridical transfer between the hemispheres. One or other tendency might predominate, depending on the conditions that prevail. For example, Hamilton and Tieman suggest that Noble might have obtained a greater degree of left – right reversal than they did because he used a different method to occlude the monkeys' eyes. Noble used a chronic procedure in which an opaque contact occluder was placed in the eye for up to a week at a time, while Hamilton and Tieman used a transient procedure in which the eye was externally blocked from seeing the stimuli. Chronic occlusion may have produced the more strongly lateralized attention processes, and therefore the greater degree of interocular mirror-image reversal. Noble's own experiments may also support Hamilton and Tieman's interpretation. The procedures that he used ostensibly to direct "attention" to the untrained hemisphere (see p. 63) may have in fact served rather to facilitate the attentional switch from one side of the stimulus patterns to the other.

Interhemispheric transfer of mirror-image discrimination has also been investigated in species other than the monkey. Berlucchi and Marzi (1970) tested interocular transfer of visual mirror-image discrimination in split-chiasm cats. Like Hamilton and Tieman, they found transfer to be either weakly veridical or at a chance level, and cats retaught the original discrimination with the untrained eye learned it faster than cats taught the reversed discrimination. However, we might nonetheless contrast these results with those of Myers and Sperry (1958), who found interocular transfer of nonmirror-image pattern discriminations in split-chiasm cats to be virtually perfect. Again, this suggests some reversal tendency in Berlucchi and Marzi's experiment which may have acted to produce conflict and prevent perfect veridical transfer.

There have been several experiments on interocular transfer of mirror-image discrimination in the pigeon. Since each eye of the pigeon projects wholly to the optic tectum on the opposite side, interocular transfer can be regarded as equivalent to interhemispheric transfer. Nancy K. Mello has reported several experiments suggesting interocular mirror-image reversal. For example, she taught monocularly viewing pigeons to peck a key displaying an oblique line, then tested for generalization to lines of different orientations with each eye in turn. When the birds viewed with the trained eye, they pecked most to the original line and less as the line was rotated away from the original. But when they were tested with the untrained eye, the generalization gradient was mirror-reversed so that maximum pecking was now to the mirror image of the original line (see Fig. 6.3; Mello, 1965, 1966a).

In another study, Mello (1966b) taught monocularly viewing pigeons various mirror-image discriminations, then tested them with only the untrained eye. There was again evidence of interocular mirror-image reversal for at least some of the discriminations, although for others there was a lack of transfer rather than a reversal. Williams (1971) found consistent interocular mirror-image reversal in discrimination of two-color circles when they were presented as left −right mirror images, but transfer was veridical when they were presented as up−down mirror images.

These results might be taken as evidence for interhemispheric mirror-image reversal caused by homotopic transfer of information from one side of the brain

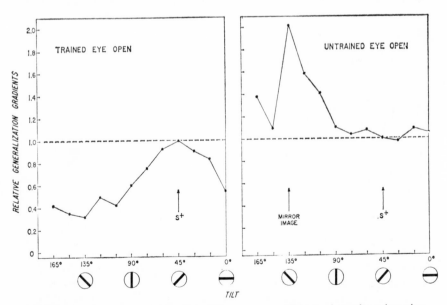

FIGURE 6.3 Relative generalization gradients on a continuum of angular orientation, obtained from pigeons trained monocularly to peck at a 45° oblique line for food reinforcement. Note that the peak for the untrained eye is at 135°. (From Mello, 1965.)

to the other. There is, however, a more plausible explanation similar to that proposed by Hamilton and Tieman to explain interocular mirror-image reversal in the monkey. A pigeon viewing with one eye tends to focus its attention on one side of an object—the right side if viewing with its right eye, the left if viewing with its left eye (Beale & Corballis, 1967). This could explain the reversal since, as we have already remarked, opposite sides of mirror-image stimuli look alike. In one experiment, we found a positive correlation between the degree of interocular mirror-image reversal and the degree to which the pigeons tended to switch their pecking from one side of the display key to the other on transfer tests (Beale & Corballis, 1968). We suggested, therefore, that reversal depended on "beak shift." Later studies have suggested that reversal does not necessarily depend very closely on where a bird actually pecks and whether there is reversal (cf. Beale & Williams, 1971), but they confirm that monocularly viewing pigeons base the discrimination of patterns on cues which are displayed on only one side of the key—the side of the seeing eye. For example, a bird viewing with its right eye might interpret a 45° line across the key as "high" and a 135° line as "low," and we have indeed found that there is almost perfect (intraocular) transfer from the discrimination of mirror-image obliques to the discrimination of a high from a low *horizontal* line (Corballis & Beale, 1970b). Similarly, discrimination of mirror-image circular discs that were red on one side and blue on the other was apparently learned by monocularly viewing pigeons as a simple color discrimination (Clarke & Beale,

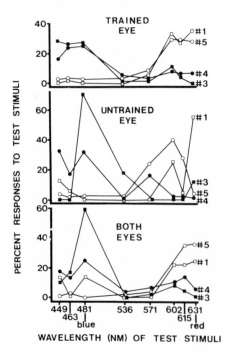

FIGURE 6.4   Percentage of responses to monochromatic stimuli by pigeons previously trained monocularly to peck at a stimulus that was red on the left and blue on the right (positive stimulus) but not at one that was blue on the left and red on the right (negative stimulus;. Pigeons 1 and 5 were trained with the left eye open; Pigeons 3 and 4 were trained with the right eye open. The results illustrate that the discrimination was based lagely on the colors appearing on the stimuli on the side of the pigeon's viewing eye. (From Clarke & Beale, 1972.)

1972; Williams, 1971; see Fig. 6. 4). Such data provide compelling evidence that interocular mirror-image reversal in the pigeon occurs simply because the birds tend to switch attention from one side of a stimulus pattern to the other.

Finally, interocular mirror-image reversal has been demonstrated in the goldfish, which, like the pigeon, has a crossed visual system. Ingle (1967) found reversals in the discrimination of sideward T's (⊣ versus ⊢) and red and green squares (red–green versus green–red), but veridical transfer of the discrimination of mirror-image obliques and mirror-image arrowheads (> versus <). He thought the discrepancy might lie in the different angles subtended by the stimuli rather than in the differences of shape. Campbell (1971) has confirmed that this was so. Using the same stimuli, he found veridical transfer in all cases when the stimuli subtended 5° and in all but one of the six cases when they subtended 10°, but there was interocular mirror-image reversal when the stimuli subtended 15°. As Ingle (1967) recognized, the wider stimuli may have been interpreted by the fish as spanning front to back rather than left to right, since the eye of the goldfish is somewhat laterally placed. This could explain the reversal, since front–back *equivalence* between the eyes represents a left–right *reversal*.

To summarize, experiments designed to test directly whether interhemispheric transfer is accompanied by left–right reversal have produced results which are equivocal, at best. The technique of training one hemisphere, then testing the other, is by nature ambiguous. Because only half of the perceptual world is represented in each half of the brain, restriction of input to one hemisphere necessarily creates a perceptual asymmetry. This asymmetry is left–right reversed when input is switched to the other hemisphere. Consequently, the technique confounds the role of external stimulus asymmetries with that of the internal commissural mechanisms. It is worth noting, in fact, that the monocular animal, when it learns to discriminate stimuli that are left–right mirror images of one another, is not learning a *true* mirror-image discrimination at all, since the fact of having one eye occluded creates a consistent asymmetry. With respect to the animal's midsagittal plane, the mirror image of a stimulus viewed through one eye is the left–right reflection of that stimulus *viewed through the other eye*. The animal that exhibits interocular mirror-image reversal is simply treating mirror images as equivalent; one could say it is confusing them. But we have still gained little information about the mechanisms which underlie this process.

EVIDENCE AGAINST HOMOTOPIC
PERCEPTUAL TRANSFER

Even if the evidence reviewed in the previous section had been less equivocal, there would still be strong grounds for doubting whether Noble's theory could be entirely correct. In particular, it makes little sense to suppose that spatial information is *perceptually* reversed in transfer across the midline. Noble's theory states that the commissures map stimulus input in mirror fashion from the projection areas on one side of the brain to the projection areas on the other side. This implies that an animal should actually *see* an object in the visual field in duplicate, both in its correct location and reflected across the vertical meridian. This is clearly absurd.

The processes of interhemispheric visual transfer must in fact be designed to maintain left – right orientation. An object moving across the visual field is perceived as the *same* object with the same left–right orientation as it crosses the vertical meridian. Matching of simple patterns across the two halves of the visual field is more rapid if they are the same than if they are left–right mirror images (Corballis, Miller, & Morgan, 1971; Corballis & Roldan, 1974). Perception of a centrally fixated object requires integration of information across hemispheres, since each half of the object would be projected to the opposite hemisphere; it makes no sense to suppose that this integration could be accompanied by left – right reversal. In general, the two halves of the visual field are so well integrated that we are not even aware of any discontinuity at the vertical meridian. *Perceptually,* there is never any ambiguity as to which way round things are in the visual field, regardless of the half-field in which they are located.

These observations apply particularly to human perception, but we have little doubt that similar principles apply to animals. For example, Mello (1967) found no evidence for interhemispheric mirror-image reversal in pigeons on a task requiring interocular *perceptual* integration. First, she trained the pigeons binocularly to discriminate crossed oblique lines from parallel ones. Then, using colored filters to keep input to the two eyes separate, she presented a different oblique line to each eye. If interocular integration involved reversal, the pigeons should have interpreted the lines as crossed when they were parallel and parallel when they were crossed But they did not; they evidently saw the crossed lines as crossed and the parallel ones as parallel. This result contrasts with the interocular mirror-image reversal effect discussed in the previous section, which occurs when pigeons are taught a mirror-image discrimination with one eye open and tested with the other eye open. It suggests that reversal is not a perceptual phenomenon.

The anatomic and physiological evidence supports these observations. Some years before Noble wrote on the topic, Sperry (1962) had raised the question of whether the commissures were homotopic or whether they were organized to produce what he called "supplemental complementary"—a left–right equivalence between hemispheres (see Fig. 6. 5). Although he concluded from the anatomic and physiological evidence that many of the commissures were homotopic, he also found evidence to suggest that the commissures linking the visual areas were not. There are more recent data which bear this out. For example, there are single neurons in the occipital cortex of the cat (Berlucchi &

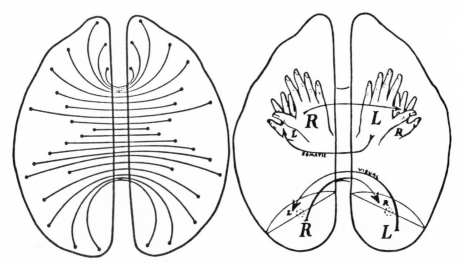

FIGURE 6.5   Two possible interhemispheric connection systems. The one on the left illustrates homotopic connections, the one on the right connections which maintain left–right equivalance, or "supplementary complementarity." (From Sperry, 1962; with the permission of Roger W. Sperry.)

Rizzolatti, 1968) and monkey (Hubel & Wiesel, 1967) which respond selectively to visual stimuli consisting of straight edges in particular orientations which span the vertical meridian of the visual field. Since opposite sides of the meridian are projected to opposite hemispheres, homotopic transfer would imply that the orientations preferred by any given cell ought to be mirror images of one another in the two half-fields. There is no evidence that this is ever so. On the contrary, such cells typically respond maximally when the edge is continuous across the meridian and is thus in the *same* orientation in each half-field. The main functions of the commissures linking the visual cortices in mammals seem to be twofold: first, to maintain the continuity of visual processing across the meridian (Hubel & Wiesel, 1967; Whitteridge, 1965), and second, to mediate depth perception when binocular disparity is such that an object appears in the left visual field of one eye and the right visual field of the other (Blakemore, 1969). Both functions are characterized by "supplemental complementarity" rather than by homotypy.

Noble (1968) had also suggested the inferotemporal cortex, which is presumed to mediate a higher level of visual analysis than the occipital cortex, as a possible site for homotopic transfer. But again the evidence is rather negative. Gross and his colleagues have recorded from many single neurons in the inferotemporal cortex of the monkey, and found some which responded to stimuli extending more than 3° into both visual half-fields (Gross, Bender, & Rocha-Miranda, 1969; Gross, Rocha-Miranda, & Bender, 1972). These cells typically responded preferentially to bars in particular orientations or to stimuli moving in particular directions. With one exception, the preferred orientations and directions of motion for any particular cell were the same for each visual half-field, indicating veridical transfer of left–right information. The exceptional cell responded maximally to opposite directions of lateral motion in the two half-fields (Gross *et al.*, 1969). This was the only cell which might be said to have suffered a mirror-image confusion.

We do not mean to rule out the possibility that homotopic connections between the hemispheres may play some role in perceptual processing. In the next chapter, in fact, we shall argue that homotopic interhemispheric mapping might mediate the perception of vertical symmetry. But we do not believe there is any reversal process which would serve to disrupt the ability to perceive objects in their correct orientations in space. We have argued at length that left –right confusion is not primarily a perceptual problem. For the source of the difficulty, we should look to the higher mental processes which are concerned with the labeling and recognition of patterns rather than with their locations and orientations in perceptual space.

INTERHEMISPHERIC REVERSAL AND MIRROR-IMAGE GENERALIZATION

Between them, Orton and Noble may have provided the ingredients for a plausible theory of mirror-image generalization based on interhemispheric mirror-image reversal. We agree with Orton that the phenomena to be explained have to do with memory rather than with perception, but his account of how the reversal comes about is not logically consistent. Noble, on the other hand, provided a consistent explanation for mirror-image reversal in terms of transfer between the hemispheres, but failed to distinguish memory reversal from perceptual reversal. We suggest, therefore, that there may indeed be a process of homotopic mapping between hemispheres, but that this has nothing to do with the transfer of perceptual input from one hemisphere to the other. Rather, its function would be to "symmetrize" the structural formation of memory traces; to lay down memory traces in both veridical and mirror-image forms so that the organism can then generalize from particular learned experiences to their mirror images (cf. Corballis, 1974; Corballis & Beale, 1970a). We propose, in short, that interhemispheric mirror-image reversal is the mechanism of mirror-image generalization.

It is important to understand that this theory does not depend on the assumption of topographic coding in the brain. Consider again the ideal case of a perfectly symmetrical brain. Suppose too that the formation of memory traces depends on structural changes in the brain. If the processes responsible for establishing structural changes on one side of the brain are mirror reversed on

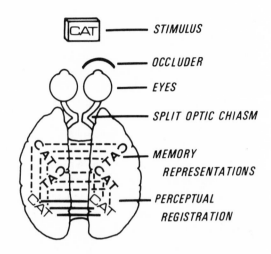

FIGURE 6.6 Schematic representation of a theory in which it is assumed that interhemispheric perceptual transfer (solid lines) is veridical, but that memory transfer (dashed lines) is left–right reversed. To facilitate comparison with Fig. 6.2, the figure is drawn for a preparation with a split optic chiasm and the right eye occluded. (From Corballis, 1974; with the permission of the Canadian Psychological Association.)

the other side, then the brain as a whole would remain structurally symmetrical. As we explained in Chapter 3, it follows that the organism could have no memory for the left–right orientation of the event that led to the structural change. This is so regardless of the nature of the structural change—whether it represents a topographic "copy" of the input or a highly encoded, abstract version of it. The point is simply that interhemispheric mirror-image reversal of the memory processes would act to preserve the structural symmetry of the brain and so serve to generalize the record of events to their left–right mirror images.

The argument applies strictly to the ideal case, of course. In truth, the brain of man, at least, is not perfectly symmetrical and neither are all memories perfectly generalized to their left–right mirror images. Most subhuman animals also appear to be able to learn specific left–right asymmetries, albeit with difficulty, as we saw in Chapter 4. This means that they must either possess some structural asymmetry or else acquire it with asymmetrical experience. But this need not invalidate our general thesis that mirror-image generalization, to the extent that it occurs, is achieved by homotopic mapping between hemispheres. The reversed record may not be so strongly established as the original one; despite the adaptive advantages of mirror-image generalization, we cannot deny that there might also be some benefit in registering the distinction between actual experience and its mirror image.

The experiments described earlier on the interhemispheric transfer of mirror-image discriminations fail to provide critical evidence for our theory. We have already explained how these experiments confound the effects of external stimulus cues with those of the internal transfer mechanisms. They fail, moreover, to distinguish perceptual transfer from the transfer of memory traces. Figure 6.6 schematically depicts the potential consequences of restricting input to one half-field, as in Noble's split-chiasm preparation. As we suggested in the previous section, the transfer of perceptual information from one hemisphere to the other is probably veridical rather than mirror reversed so that both hemispheres are correctly informed about the left–right orientations of events and objects in the world. Consequently, one might expect both hemispheres to establish veridical memory traces. But our hypothesized process of mirror-image generalization would *then* create reversed structural changes across hemispheres, so that *both* hemispheres would record the reversed trace (as well as the veridical one). Clearly, this is a more complex chain of events than Noble envisaged (compare Fig. 6.6 with Fig. 6.2).

In experiments on the transfer of *visual* information from one hemisphere to the other, it may be virtually impossible to separate the effects of perceptual transfer from the effects of memory transfer. Perceptual integration across the visual half-fields appears to be highly efficient and virtually automatic; as we noted earlier, one is not normally even aware of any perceptual discontinuity at the vertical meridian, even though information to either side of it is projected to opposite hemispheres. Presumably, however, there is less ambiguity in experiments on the bilateral transfer of *motor* learning. Milisen and Van Riper (1939) found, in fact, that transfer of training from one hand to the other was more effective if the untrained hand was tested on the mirror image of the skill the trained hand was taught. They taught people to move a stylus rapidly round a slot shaped somewhat like a clover leaf, using their right hands. Half of the group moved the stylus clockwise, the other half counterclockwise. When they were subsequently tested with their left hands, the subjects were reliably better if they moved the stylus in the opposite direction to that required during training. This could be taken as evidence for a left–right reversal in the transfer of motor learning from the left hemisphere to the right.

We may remind the reader, too, of the mirror writer described by Ireland (1881), whom we quoted at the beginning of this chapter. Mirror writing is a widely documented phenomenon and has been discussed in some detail in a classic monograph by Critchley (1928). We shall have more to say about it in Chapter 12, but for the present we may note that mirror writing is commonly associated with injury to the dominant cerebral hemisphere. Again, this is at least consistent with the proposition that motor habits established primarily in one hemisphere tend to be mirror reversed in the other.

The transfer technique is not the only method for testing our hypothesis of interhemispheric mirror-image reversal. An alternative is to compare normal with split-brained animals on their ability to tell left from right. For if the commissures are indeed involved in the "symmetrization" of memory traces, then the split-brained preparation should neither suffer mirror-image confusion nor enjoy mirror-image generalization. We described two relevant experiments in Chapter 4. One was the study reported by Pavlov (1927) in which it was found impossible to teach an intact dog to discriminate mirror-image touches, but trivially easy to teach a split-brained dog to do so. The other was the experiment on mirror-image generalization, reported by Beale *et al.* (1972). Normal pigeons showed generalization from a particular line tilt to its mirror image, but split-brained birds did not.

Even this last result fails to prove conclusively that the commissures produce interhemispheric reversal of memory. As Hamilton and Tieman (1973) again point out, it can be explained in terms of stimulus control. The eyes of the pigeon are somewhat laterally placed so that the visual field of each extends only about 12° past the beak. Moreover, each eye projects only to the opposite optic tectum. In the split-brained bird, therefore, each hemisphere might "attend" only to cues on one side of the stimulus pattern. In learning to respond to an oblique line, one hemisphere might register simply that it is in the upper quadrant, while the other registers simultaneously that it is in the lower quadrant. Since the hemispheres are disconnected there would be no confusion. The generalization gradients might therefore represent stimulus control along an up–down dimension rather than along an angular one, which could explain why they differ from those obtained with normal birds.

In the final analysis, behavioral experiments have so far failed to provide unequivocal support for the hypothesis of interhemispheric mirror-image reversal. Although more exacting experiments are certainly possible, it is perhaps doubtful that the hypothesis can ever be verified by experiments of the type we have discussed. These experiments are a considerable inferential step away from the hypothesis, which is ultimately neural rather than behavioral. Even so, we think there are excellent reasons for retaining the hypothesis, at least as a heuristic, for it expresses concisely what we have maintained to be the essence of the left–right problem. The hypothesis stresses that the problem is one of memory rather than one of perception. It relates the problem explicitly to the structural symmetry of the nervous system. It emphasizes that mirror-image generalization need not involve a loss of other kinds of spatial information—we may remember virtually everything about Whistler's portrait of his mother except the direction of her profile. Finally, homotopic transfer would be a logical and natural way for the brain to accomplish mirror-image generalization, the more so given that homotopic connections are thought to exist. We can think of no more simple way the brain *could* generalize memories to their mirror images.

7

The Perception of Symmetry

Symmetry is a human concept, because
with all our irregularities we are more or
less symmetrical and the balance of a
mantlepiece by Adam or a phrase by
Mozart reflects our satisfaction with our
two eyes, two arms and two legs.

—*Civilisation: A Personal View*
KENNETH CLARK

From ancient times, men have used symmetry, particularly left – right symmetry, as an organizing principle in painting, sculpture, architecture, and
design. Figure 7. 1 shows, for example, a design segment from the silver vase
of King Entemena (c. 2700 B.C.). Notice that the bilateral symmetry of the
lion-headed eagle which dominates the segment is carried through the rest of
the design so that the other animals are duplicated in mirror-image profiles.
Weyl (1952) observes that it was not much later in the history of design that the
eagle was itself given two heads, each facing in opposite directions. The
two-headed eagle can be traced through Persian, Syrian, and Byzantine
cultures, and appeared in the coats-of-arms of Czarist Russia and the Austro-
Hungarian Empire right up to modern times. It is a striking illustration of the
way in which the principle of symmetry can so dominate a design as to distort
reality.

Experiments on aesthetic preferences among meaningless shapes indicate
that most people judge symmetrical shapes to be more interesting and pleasing
than asymmetrical ones (e.g., Day, 1967, 1968; Eisenman, 1967), although the
reverse may be true of artists or of people who are deemed to be more than
usually creative (Barron, 1958, 1965). Moreover, few works of art are
perfectly symmetrical, although there is often a rough symmetry which lends
coherence or balance to a work. Weyl (1952) remarks that " . . . seldom is
asymmetry merely the absence of symmetry. Even in asymmetric designs one

74

FIGURE 7.1   Design segment from the silver vase of Entemena (c. 2700 B.C.), illustrating left–right symmetry. (Photograph courtesy of le Secretariat d' État à la Culture,
Museé de Louvre, Paris.)

feels symmetry as the norm from which one deviates under the influence of
forces of a non-formal character [p. 13]." Later (p. 16), he translates from
Dagobert Frey: "Symmetry signifies rest and binding, asymmetry motion and
loosening, the one law and order, the other arbitrariness and accident, the one
formal rigidity and constraint, the other life, play and freedom [Frey, 1949,
p. 276]."

Whether or not we find symmetry to be pleasing, however, we seldom fail to
notice that a pattern is symmetrical, especially if it is symmetrical about a

vertical axis. One possible reason for this is that we have learned to attach importance to symmetry because it is so common a feature of the everyday world. Objects which are symmetrical, or nearly so, include chairs, lamps, bottles, cars, airplanes, trees, animals, and people. Alternatively, one might argue that sensitivity to left–right symmetry is a product of evolution rather than of learning and, more particularly, that it can be attributed in some way to the bilateral symmetry of the nervous system.

Although the perceptual salience of symmetry need not depend exclusively on either learning or on evolution, we shall attempt to argue the case for the bilateral symmetry theory. This, of course, is in keeping with our general theme. Once again, we turn first to the pioneering observations of Ernst Mach.

MACH'S VIEWS

Mach made much of the observation that vertical (or left–right) symmetry is more salient than horizontal (or up–down) symmetry:

> The vertical symmetry of a Gothic cathedral strikes us at once, whereas we can travel up and down the whole length of the Rhine or Hudson without becoming aware of the symmetry between objects and their reflexions in the water. Vertical symmetry pleases us, whilst horizontal symmetry is indifferent, and is noticed only by the experienced eye [Mach, 1898, p. 94].

Perhaps to show that the phenomenon is not simply a product of specific learning, he also made the point by drawing attention to the impressions induced by various systematic juxtapositions of a meaningless shape (Mach, 1897). These are reproduced in Fig. 7.2. Mach noted that repetition of the pattern produces an "agreeable" impression which is lost if one pattern is rotated 90° relative to another. But if the pattern is mirrored about the vertical the affinity between the forms is again strikingly apparent. Symmetry about the horizontal is not so obvious. Finally, Mach observed that the affinity is again apparent if one pattern is rotated through 180° in the same plane to produce so-called centric symmetry. These arrangements are all shown in Fig. 7. 2, so the reader can compare his own impressions with Mach's.

As we saw from the quotation in Chapter 1, Mach thought that the perceptual salience of left–right symmetry was related to the confusion of left and right, and that both arose as a consequence of the bilateral symmetry of the visual system. Symmetrical innervation of a symmetrical apparatus, he maintained, would produce an effect much like that of repetition. Thus, after discussing the sensation induced by a left–right repetition of a pattern, he wrote:

> In a figure symmetrical with respect to the median plane, *similar* space-sensations corresponding to the symmetrical directions take the place of *identical* space-sensations. The right half of the figure stands in the same relation to the right

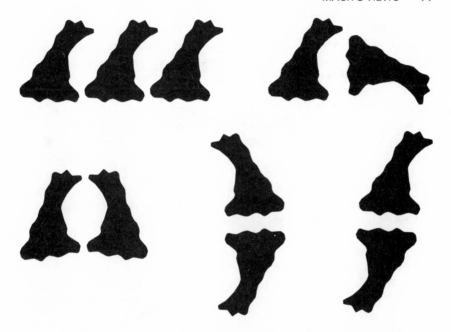

FIGURE 7.2   Various juxtapositions of a meaningless shape to illustrate repetition (top left), 90°
rotation of one relative to another (top right), left–right or vertical symmetry (bottom left), up–
down or horizontal symmetry (bottom center), and centric symmetry (bottom right). (From Julesz,
1969; after Mach, 1897; with the permission of the Bell Telephone Laboratories Inc., New Jersey,
and Bela Julesz.)

half of the visual apparatus as the left half of the figure does to the left half of the
visual apparatus [Mach, 1897, p. 53].

This account is not altogether satisfactory. For one thing, it is not likely that
the salience of symmetry is so closely related to the confusion of mirror images
as Mach suggested. If an observer were actually confused about which way
round each half of the pattern was, then he should confuse symmetry with
repetition, or at least perceive them as similar. Yet symmetrical patterns need
not look particularly like repeated ones (see Fig. 7. 2, for example). In any
case, we have already argued that the confusion of mirror images is not so
much a problem of perception as it is one of labeling. By contrast, the salience
of vertical symmetry appears to be an immediate, holistic perceptual experience.

"Symmetry," wrote Pascal in his celebrated *Pensées,* "is what you see at a
glance,"[1] and there are some recent experimental observations which bear him

[1]Translation from H. F. Stewart, *Pascal's Pensées.* London: Routledge & Kegan Paul,
Ltd., 1950, p. 491.

out. For example, Locher and Nodine (1973) recorded the eye movements of subjects while they rated the complexity of various nonrepresentational shapes and found that when the shapes were vertically symmetrical the subjects typically scanned only one side of them. They evidently knew before they began to scan the shapes that they were symmetrical and so did not have to scan both sides. Perception of symmetry must therefore be fairly immediate: we may know that a shape is symmetrical before we know what else it is.

The same conclusion is suggested by other studies in which subjects were required to respond to symmetrical displays. Fitts, Weinstein, Rappaport, Anderson, and Leonard (1956) found people to be faster at recognizing left–right symmetrical patterns than either left–right repeated ones or up–down symmetrical ones. Similarly, Deregowski (1971) reported that children were better able to recall left–right symmetrical patterns than left–right repeated ones. However, some of our own work suggests that the advantage of symmetry over repetition depends on how the subjects interpret the displays. For example, Corballis, Miller, and Morgan (1971) found that subjects were faster at deciding when two left- or right-pointing arrowheads were pointing in the same direction than when they were pointing in opposite directions; here, the advantage lay with the repeated arrangement, not the symmetrical one. In a later study, Corballis and Roldan (1974) showed that the relative speeds of detecting symmetry and repetition could be influenced by instructions and by the spatial separation of the patterns. When the stimuli were pairs of arrowheads or simple C shapes, the subjects were faster at judging each pair to be the same than at judging them to be mirror images; however, when they were required to judge each configuration as a whole to be either symmetrical or asymmetrical (or repeated), the advantage lay with the symmetrical arrangements. With more complex dot patterns instructions had no such effect, but the spatial separation of the two halves of the patterns proved to be critical. When the two halves were close together so as to encourage unitary perception, symmetry was detected more rapidly than repetition. The advantage of symmetry was lost, however, when the two halves of the pattern were distinctly separated. These results suggest that symmetry is most salient when the pattern is perceived holistically, and less so when it is perceived as two distinct half patterns. Perceptually, the impression of symmetry is not so much an awareness of the relation between the two halves of the pattern, as Mach seemed to imply; rather, it is an immediate awareness of the symmetry in the pattern as a whole.

Another difficulty with Mach's analysis is that it seems to demand that, if one is to perceive the symmetry of a figure, its axis of symmetry must be perfectly aligned with the meridian plane of the observer. Yet we can perceive symmetry without central fixation or when the axis of symmetry departs from the vertical. For example, Corballis and Roldan (1974) found that the relative speeds of detecting symmetry and repetition were little affected if the patterns

were presented unilaterally rather than bilaterally. And Mach himself acknowledged that we *can* perceive horizontal symmetry, even though it is less salient
than vertical symmetry (Mach, 1897). Such observations pose a problem for
Mach's theorizing, and we shall have more to say on this issue later in the
chapter. As we shall see, it was again Mach himself who hinted at a possible
solution.

Mach raised one further difficulty for his theory:

> The presence of a sense for symmetry in people possessing only one eye from
> birth, is indeed a riddle. Of course, the sense of symmetry, although primarily
> acquired by means of the eyes, cannot be wholly limited to the visual organs. It
> must also be deeply rooted in other parts of the organism by ages of practice and
> can thus not be eliminated forthwith by the loss of one eye.[2] Also when an eye is
> lost, the symmetrical muscular apparatus is left, as is also the symmetrical
> apparatus of innervation [Mach, 1898, p. 99; footnote inserted].

The last phrase contains the key to the riddle, since it is the visual *fields* rather
than the eyes which are mapped symmetrically in two halves of the brain; the
left field is projected to the right visual cortex and the right field to the left
visual cortex regardless of which eye is viewing. Mach has surely overem-
phasized the importance of the symmetry of the two eyes and has insufficiently
stressed the importance of the symmetry of the brain.

MACH'S THEORY MODIFIED: JULESZ'S THEORY

Let us now look more closely at Mach's suggestion that the salience of left–
right symmetry arises as a consequence of the symmetry of the visual system
and is but an example of the confusion of left–right mirror images. It is true, as
we showed in Chapter 3, that a perfectly symmetrical system would be unable
to discriminate mirror images. However, the logic of that argument does not
apply in any obvious way to the perception of symmetrical patterns. Mach
argued, in effect, that a symmetrical system would treat left–right symmetry as
equivalent to repetition, but there is no compelling reason, based on symmetry
per se, why this should be so. One could easily construct a symmetrical device
which would respond differently to symmetrical and repeated patterns. We
have already noted that symmetry bears no striking resemblance to repetition;
one would be unlikely to confuse them.

However, there is some recent evidence which nonetheless lends support to
Mach's idea that the perception of symmetry may depend on the structural
symmetry of the visual system. This evidence comes from the work of Julesz

---

[2]There is an interesting inconsistency here. Mach began by raising the problem of
people missing an eye *from birth*, but then, to ease the burden of explanation,
conveniently discusses the potential consequences of *losing* an eye.

FIGURE 7.3 Random-dot patterns illustrating up–down symmetry (left) and left–right symmetry (right). (From Julesz, 1969; with the permission of Bela Julesz.)

(1971) on the perception of complex line and dot patterns. Examples are shown in Fig. 7.3. These patterns are generated by computer to exhibit certain regularities, including symmetry or repetition about an axis, but they are otherwise random and without coherent shape or form. Repetition about an axis is difficult to detect, as is symmetry about the horizontal axis. Left – right symmetry is much more salient and can in fact be detected even when exposure is as brief as 40 msec. However, one cannot discern left–right symmetry if one fixates away from the axis of symmetry, or if one half of the pattern is dilated relative to the other; that is, the perception of left – right symmetry seems to require projection that is symmetrical with respect to the center of the fovea.

These observations suggested to Julesz that the symmetry of these patterns, which are characterized by "high spatial resolution," is perceived by means of point-by-point comparison process in a brain area that is itself organized symmetrically with respect to the fovea. However, he noted that one can readily detect symmetry in simple shapes, like those of Fig. 7. 2, without central fixation. In the case of patterns with "low spatial frequencies," therefore, he proposed that the perception of symmetry must depend on some different, perhaps more cognitive, mechanism. Later on, we shall question whether it is really necessary to postulate separate processes for the perception of symmetry in the two cases. But, for complex patterns at least, we may note that Julesz's theory of the perception of symmetry is essentially an extension of Mach's. The component that was missing from Mach's theory was the comparison process, which is necessary for the integration of information between the two halves of the figure.

Since opposite halves of a left–right symmetrical pattern, fixated centrally, would project to opposite sides of the brain, one must infer that the "point-by-point comparison process" envisaged by Julesz involves homotopic comparisons between symmetrically opposite points in the brain. In support of this, Julesz cites an observation by Brindley and Lewin (1968). These authors were able to evoke visual phosphenes in a blind woman by directly stimulating her visual cortex. When unilateral stimulation exceeded a certain level, the woman reported seeing a new phosphene at a point in her visual field symmetrically located with respect to an earlier phosphene. This implies a homotopic transmission between mirror-image regions of the brain.

In the previous chapter, however, while discussing Noble's theory of interhemispheric mirror-image reversal, we concluded that the neurophysiological evidence was mostly contrary to the notion of homotopic transfer between the visual (that is, occipital and inferotemporal) areas of the cortex, at least in cat and monkey. Rather, the commissures in these areas seemed to be organized so as to preserve left–right orientation in the transmission of spatial information between hemispheres. In animals with frontal vision, this is what one would expect, since there must be continuity and left – right equivalence between the two half-fields. But this may not be true of animals with nonoverlapping visual fields. In certain birds and fish, for example, the eyes are laterally placed and movement across the field of an eye would be interpreted as movement in front–back plane. Now, front–back equivalence between the two visual fields would demand a left–right *reversal*. For example, back-to-front movement across the left visual field would be left-to-right movement, but across the right visual field it would be right-to-left movement. Moreover, front–back equivalence would be mediated by homotopic mapping across the midline. Julesz suggests that it may be the residual of this homotopic mapping which explains the perception of symmetry even in higher mammals, including man: "Perhaps," he writes, "it is the remainder of the back–front movement symmetries that animals with nonoverlapping visual fields experience [Julesz, 1971, p. 133]."

If the mechanism underlying the perception of symmetry is indeed as primitive as Julesz believes, it is reasonable to suppose it may even be mediated subcortically rather than via the corpus callosum. Observations of human patients with section of the corpus callosum lend support to this possibility. For example, Trevarthen (1970) has observed that these patients tend to interpret diagonal lines in each visual half-field as being "in line" when they in fact form a V-shaped configuration, symmetrical about the vertical meridian. They are more sensitive to symmetry about the meridian than to contiguity or alignment across it. Similar observations have been reported by Trevarthen and Sperry (1973). Levy, Trevarthen, and Sperry (1972) have also reported striking evidence that commissurotomized patients accomplish a mirror-image completion of half-pictures of familiar symmetrical objects presented in a single half-field. For instance, a composite stimulus consisting of half a bee in the left field and half a rose in the right is "interpreted" by the right cerebral hemisphere as a *whole* bee and by the left hemisphere as a *whole* rose.

In summary, then, it appears that there may be at least two different kinds of neural mapping involved in perceptual integration across the vertical meridian. One is a process which preserves left–right orientation and which serves to maintain perceptual continuity across the visual field. The other is a more primitive, possibly subcortical process which involves homotopic mapping and which enables us to rapidly detect left–right symmetry.

PERCEPTION OF SYMMETRY AS A
FUNCTION OF ORIENTATION

The question that remains is whether it is really necessary to suppose, as Julesz (1971) did, that there are two mechanisms for the detection of symmetry—one relatively primitive mechanism that involves homotopic mapping and demands that the stimulus be aligned exactly with the symmetry of the nervous system itself, and a higher-level, more cognitive mechanism that can detect symmetry regardless of the orientation or location of the stimulus in the receptive field. We shall focus the discussion on the role of orientation in the detection and perception of symmetry.

As described above, the case for the more primitive mechanism rests on Julesz's observations concerning the perception of symmetry in his complex, computer-generated patterns. These observations seem to suggest that symmetry is readily detected only when the axis of symmetry of the pattern is aligned with the vertical meridian of the eye. We may contrast this conclusion with that reached by Rock and Leaman (1963) in their experiments on the perception of symmetry. These authors adapted a technique developed originally by Goldmeier (1936, 1972). Observers would be shown a shape that was symmetrical about both the horizontal and the vertical and asked to compare it with two modified versions, one symmetrical about the horizontal only and the other symmetrical about the vertical only. They overwhelmingly chose the vertically symmetrical shape as the more similar to the doubly symmetrical one, which is further testimony to the salience of left – right over up – down symmetry (see Fig. 7.4). However, the advantage of vertical symmetry applied not to the *retinal* vertical, but rather to the *phenomenal* or *perceptual* vertical. For example, when the observers tilted their heads through 45°, patterns symmetrical with respect to the true, gravitational vertical were still seen as more salient than those that were symmetrical with respect to the true horizontal, even though both were equally inclined with respect to the retinal vertical. Similarly, if the shapes were tilted through 45° and the observers were asked to imagine them as upright, the advantage lay with the shapes that were imagined as vertically symmetrical, although again both axes of symmetry were equally inclined on the retina.

On the basis of these results, Rock and Leaman argued that the salience of left–right symmetry cannot depend in any simple way on the anatomic symmetry of the nervous system. They proposed instead that it simply reflects the influence of the environment:

> Symmetry about a vertical axis is widespread in the sphere of animal and plant life. It is also common in man-made objects. These facts about the environment are compatible with a theory that we learn to become sensitized to vertical symmetry or with a theory that such sensitization has come about through biological evolution [Rock & Leaman, 1963, p. 182].

Rock and Leaman's observations need not contradict Julesz's theory, however, since the patterns studied by Rock and Leaman were relatively simple and amorphous, whereas Julesz's notion of a strict topographic mapping process was applied only to patterns with high spatial frequencies.

Yet Rock and Leaman's results need not rule out the possibility that the perception of symmetry, even in simple patterns, may depend on fixed homotopic mapping somewhere in the brain. We need only suppose that there

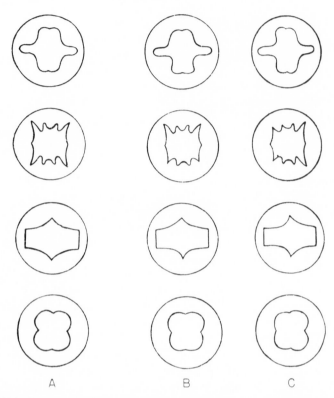

FIGURE 7.4   Four sets of patterns illustrating Goldmeier technique. The patterns labeled A are symmetrical about both the vertical and the horizontal axis; those labeled B are symmetrical about the vertical only; those labeled C are symmetrical about the horizontal only. Subjects choose which of B and C is most like A. (From Rock & Leaman, 1963; with the permission of the North-Holland Publishing Company and Irvin Rock.)

are analog processes of rotation, and perhaps of translation, dilation, and so on, that serve to compensate for such factors as head tilt, eccentric eye fixation, and so on, and might allow a subject to bring some internal representation of a symmetrical pattern into alignment with the symmetry of the brain. As we saw in Chapter 5, the work of Shepard and his colleagues has indeed shown that subjects can perform rigid mental rotations of simple two- and three-dimensional rectangular figures, and of familiar symbols such as letters and digits. Moreover, Cooper and Shepard (1973) have argued explicitly that the physical representation of a mentally rotated pattern is, at some level in the brain, identical to that of the same pattern *actually* rotated. Consequently, one might suppose that the physiological representation of a symmetrical pattern could be aligned with the symmetry of the brain even if the pattern is not projected symmetrically onto the retina.

This possibility was anticipated by Mach. Discussing how it is that we can detect horizontal symmetry, he wrote that, in this case, "the affinity of form is recognizable only by turning the figure round or by an *intellectual* act [Mach, 1897, p. 46; his italics]." This actually makes little sense in the context of Mach's own theoretical discussion, since the mechanisms he postulated were too peripheral to be preceded by processes of mental rotation, but the idea becomes plausible enough if we suppose that the detection of symmetry is central rather than peripheral. And we see no essential contradiction between supposing that the detection of symmetry is at once central to the various analog processes that serve to adjust for head tilt and to create imagined changes in orientation, but at the same time depends on fairly primitive, possibly subcortical mapping between hemispheres.

In order to pursue the idea that the detection of symmetry may depend on analog rotations of the input, Corballis and Roldan (1975) have investigated the time it takes to detect symmetry as a function both of the orientation of the pattern and the tilt of the subject's head. Examples of the patterns they used are shown in Fig. 7.5. Note that the axis is clearly marked with a line and the pattern is either mirrored about the line or repeated across it. The center panel of Fig. 7.6 shows the typical result that is obtained with the head upright; the time taken to judge a pattern either symmetrical or not increases as the axis departs from the vertical. Thus, decision time is fastest for vertical symmetry, slowest for horizontal symmetry, and intermediate when the axis is oblique. This result is consistent with the idea that the subjects mentally rotated the

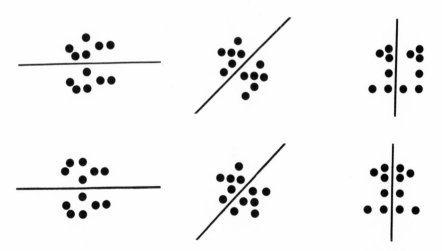

FIGURE 7.5   Examples of symmetrical and repeated patterns in an experiment by Corballis and Roldan. The patterns shown here as photographic negatives of originals. (From Corballis & Roldan, 1975. Copyright 1975 by the American Psychological Association. Reprinted by permission.)

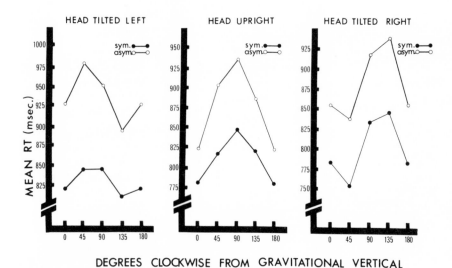

DEGREES CLOCKWISE FROM GRAVITATIONAL VERTICAL

FIGURE 7.6   Mean reaction time to judge patterns symmetrical or not, as a function of the angular oriéntation of the axis, shown separately for head tilted left (left), head upright (center), and head tilted right (right). (From Corballis & Roldan, 1975. Copyright 1975 by the American Psychological Association. Reprinted by permission.)

patterns to the vertical before judging their symmetry, although it does not, of course, prove it.

Goldmeier (1972) has written that "geometric symmetry is *preferentially realized* with a vertical orientation of the axis of symmetry; second in effectiveness is a horizontal orientation; and least effective are oblique axes [p. 90; his italics]." The results of Corballis and Roldan contradict this assertion, at least insofar as symmetry about the obliques was detected more rapidly than symmetry about the horizontal. Goldmeier reached his conclusion on the basis of certain perceived similarities among square- and diamond-like shapes subjected to slight asymmetric distortions. These similarities may have been influenced by the familiarity of the shapes. More likely, however, the discrepancy between his observations and those of Corballis and Roldan have to do with the salience of the axis of symmetry. As Fig. 7.5 illustrates, the axis was clearly indicated in the patterns Corballis and Roldan presented to their subjects. But in the absence of any information as to where the axis of symmetry might lie, an observer might well be expected to look for symmetry about the horizontal and vertical before seeking an oblique axis. Thus Goldmeier notes that a square is more likely to be spontaneously perceived as symmetrical about the vertical or horizontal than about a 45° oblique. But if an oblique were to be actually drawn in, the symmetry about it would then be obvious.

The effect of head tilt on the orientation function in the Corballis and Roldan experiment is shown in the left and right panels of Fig. 7.5. The observers' heads were tilted 45° to the left (counterclockwise) and right (clockwise), respectively. The orientation functions have clearly been shifted in the direction of the head tilt, indicating that the effect of orientation on the detection of symmetry is more nearly constant when measured on retinal than on gravitational coordinates. It is important to note that this is counter to the evidence of Rock and Leaman (1963), who found that when observers tilted their heads the salience of vertical over horizontal symmetry was tied to gravitational rather than retinal coordinates. The discrepancy probably has to do with the nature of the correction for head tilt and the speed with which the subjects performed their tasks. In Rock and Leaman's experiment there was no premium on speed, and the subjects almost certainly made their judgments after correcting their perceptual coordinates to compensate for head tilt. As we saw in Chapter 5, Rock himself has suggested that compensation for head tilt cannot begin until there is a retinal image to correct, so that the first fleeting impression of a figure is framed in retinal rather than gravitational coordinates (Rock, 1973). In Corballis and Roldan's experiment, therefore, where the subjects had to respond as quickly as possible, the reference frame would still have been primarily retinal, although it is possible to detect in Fig. 7.5 a slight lean in the direction of gravitational axes (see Corballis & Roldan, 1975).

We have suggested, then, that the perception of symmetry may indeed depend on a representation that is at some level isomorphic with the vertical symmetry of the brain itself. With fairly simple patterns, this may be achieved by mental rotation, and possibly by comparable processes of mental translation, or of dilation of one half of a pattern relative to the other, or of even more complex elastic transformations. With complex patterns, however, these mental operations may be impossible, or at least severely restricted. For example, Rock's (1973) observation that we cannot recognize familiar faces or cursive script upside down implies that these patterns are too complex for mental rotation. Julesz (1971) may therefore have been mistaken in supposing that different principles underlie the detection of symmetry in complex and simple patterns. The difference may lie instead in the relative ease with which we can mentally transform them. In particular, Julesz's patterns are so complex and formless that they must surely defy even the most elementary of mental transformations.

Finally, it is worth repeating that mental rotation to the vertical or upright position appears to be necessary both for the perception of symmetry and (as we saw in Chapter 5) for the discrimination of letters and digits from their mirror images. To this extent, at least, Mach may have been correct in identifying the two problems and in relating both to the symmetry of the visual system. Symmetry and left – right orientation are both egocentric concepts fundamentally linked to our own body coordinates and perhaps to the homotopic connections which project mirrorwise between the two halves of the brain.

CONCLUSION

In summary, we have been able to sustain the argument, originated by Mach and pursued by Julesz, that the perception of symmetry depends ultimately on the structural symmetry of some projection area in the brain. It does not necessarily follow, of course, that the mechanisms involved are wholly "built in," or are unaffected by learning. We are surrounded by symmetries in the everyday world, so it is likely that our knowledge and understanding of symmetry is at least partly conditioned by experience. Even so, it is of interest to speculate as to the contingencies which might have favored the evolution of mechanisms for detecting symmetry. Perhaps, as Julesz (1971) suggests, the symmetrical structure of the brain, together with homotopic mapping between symmetrical points, might have evolved for quite different reasons, and sensitivity to symmetrical stimulation is simply a by-product. But there is also the possibility that the ability to detect symmetry serves its own adaptive function. The frontal aspect of other faces or bodies is more or less symmetrical, so that awareness of symmetry might alert an animal to the possibility that it is being approached or watched. A preexisting sensitivity to symmetry might also facilitate the process whereby animals and men learn to characterize the facial and bodily characteristics of others. Finally, a primitive awareness of symmetry might play a useful role in directing the eye to the center of a pattern. This might be accomplished by a preattentive mechanism which seeks to maximize the symmetry of excitation.

We shall leave the last word to Pascal, by completing the quotation we made earlier. Symmetry, he said, "is founded on the fact that there is no reason for any difference, and likewise on the shape of the human face. Whence it comes that we do not ask for symmetry in height or depth, but only in breadth."

8

The Evolution of Symmetry and Asymmetry

Tiger! Tiger! burning bright
In the forests of the night,
What immortal hand or eye
Could frame thy fearful symmetry?

—*The Tiger*
WILLIAM BLAKE

Thus far in this book, we have emphasized the psychological consequences of structural bilateral symmetry. In later chapters, our emphasis shifts more to the implications of asymmetry rather than symmetry. This is an appropriate point, therefore, to examine the nature of symmetries and asymmetries themselves. In this chapter, we do so from a somewhat speculative, evolutionary point of view, emphasizing the potential importance of symmetry and asymmetry for survival and adaptation to the environment. We discuss the more specific biological mechanisms governing symmetry and asymmetry in the following chapter.

To the psychologist, and indeed to the casual eye, living animals seem to be characterized by symmetry rather than asymmetry. Asymmetries are commonly seen as the exception rather than the rule, of interest primarily because they seem to distinguish man from the lower animals. A. R. Luria expresses what is probably a typical neuropsychological perspective when he writes as follows of the evolution of the human brain:

> With the appearance of *right-handedness* . . . , and later with the appearance of another related process, namely *speech*, some degree of *lateralization of function* begins to take place, which has not been found in animals but which in man has been an important principle of the functional organization of the brain [Luria, 1973, p. 77; his italics].

Luria is not quite correct when he asserts that lateralization of function does not occur in animals; as we shall later see, animals have been shown to display both paw preferences and some degree of cerebral lateralization of function. There may be less of a discontinuity between man and the lower animals than Luria seems to imply. Nevertheless it is probably fair to say that these functional asymmetries reach full and significant expression only in man and that from a neuropsychological viewpoint most animals are characterized by symmetry rather than by asymmetry.

From a broader biological perspective, however, asymmetry appears to be the rule rather than the exception. Early in the nineteenth century, Louis Pasteur discovered that the molecules of living matter possess a fundamental asymmetry, or "handedness" (Dubos, 1960). Indeed, Pasteur thought it was precisely this quality which most clearly distinguished the organic from the inorganic. In a much more recent discussion of the role of symmetry in biological systems, the biologist J. Monod is contemptuous of the apparent symmetry which seems to pervade animal life:

> The truth of course is that these morphological, macroscopic symmetries are superficial, and do not reflect the fundamental order *within* living things. I am not even referring now to the fact that we possess only one heart, on one side, and a single liver, on the other, although this is enough to show that our outwardly "bilateral" appearance is something of a fake. I am referring to the microscopic structures which are responsible . . . for all the properties of living things, namely proteins and nucleic acids [Monod, 1969, pp. 16–17].

Even gross anatomic asymmetries are to be found in species of all levels. Gardner (1967) reminds us of such creatures as the hermit crab with one large and one small pincer; the anableps, a fish with its sex organs on the side of the body; and of various asymmetrical helical structures among shellfish and climbing plants. Aside from the lateral displacements of the heart and stomach, the human body exhibits several more subtle asymmetries. The right arm is generally a little longer than the left, but the bones of the left leg are slightly longer than those of the right (Ingelmark, 1947). It has often been observed that the two halves of the face are not mirror images (e.g., Wolff, 1933); moreover, the right half is usually said to look more "like" the person's face than the left half, an asymmetry which lies as much in the observer as in the observed (Gilbert & Bakan, 1973). Von Bonin (1962, p. 1) goes so far as to remark that "asymmetries of paired organs are the rule, rather than the exception, in the human body," although he also admits (p. 6) that the differences are usually small.

The point is that symmetry per se is not a fundamental biological principle, and there is no a priori reason to expect it. Rather, symmetry is an evolutionary adaptation to an environment which is itself without systematic left–right bias. Asymmetries readily evolve in structures which are not directly influenced by the external environment. The survival value of symmetry thus applies particularly to those structures which are concerned with perception of the world and movement through it, and with the internal representation of these functions. Let us elaborate.

THE EVOLUTION OF SYMMETRY

Broadly speaking, the bodies and nervous systems of animals have evolved from spherical symmetry to radial symmetry to bilateral symmetry. Hermann Weyl, in the first of his series of lectures on symmetry, gave a succinct and lucid account of how this progression was shaped by environmental influences (Weyl, 1952). The lowest forms of animals, he noted, were small creatures suspended in water where stimulation could impinge from any direction. These creatures were therefore more or less spherical. For forms fixed at the bottom of the ocean, however, gravity would have provided a consistent directional influence, narrowing the set of symmetrical influences to those about the vertical axis. These creatures were radially symmetrical. Animals capable of propelling themselves, whether through water, air, or on land, created for themselves another consistent directional influence along the direction of motion itself. Hence the anteroposterior axis was added to the dorsoventral one to define a midsagittal plane and the environmental influences were then indifferent only with respect to left and right. The freely moving animal is therefore characterized by bilateral symmetry. Weyl writes:

> Factors in the phylogenetic evolution that tend to introduce inheritable differences between left and right are likely to be held in check by the advantage an animal derives from the bilateral formation of its organs of motion, cilia or muscles and limbs: in case of their asymmetric development a screw-wise instead of a straightforward motion would naturally result. This may help to explain why our limbs obey the laws of symmetry more strictly than our inner organs [Weyl, 1952, p. 27].

Most forms of locomotion—legs for walking, fins or flippers for swimming, wings for flying — are indeed characterized by bilateral symmetry, although there are rare exceptions such as the sideways crawl of the crab or the asymmetrical gallop of the horse. Gardner (1967) also comments that different species have independently evolved the same basic locomotory mechanisms; for example, birds, reptiles, insects, mammals, and even a species of fish have all evolved wings. Gardner points out, too, that the advantages of bilateral symmetry are not confined to motor systems, but apply equally to the sensory apparatus, especially in a world where there are unlikely to be systematic biases in the stimuli impinging on one or other side. "The slightest loss of symmetry, such as the loss of a right eye," he writes, "would have immediate negative value for the survival of any animal. An enemy could sneak up unobserved on the right [Gardner, 1967, p. 70]!"

Given the advantages of possessing motor apparatus and sensory organs that are bilaterally symmetrical, it is not surprising that the associated neural structures should also be symmetrical. This applies not only to the peripheral nervous system, but also to the central nervous system and brain. Young (1962) notes that sensory and motor representation in the brain is to a large extent topographic or maplike. As one would expect, these internal maps reflect the symmetry of the external structures they represent—namely, the musculature, the body surface, and the visual and auditory fields. The primary sensory and motor areas of the mammalian cortex are located in corresponding regions on either side of the brain and appear to be organized in mirror-image fashion across the midsagittal plane.

Young also points out, however, that representation in the brains of higher organisms is to some extent "abstract" rather than topographic. Abstract representation is presumably more appropriate when the emphasis is on rapid or complex computation, such as sequential planning or prediction. For example, language is surely represented in an abstract rather than a topographic fashion. Even spatial information may be for certain purposes better represented as a set of coordinates or descriptions than as a topographic map, especially for pattern recognition or for the extraction of higher-order perceptual constancies. Thus, Pylyshyn (1973) is severely critical of what he calls the "picture metaphor" of mental imagery, arguing that images must be coded abstractly as sets of descriptions rather than literal pictures. Yet the work of Shepard and his colleagues, which we have already discussed in detail in Chapter 5, suggests that there is also, at some level, a fairly close isomorphism between an image and its external form. We suspect that spatial images are indeed stored in an abstract way but can be internally generated or "displayed" in a topographic fashion, just as a television signal can be decoded and displayed spatially on the screen. The brain may therefore make use of both kinds of representation, abstract and topographic, as alternative ways of coding the same information.

Although the advantages of symmetry are perhaps less compelling in the case of abstract than of topographic representational systems, there are still plausible enough reasons why symmetry has been largely preserved in the mammalian brain. For one thing, we argued in earlier chapters that it would be of advantage to animals in the natural world to be able to generalize events and experiences to their left–right mirror images. We suggested in Chapter 5 that this might be accomplished by a process of interhemispheric mirror-image reversal which requires symmetrical organization but which does not necessarily depend on topographic representation. Dimond (1972) has emphasized that the brains of higher animals are not only symmetrical, they are also "double"; each half of the brain can function to a large extent autonomously, with its own powers of thought, emotion, even volition (see also Gazzaniga, 1970). Yet there must also be effective communication between the two halves if the individual is to achieve singleness of purpose, and this implies both a common organization and a coherent system of interhemispheric mapping. Given the contingencies which already predispose the nervous system to be bilaterally symmetrical, it is not surprising that the equivalences between the two halves of the brain should also be based on symmetry. Opposite regions typically perform the same functions so that interhemispheric integration can be based to a large extent on the simple principle of homotopic mapping. Of course, homotopic mapping may not be appropriate for every purpose, as we saw in Chapter 5; but even in the case of the heterotopic mapping neccessary to create continuity and left–right equivalence across the vertical meridian of the visual field, we suspect that the basic organization is symmetrical. Whatever its disadvantages, symmetry remains a powerful principle of organization and communication within the brain.

THE EMERGENCE OF ASYMMETRY

In Plato's *Symposium*, Aristophanes says that men were originally spherical, with their faces pointing up to heaven and their round bottoms on the ground. But they grew proud, so Zeus split them through the middle from top to bottom and had Apollo turn their faces and genitalia around. He then made a further threat that if they continued to be insolent, he would split them again so that they would have to hop around on a single leg. Surreptitiously, Zeus seems to be carrying out his threat, if not to split us, at least to deprive us of our symmetry.

We shall be primarily concerned with handedness and cerebral lateralization of function. In man, both phenomena are well known: most people prefer to use the right hand rather than the left for most unimanual tasks, and show the greater strength and skill with the right hand. In an even higher proportion of individuals, the left cerebral hemisphere is primarily responsible for verbal processing, while the right hemisphere is the more specialized for nonverbal functions, including spatial perception. We shall discuss these phenomena in more detail later in this chapter and in the following chapter. First, however, it is pertinent to inquire whether comparable asymmetries are to be observed in species other than man.

Manual and Cerebral Asymmetries in Animals

Rats and mice. Both rats and mice have been observed to maintain consistent preferences for one or other paw. Individual mice, for instance, will typically reach for food in a glass tube with the same paw on successive trials and even over successive days, and the preferred paw is usually also the one with the stronger grip. Unlike man, however, individuals are as likely to be left-pawed as right-pawed (Collins, 1970). Moreover, Collins (1969) found that the proportions of left and right paw preferences remained approximately equal after three generations of selective breeding for sinistrality. Basically the same results have been obtained with rats. Although Tsai and Maurer (1930) declared that white rats showed an overall preference for the *right* paw in reaching for food, this does not seem to have been corroborated by subsequent studies. In fact, Peterson (1934) found that left-pawed and right-pawed rats persisted in approximately equal numbers even after eight generations of selective breeding for pawedness. In rats and mice, therefore, the direction of paw preference seems to be established on an entirely random basis.

In mice, however, there is some evidence for a cerebral asymmetry which may be partly under genetic control. Collins and Ward (1970) found that audiogenic seizures were induced more rapidly, on average, by sound in the left ear than by sound in the right ear among one inbred strain of mice, but there was no such asymmetry among another strain.

Birds.   Nottebohm (1970, 1971, 1972) has shown that the pattern of song in chaffinches and canaries is largely destroyed if the left hypoglossal nerve is cut, but remains more or less intact if the right hypoglossal nerve is cut. It is a reasonable inference that birdsong is primarily under the control of the left side of the brain. The analogy with the left-hemisphere control of speech in humans is striking.

Cats.   In cats, there is some evidence for an overall preference for the left paw. Cole (1955) found that about twice as many cats preferred the left as preferred the right paw in performing manipulative acts, although a good proportion also showed no consistent preference. There is also evidence for an association between pawedness and cerebral lateralization. Webster (1972) taught eight cats various visual discriminations, then sectioned their corpus callosums so that he could test each cerebral hemisphere separately. In seven of the eight cats, postoperative retention of some problems was better when the relevant input was projected to the hemisphere ipsilateral to the animal's preferred paw than to the contralateral hemisphere. This finding is somewhat analogous to the fact that humans typically show lateralization of spatial information in the minor hemisphere—the hemisphere that is usually ipsilateral to the preferred hand.

Primates.   Neither monkeys (Cole, 1957) nor chimpanzees (Finch, 1941) appear to display any overall preference for either the left or the right hand, although individuals may maintain consistent preferences. Several authors have suggested, however, that monkeys may show cerebral asymmetries which consistently favor one or other side.

Ettlinger, Blakemore, and Milner (1968) observed that four monkeys spontaneously switched preference from the left hand to the right, depending on whether they were performing a visual or a tactile discrimination task. This suggests a right-hemisphere specialization for visual performance and a left-hemisphere specialization for tactile performance. Although Gautrin and Ettlinger (1970) could find only weak support for this hypothesis, a study by Gazzaniga (1963) appears to confirm that visual learning is localized primarily in the right hemisphere. He trained three intact monkeys on a visual discrimination task, then cut their corpus callosums and optic chiasms. Retention of the task was better when input was to the right eye than to the left, suggesting that the original discrimination was localized more in the right hemisphere than in the left.

In seeming contradiction to this, Hamilton, Tieman, and Farrell (1974) found that split-brained monkeys learned some visual discriminations more rapidly when input was to the left hemisphere than to the right, although for other visual discriminations there was no such asymmetry. The critical difference may lie in whether learning is pre- or postoperative, since Gazzaniga also found that postoperative learning was in some cases faster when input was to the left hemisphere. The mechanisms by which lateralization is normally established may be impaired when the corpus callosum is sectioned.

Perhaps the closest analogy to human laterality will come from the African mountain gorilla. Schaller (1963) reports that he saw eight of these gorillas giving chest-beating displays, and all favored the right hand. Groves and Humphrey (1973) also report the mountain gorillas often have asymmetrical skulls, with the left side longer than the right, although there appears to be no such asymmetry in the gorillas found near the coast.

Conclusions.   The evidence we have reviewed suggests that there is perhaps less of a discontinuity between man and the lower animals than many authors have assumed. With respect to handedness, or pawedness, the most obvious difference is that animals do not seem to show marked preferences across individuals for left or right paw, whereas humans are predominantly right-handed. Yet even this may be a difference of degree rather than kind; we saw some evidence for an overall bias in the case of cats and of mountain gorillas. Annett (1972) has also shown that animals resemble humans in that the proportions of individuals classified as right-, mixed-, and left-handers fall very close to those predicted by a binomial distribution. This is true of mice, rats, cats, monkeys, and chimpanzees, as well as of humans. Annett attributes these binomial proportions to an underlying normal distribution of intermanual differences in skill, common to man and lower animals. In man, the distribution is shifted as a whole to the right, so that the right hand is favored overall. In cats, it may be shifted slightly to the left. Annett (1972) writes that her observatons "suggest that in all samples, human and nonhuman, the distribution of lateral asymmetry differs in only one significant respect, the *extent* to which the distribution is shifted to the right [p. 352; italics added]."

There was somewhat better evidence that cerebral lateralization in animals may be consistently biased in one or other direction. In particular, the left-hypoglossal control of song in passerine birds presents a tantalizing parallel to the left-hemispheric control of human speech. We also found evidence for consistent asymmetries in mouse, cat, and monkey, although the direct parallels with cerebral asymmetry in man were somewhat less clear. Even so, it is apparent that man is by no means unique in possessing a cerebral organization which exhibits some consistent asymmetries common to the majority of individuals.

We now return to our evolutionary theme and discuss the possible adaptive advantages which may have been responsible for the evolution of these asymmetries.

The Advantages of Asymmetry

We have seen that the advantages of symmetrical organization have much to do with the fact that the natural world is without systematic left–right bias. These advantages would apply most particularly to functions associated with direct reactions or responses to spatial aspects of the environment, such as escape or pursuit, reactions to noxious stimulation on the body surface, or simple linear propulsion through some environmental medium. However, there are many overt behaviors in the repertoires of higher animals which are relatively unconstrained by the environment, or which represent operations on the environment rather than reactions to it. Such behaviors are often what we call *manipulative*. Most of them involve the use of the hands or forepaws rather than the feet or hindpaws, and many involve the use of tools. The evolution of an upright stance and bipedal method of locomotion was obviously an important step in the development of manipulative skills, since it frees the hands from any involvement in locomotion.

Unlike locomotory or reflex acts, many manipulative acts put no special premium on a symmetrical system and are in some respects better served by an asymmetrical one. For skills that are essentially unimanual, it may be unnecessary and wasteful to have both hands or forepaws specialized. For example, the mouse reaching for food might just as well use one paw as the other. Once the choice is made, however, it is perhaps in the mouse's interests to continue to use the same paw, so that it can most profit from further experience and training. Perhaps this is why most species seem to be readily capable of the simple left–right differentiation which enables them to consistently respond with the same paw. Yet there must also be some advantage in retaining a degree of ambilaterality in case the object the mouse is reaching for is accessible only to the nonpreferred paw.

Woo and Pearson (1927) comment amusingly on the relative merits of unilaterality and ambilaterality for primitive man:

> There seems . . . to be a number of cases in which ambilaterality might be more advantageous to primitive man than unilaterality. Thus equality of both hands in ascending or descending a tree might be more valuable than increased adroitness in a single hand. Again, it might be more advantageous to throw two stones, one from either hand, than one stone from a single hand, even with slightly greater weight and celerity. The ''feeling'' that we now recognize that we could not

possibly do two things at one time—take two aims at once—even if it not be a result of our unilaterality—i.e., a measure of our loss of ambilaterality—throws us back on something of a psychological character, which may possibly be the source of unilaterality (but not of dextrality), namely that thought as a mental process is unique, thoughts may be rapidly successive, but cannot be contemporary. Yet an ambilateral man with two stones aimed in rapid succession might have certain advantages over a unilateral man who had to recharge, even if his other hand was his magazine [p. 168].

The advantage of manual asymmetry is perhaps more decisive in the case of skills which are bimanual, but which require different complementary contributions from two hands. Bruner (1968) has pointed out that these complementary roles can often be characterized as those of *holding* and *operating*—one hand holds the banana while the other peels it, one holds the nail while the other swings the hammer, or one steadies the paper while the other wields the pen. Even in these cases, however, the role of holding is seen as subordinate to that of operating, and in most people the hand that is preferred for unimanual skills is also the operating hand for bimanual ones.

So far as the individual in the natural environment is concerned, the *direction* of manual asymmetry is unimportant. It does not normally matter whether a mouse prefers the left or the right paw in reaching for food, or whether a monkey peels a banana with its left or its right hand. Consistency between individuals becomes important only when there are interindividual elements, such as those involved in sharing or communication. For example, tools and weapons may be constructed for use with one or other hand. If they are to be shared among members of a group, then, there is clearly some advantage to be gained if all members are of the same handedness. A simple communicative gesture like shaking hands requires that each individual offer the same (left or right) hand. These considerations help us understand why humans, among the most manipulative, cooperative, and communicative of species, are predominantly right-handed.

Why the right hand rather than the left? Some authors, such as Blau (1946), have implied that the initial choice may have been arbitrary, but once established was maintained by cultural pressures. Annett (1972) has argued against this on the grounds that there have been no cultures known to have preferred the left hand. Blau thought that there may have been left-handed cultures, but the evidence is tenuous indeed. For example, he revived an idea advocated by Erlenmeyer in the 1880s that the ancient Hebrews may have been predominantly left-handed because they wrote from right to left. This inference is almost certainly false (Hewes, 1949). Blau also drew attention to the 700 left-handed men in the army of Benjamin, referred to in the Old Testament (Judges 20:16), but he neglected to mention that these were but a fraction of the total army of 26,000. Other evidence, drawn from legends or pictures, appears equally without solid foundation. In general, one cannot but be impressed at the extent to which right handedness prevails in cultures as diverse as the Maoris, the

North American Indians, the Chinese, various African tribes, and several others, all discussed in the collection of readings by Needham (1973).

Another idea, first attributed to Thomas Carlyle, is that the choice of the right hand as the preferred one might have been dictated by the fact that the heart is displaced slightly to the left so that the left hand was assigned the passive, protective role of holding the shield while the right hand wielded the stick or sword. However, the displacement is so slight that it is unlikely that the choice of hands would have significantly affected survival rate. The hypothesis also fails to account for the survival of a small proportion of left-handers, or to explain why the proportion of right-handers is if anything slightly higher among women than among men (Clark, 1957). Blau (1946) seemed to give some credence to the possiblity that the displacement of the heart may have influenced early man to be right-handed, but that the choice has long since become rooted in custom and in man's mechanical contrivances.

Our own view, which we shall document in the following chapter, is that right-handedness is an expression of a general biological gradient which favors development on the *left*. This gradient underlies both left-cerebral dominance and the leftward displacement of the heart. Right handedness reflects the dominance of the left hemisphere, since the movements of the hands are controlled primarily, if not exclusively, by the contralateral hemisphere (e.g., Brinkman & Kuypers, 1973). Note that cerebral dominance in this sense need have nothing to do with speech, but is concerned rather with the control of complex manipulative behavior. We may observe that damage to the left hemisphere often results in a class of disturbance known as *apraxia*, which is in fact nonverbal. Although apraxia is not always clearly or precisely defined, it generally refers to the inability to perform motor acts or respond to motor commands, where the inability is not attributable to muscle paralysis. It is often said to reflect an ideational or symbolic deficit (e.g., Geschwind, 1967). However, Kimura and Archibald (1974) have argued instead that the impairment may be one of motor sequencing. They found, for example, that patients with left-hemisphere lesions performed poorly compared with patients with right-hemisphere lesions on a task requiring them to copy visually presented, meaningless hand movements. There was no such deficit on tasks involving individual finger flexions or the copying of static hand positions.

Quite apart from the implications of handedness, however, there is another reason why one might expect complex, internally initiated motor actions to be controlled by an asymmetrical system. We remarked earlier that the brain is in many respects a double organ, and each cerebral hemisphere seems to possess considerable autonomy (Dimond, 1972; Gazzaniga, 1970). If both were equally disposed to initiate complex action sequences there would surely be potential conflict between them, particularly when there is no overt asymmetry in the actions themselves to lend the advantage to one or other side. These conditions would surely favor the evolution of some internal mechanism to bestow executive motor functions on just one hemisphere (cf. Levy, 1969).

Thus, birdsong and human speech are both overtly symmetrical, but are controlled predominantly by the left side of the brain. It is noteworthy that cerebral lateralization in humans is more pronounced with respect to the *expression* of language than with respect to its *reception* (Gazzaniga & Sperry, 1967). It has been argued, moreover, that stuttering is caused by interhemispheric conflict in persons without clear lateralization (Orton, 1929; Travis, 1937). Although this contention is somewhat controversial, Sussman and MacNeilage (1975) have reported evidence that stutterers display little or no lateralization for speech production but the usual left-hemisphere superiority for speech perception. The phenomenon of eye dominance may provide another example of the lateralization of executive functions. Although the dominance of one eye over the other is usually established in terms of sighting or aiming (e.g., Miles, 1929, 1930), Walls (1951) has proposed that its true basis has to do with eye movements. Voluntary changes in fixation are initiated through the dominant eye, while the nondominant eye simply makes reflexive adjustments to maintain binocular fusion. Experiments have shown that the dominant eye is the more rapid and accurate in visual tracking or scanning tasks, which lends support to Walls' theory (e.g., Corballis, 1964; Money, 1972).

The Relation between Cerebral and Manual Asymmetries in Man

Although the lateralization of birdsong suggests that cerebral asymmetry can arise independently of any motor asymmetry, there has been much speculation that the lateralization of speech representation in the human brain is related in some way to handedness. The neurological evidence suggests that nearly all right-handers have speech represented in the left cerebral hemisphere (Branch, Milner, & Rasmussen, 1964; Rossi & Rosadini, 1967). We should also note that somewhat less than half of the population of left-handers have speech localized primarily in the right hemisphere (e.g., Goodglass & Quadfasel, 1954), and lateralization of cerebral function is in general less extreme among left-handers than among right-handers (Hécaen & Sauguet, 1971; Zangwill, 1960). We shall see, however, that additional factors may complicate the issue among left-handers, so that the characteristic pattern of asymmetry among right-handers may give the truer picture of evolutionary trends.

Some writers have urged that handedness is governed by the lateralization of speech mechanisms. For instance, Brain (1945) argued that because animals appear to be divided about equally in their preference for one or other hand (or paw), it must have been the appearance of a "motor speech centre" in the left hemisphere of man which brought about his preference for the right hand. W. W. Roberts gave the argument a more ontogenetic emphasis, but with an evolutionary undertone:

> It is not improbable that the infant passes through an earlier, fleeting, simian phase [in which] rudimentary handedness may be detected. But true human handedness occurs only after the beginnings of speech, by which it is directed and to which it is linked. Its essential quality is its determination by speech [Roberts, 1949, p. 567].

We think it more plausible, however, that cerebral lateralization of speech evolved from handedness rather than the other way about. Hewes (1973) has revived the old theory, which dates back at least to the eighteenth century French philosopher, Etienne de Condillac, that man's first language was basically gestural, carried on with signs of the hand and arms. As new evidence for this, he notes that chimpanzees cannot be taught vocal speech, but quite readily learn a form of sign language (e.g., Gardner & Gardner, 1969, 1971). Hewes speculates about the origins of signs associated with early tool-making, the involvement of the mouth and tongue in some expressive gestures, and the reasons why a vocal sound system might have gradually replaced an earlier gestural one. We need not go into details; the reader is referred to Hewes' paper and the variety of comments from other experts which follow it. For our purposes, the important point is the implication concerning lateralization of function. We quote from Hewes:

> The peculiarly human association of right-handedness and left-hemispheric dominance for both language skills and precise manual manipulations could well be the outcome of a long selective pressure for the clear separation of the precision grip from the power grip, combined with manual-gesture language exhibiting a similar (and related) asymmetry. If tool-making and tool-wielding already had a pronounced dextral bias, one would expect gestures derived from tool- and weapon-making and wielding to present the same preference for the right hand. . . . I believe that the phenomenon of cerebral lateralization can best be envisaged as the joint selective product of more precise tool and weapon manipulation, pressures for much greater terrain cognizance, involving right–left cognizance with respect to responses to visible landmarks, and the growth of a manual-gesture language; in other words, I think lateralization precedes the development of speech [Hewes, 1973, p. 9].

Kimura has reported some data which lend further credence to Hewes' speculations. People commonly gesture with their hands as they speak. Kimura classifies hand and arm movements into two types, free movements and self-touching movements. Self-touching movements occur at all times and are probably nongestural. However, free movements occur with significant frequency only when a person is talking. Right-handers make many more such gestures with their right hands than with their left (Kimura, 1973a). Left-handers make more bilateral free movements, which is consistent with other evidence (cited earlier) that left-handers show less cerebral lateralization than right-handers do. Even so, a more detailed analysis suggested that even in left-handers the majority of free movements were made with the hand contralateral to the hemisphere dominant for speech (Kimura, 1973b).

A common element which characterizes many of the functions of the left hemisphere in man is therefore its specialized involvement in complex movement. The right hand is usually not only the preferred hand, it is also the more skilled at making precision movements, as in such activities as repetitive tapping (Bryan, 1892), dowel balancing (Barnsley & Rabinovitch, 1970), and writing. The production of speech sounds also requires motor control of great delicacy and precision (MacNeilage, 1972). Specialization of one cerebral hemisphere in motor control is exactly what one might expect, since the most compelling arguments for lateralization apply to motor rather than to receptive functions, and particularly to those motor acts that are internally generated rather than those that represent reactions to spatial features of the environment.

Yet it would be wrong to insist that the specialization of the left hemisphere is exclusively motor. We have already noted that there is some degree of left-hemispheric specialization for the *perception* of speech stimuli, although it is less pronounced than that for language expression. A great many investigators have demonstrated a left-hemispheric superiority for the perception of speech sounds (e.g., Kimura, 1967; Studdert-Kennedy & Shankweiler, 1970), whether or not the sounds are meaningful (Kimura & Folb, 1968). Similarly, in visual perception, there is evidence for the superiority of the right over the left visual field in the detection of unilaterally presented letters (e.g., Heron, 1957; Kimura, 1966), and even of mirror-image letters (Bryden, 1966), implying a left-hemisphere advantage in the visual perception of verbal material (see White, 1969, for a review and critique). Thus, although the origins of cerebral lateralization in man lie in the evolution of manipulative behaviors, the actual distribution of specialized functions between the two hemispheres may depend on more complex principles.

The Duality of the Brain

For many years, attention was focused on the hemisphere in which speech was localized — the so-called "dominant," "leading," or "major" hemisphere. Yet Hughlings Jackson recognized very early on that the other hemisphere, the "minor " hemisphere, might also possess specialized capacities of its own: "If, then, it should be proven by wider experience that the faculty of expression resides in one hemisphere," he wrote, "there is no absurdity in raising the question as to whether perception — its corresponding opposite — may be seated in the other [Jackson, 1864; quoted in Taylor, 1958, p. 220]." These were prophetic words. Yet even in a conference held as late as 1961, J. Z. Young could still wonder whether the minor hemisphere might be merely a "vestige," although he allowed that he would rather keep his than lose it

(Young, 1962, p. 24).[1] It is really only in the last decade that the extent of specialization in the so-called minor hemisphere has become apparent.

Although we shall not attempt a complete review, it is instructive to consider something of the range of functions that are typically localized more in the right than in the left hemisphere. Studies of the effects of right-hemisphere lesions show that these include the ability to remember music, nonsense figures, and faces, and to perform a variety of nonverbal, visuospatial tasks (see Milner, 1971, for a review). There are several known cases of musicians, among them the composer Ravel, who have suffered damage to the left hemisphere with loss of speech or other language functions, yet who have retained their musical ability (Alajouanine, 1948; Luria, Tsvetkova, & Futer, 1965). Commissurotomized patients write much better with their right hands than with their left, but the left hand is superior at copying or drawing pictures or at arranging blocks to match a visual pattern (see Gazzaniga, 1970, for a review). This is striking testimony to the visuospatial ability of the right hemisphere, since the patients had had little or no previous experience at drawing with the left hand. It is also possible to demonstrate lateralization of perceptual processing in normal individuals. Studies of auditory perception indicate a right-hemisphere specialization for the perception of melodies (Kimura, 1964), musical chords (Gordon, 1970), sonar sounds (Chaney & Webster, 1966), and environmental sounds (King & Kimura, 1972); in visual perception, there is a left-hemifield advantage, implying a right-hemisphere specialization, for the perception of faces (Geffen, Bradshaw, & Wallace, 1971), spatial configurations (Kimura, 1969), and even the judgment of depth (Durnford & Kimura, 1971); in tactile perception, the right hemisphere seems to be specialized for the perception of meaningless shapes (Witelson, 1974).

---

[1]Young's comment echoes a remarkable poem by Rudyard Kipling, entitled "The Two-Sided Man." Here is an abbreviated version:

> Much I owe to the Lands that grew—
>   More to the Lives that fed—
> But most to the Allah Who gave me two
>   Separate sides to my head.
>
> Much I reflect on the Good and the True
>   In the faiths beneath the sun
> But most upon Allah Who gave me two
>   Sides to my head, not one.
>
> *I* would go without shirt or shoe,
>   Friend, tobacco or bread,
> Sooner than lose for a minute the two
>   Separate sides of my head!

> *Rudyard Kipling's Verse*
> (London: Hodder & Stoughton, 1927,
> p. 568)

The principal characteristic which these right-hemisphere functions share, and which distinguishes them from the corresponding left-hemisphere functions, is that they are nonverbal. Otherwise, they seem simply to represent a cross section of normal perceptual and cognitive processes. They include the auditory, the visual, the somesthetic; the temporal, as well as the spatial. One might conclude from this, not that the right hemisphere is intrinsically specialized for these functions, but that the left hemisphere is deficient in them, presumably because of its specialization for language and verbal processes (cf. Levy, 1969). If this is so, then there is no need to assume that right-hemisphere specialization evolved separately from left-hemisphere specialization. Rather, it is acquired by default, a by-product of the lateralization of language representation.

Some authors have nevertheless tried to define a more profound duality distinguishing the two hemispheres. Bruner (1968), for example, seeks an analogy between speech and manual skill. Just as the left hand holds the screw while the right hand operates the screwdriver, he suggests, so the right hemisphere "holds" the context of an utterance while the left hemisphere "operates" upon it to produce the actual speech. The analogy surely goes too far. In fact, the ability to speak coherently, and in context, is little impaired by surgical separation of the hemispheres (Gazzaniga, 1970) or even by total removal of the right hemisphere (Mensh, Schwartz, Matarazzo, & Matarazzo, 1952; Rowe, 1937). There may be, if anything, a limited sense in which the right hemisphere acts as a holding mechanism for the left. Gazzaniga (1970) cites evidence that split-brained patients may be deficient in short-term memory, and suggests that the right hemisphere may function as a reverberatory device, or "echo box." One of its functions may be to monitor statements initiated by the left hemisphere, and to signal qualifications or modifications (MacKay, personal communication to Gazzaniga, 1970). As weak evidence for this, it has been reported that patients with right-cerebral lesions did not qualify their utterances as often as patients with left-cerebral lesions (Hall, Hall, & Lavoie, 1968).

Other writers have sought an interhemispheric duality not so much in the way the two hemispheres cooperate as in the different cognitive styles represented by each. There has been a long history of attempts to define this duality and in Table 8.1 we reproduce from Bogen (1969b) a list of the different characterizations that have been proposed. A pattern clearly emerges; the left hemisphere is seen as the more rational, logical, analytic, the right hemisphere as the more intuitive, synthetic, holistic. Bogen himself goes further and suggests that the duality is one that has pervaded experience and philosophy throughout history, independently of any association with the two sides of the brain. To take just a few examples, we may note the pre-Confucian Chinese concepts of Yin and Yang, the Hindu distinction between "buddhi" and "manas," or C. P. Snow's (1959) "two cultures" of the sciences and the

TABLE 8.1
Dichotomies Associated with Cerebral Lateralization[a]

Author(s)	Major hemisphere	Minor hemisphere
Jackson (1864)	Expression	Perception
Jackson (1874)	Auditoarticulary	Retinoocular
Jackson (1878-1879)	Propositioning	Visual Imagery
Weisenberg and McBride (1935)	Linguistic	Visual or kinesthetic
Anderson (1951)	Executive	Storage
Humphrey and Zangwill (1951)	Symbolic or propositional	Visual or imaginative
McFie and Piercy (1952)	Relations	Correlates
Milner (1958)	Verbal	Perceptual or nonverbal
Semmes, Weinstein, Ghent, and Teuber (1960)	Discrete	Diffuse
Zangwill (1960)	Symbolic	Visuospatial
Hécaen, Ajuriaguerra and Angelergues (1963)	Linguistic	Preverbal
Bogen and Gazzaniga (1965)	Verbal	Visuospatial
Levy-Agresti and Sperry (1968)	Logical or analytic	Synthetic perceptual
Bogen (1969b)	Propositional	Appositional

[a] After Bogen (1969b).

arts. Some writers have urged that our materialistic Western culture has forced too great an emphasis on the rational, analytic mode of thought, to the neglect of the intuitive and the holistic. Bruner (1965), for example, suggests that the right hemisphere provides the necessary ingredient for creative thought, an idea enthusiastically pursued and elaborated by Bogen and his colleagues (Bogen, 1969a, b; Bogen & Bogen, 1969; Bogen, DeZure, Tenhouten, & Marsh, 1972). Yet hard evidence is lacking, as Bogen and Bogen (1969) admit.

Bever and Chiarello (1974) have recently claimed to have demonstrated experimentally that the duality underlying interhemispheric differences lies deeper than the verbal – nonverbal distinction. They found that although musically naive listeners show the expected right-hemisphere advantage in the recognition of melodies, musically experienced listeners show a *left*-hemisphere advantage. Their result indicates, they claim, that the musically sophisticated perceive music analytically and are aware of internal relations among segments, while the naive are only aware of the overall pattern or tune. Yet this finding is difficult to reconcile with the reports of musicians who have retained their talent despite damage to the left hemisphere. (Alajouanine, 1948; Luria *et al.*, 1965). It is conceivable that Bever and Chiarello's musically sophisticated subjects used a verbal coding strategy, perhaps using letter labels for the notes, to perform the tasks required of them.

The notion of a fundamental duality between the two sides of the brain has also been invoked to explain a difference in cognitive style between individuals. The difference depends on whether the individual relies mainly on the left or the right hemisphere, and is thought to be manifest in the direction he first looks when asked a question. People who look to the right, it is said, rely mainly on the left hemisphere, and are typically rational, logical, analytic, resistant to suggestion; those who look to the left rely mainly on the right hemisphere, and tend to be intuitive, holistic, suggestible (e.g., Bakan, 1969; Singer & Singer, 1972).[2] Kinsbourne (1972) has also shown, however, that the direction of initial gaze depends on the kind of question asked. Among right-handed subjects, questions which elicit verbal processes tend to elicit rightward shifts, while questions which elicit spatial imagery tend to elicit leftward shifts. At the time of writing, therefore, it is not clear to what extent lateral eye shifts are determined by different cognitive styles, or by different kinds of questions, or by other unknown factors (cf. Ehrlichman, Weiner, & Baker, 1974).

Even if there is a case for supposing that the duality between the cerebral hemispheres transcends the distinction between verbal and nonverbal processing, we suspect that it probably evolved from the lateralization of language function. Given the initial lateralization of mechanisms for the *production* of speech, it could then have proved advantageous for the processes of speech *perception* to be localized in the same hemisphere. The so-called "motor theory" of speech perception reinforces this view, for it advocates that speech sounds are perceived with reference to the motor command system responsible for producing them (Cooper, 1972; Liberman, Cooper, Shankweiler, & Studdert-Kennedy, 1967). Yet the lateralization of speech perception may have been held partly in check by the fact that the referents of speech are usually nonverbal — things rather than words. Perhaps this explains why the minor hemisphere retains some ability to understand language, but in a more limited and concrete way than the major hemisphere (e.g., Gazzaniga, 1970). Moreover, some thought processes are probably more readily expressed in language than others; these include analytic or logical processes which mirror

---

[2]It has been said that there are two kinds of people: those who think there are two kinds of people, and those who do not.

the properties of language itself and which gain in power and precision when expressed in symbols. Such processes would naturally tend to involve the more verbal hemisphere. Other thought processes, more intuitive, holistic, creative perhaps, but also more difficult to define, lend themselves more readily to nonverbal expression, as in art, or sculpture, or music. These processes would naturally be localized in the minor, or nonverbal hemisphere.

These speculations aside, there are other, more general reasons why lateralization, once established, may have been maintained and elaborated. One is that lateralization would increase storage capacity, which probably became progressively more important as the brain evolved more symbolic and less stimulus-bound functions. At the same time, as Young (1962) points out, the advantages of symmetry would become less important. One aspect of this change of emphasis concerns the left–right dimension itself. One of our main themes so far has been that it is important for animals in the natural environment to be able to generalize experiences to their left–right mirror images. But with the evolution of tools, symbols, and man's artificial environment, mirror-image generalization becomes unnecessary, even a hindrance. It becomes important to be able to tell left from right.

Our Right-Handed World, and the Problem of Left-Handers

The asymmetries of man and his artificial world presumably reinforce each other, thus maintaining and furthering the evolution of asymmetry. The more man fashions asymmetrical tools and establishes asymmetrical conventions, the more important it is for him to be asymmetrical himself. There are many ways in which we exploit the difference between left and right; the very fact that we have different words to designate them is testimony to that. In some cases, the particular left–right polarity is essentially arbitrary. In Britain one drives on the left-hand side of the road, but in the United States one drives on the right. We know of no evidence that one system is intrinsically preferable to the other, at least from a psychological viewpoint.[3] In a great many ways, however, our asymmetrical world distinctly favors the right-handed. The range of tools and instruments with a right-handed bias may surprise the right-hander, but is probably well known to the frustrated left-hander; these include scissors, potato

---

[3]But from a meteorological point of view, there is a case to be made for driving on the left in the northern hemisphere and on the right in the southern hemisphere. Opposing streams of traffic driving on the right would create an anticlockwise vorticity in the atmosphere which might combine with the natural cyclonic vorticity of the northern hemisphere, increasing the number of tornadoes. There is evidence that the frequency of tornadoes in the United States is indeed influenced by traffic flow — another instance of the polluting influence of the motor car (Isaacs, Stork, Goldstein, & Wick, 1975).

peelers, can openers and corkscrews, fountain pens, firearms, and musical instruments. Even books and magazines are made for right-handers, since the pages are turned from the right. Sometimes there is compensation. Mr. Charles Chaplin, a left-hander, is said to have used a left-handed violin (Oldfield, 1969), and Barsley (1970) chronicles the success of the first shop in the world catering exclusively to left-handers, which opened in London in 1968.

It has also been argued that the left-to-right direction of writing is natural for right-handers, and thus unnatural for left-handers. We quote from Sir Cyril Burt:

> In writing with the right hand, the natural tendency is to begin at the left-hand margin and proceed towards the right: this, in fact, is the direction which English handwriting follows. The reasons are clear: first of all, it is easier to pull the pen than to push it; and, secondly, the hand in moving thus does not obstruct the view of what it has just written. When the left hand holds the pen, the reverse direction is more natural; to work from the left-hand margin towards the right would now involve a clumsy shove [Burt, 1957, pp. 346–347].

Left-handers often compensate by adopting a style of writing known as the "hook," in which the hand is held above the line of script. In this way, what has been written is not covered up and the pen can be pulled instead of pushed across the page (Barsley, 1970).

Yet the argument that left-to-right script favors right-handers may have been overstated. Arabic and Hebrew, for example, are still written from right to left, even though most of the people who write them are right-handed. Until about A.D. 1500, in fact, right-to-left scripts were about as common as left-to-right ones, and the gradual predominance of the left-to-right convention can be attributed as much to historical factors as to any intrinsic superiority (Hewes, 1949). It has been argued, moreover, that the hook style of writing is not an adaptation to an unnatural direction of writing, but is rather a consequence of ipsilateral control of the writing hand. Levy (1971) describes evidence that those left-handers who adopt the hook style have language functions represented primarily in the left hemisphere, while those who do not have language localized mainly in the right. She even mentions an instance of a *right*-hander, who is supposedly right-hemisphere dominant for language, who also uses the hook style. Although the evidence that Levy describes must be considered preliminary and the rationale for the argument that the hook style compensates for ipsilateral control is unclear, her observations raise further doubt as to whether there is a truly natural direction in which to write.

In any event, it is clear that left-handers do suffer prejudice and discrimination, both mechanical and social, in our right-handed world (Barsley, 1970). It is often claimed, moreover, that left-handers suffer specific cognitive deficits. Yet the proportion of left-handers has apparently remained approximately constant throughout the ages; recall that there were 700 left-handers alongside the 26,000 right-handers in the tribe of Benjamin, a proportion that is not out of line with some present-day estimates (Clark, 1957). Given that left-handers seem so poorly adapted to our right-handed world, and perhaps suffer additional cognitive deficits besides, one may wonder why they continue to survive!

Let us consider more fully the relations between handedness and cognitive abilities. It is often noted that left- and mixed-handers make up a disproportionately large number of cases of language and reading disabilities (e.g., Burt, 1957; Orton, 1937). No doubt the proportion is somewhat inflated, for parents and teachers may regard left-handedness as an additional symptom of disorder and refer a left-hander for treatment when they would not refer a right-hander with a comparable disability. Nevertheless, we shall argue in Chapter 11 that there may indeed be a higher incidence of reading disability among left- and mixed-handers than among right-handers. However, it does not necessarily follow that left- and mixed-handers *as a whole* are below right-handers in language skills. For example, Annett (1970) found that there was an excess of mixed-handers among children with IQs of below 70 on the Peabody Picture Vocabulary Test (Dunn, 1959), but this was matched by a disproportionate number of mixed-handers among those with IQs of above 130. She also found that left-handed children had generally *higher* verbal IQs than either right- or mixed-handers, although the differences were not statistically significant. Newcombe and Ratcliff (1973) found no relation between handedness and either verbal or performance IQ among persons selected at random from the population at large.

Levy (1969) has maintained, however, that left-handers are inferior to right-handers on perceptual or nonverbal skills. This results, she argues, from the fact that language functions are represented more bilaterally in the brains of left-handers than of right-handers (e.g., Goodglass & Quadfasel, 1954; Zangwill, 1960), and therefore tend to invade the hemisphere that would otherwise be specialized for nonverbal skills. To prove her point, Levy showed that a group of left-handed graduate students were significantly inferior to a group of right-handed graduate students on the performance subscale of the Wechsler Adult Intelligence Scale (Wechsler, 1955), although the groups were matched on the verbal subscale. Miller (1971) reported a similar finding among university undergraduates.

Both Levy's and Miller's results were probably biased by their selection of subjects. Recall that Newcombe and Ratcliff (1973) found no evidence for a deficit in performance IQ among left-handers in the population at large. To complicate matters further, Peterson and Lansky (1974) report a disproportionately large number of left-handers among architects and students of architecture. They also found that left-handed architectural students were somewhat *better* than their right-handed peers at designing spatial mazes according to written specifications. We might surmise that Levy's group of left-handed graduate science students was biased by the absence of those with superior spatial ability, who were perhaps hard at work studying architecture!

In the following chapter we shall document evidence that there are two different categories of left-handers. First, some people may be left-handed because of brain injury, perhaps sustained at birth (e.g., Bakan, 1971; Bakan, Dibb, & Reed, 1973). One might expect to find some cognitive deficits among this group, not because of left-handedness per se, but because of the brain damage. Second, there may be a category of individuals who inherit, not left-handedness per se, but the *absence* of any consistent predisposition to be left- or right-handed (cf. Annett, 1972). Because of random influences during development, some of these individuals will be left-handed, some right-handed, and many will display mixed preferences. We shall suggest in Chapters 11 and 12 that these "bilateral" individuals may show some specific deficits in reading, writing, or in telling left from right, but they may compensate by showing *superior* ability on other cognitive skills. Since some proportion of these individuals will be left-handers, this could explain why left-handers sometimes excel on certain tasks.

Among those we have termed "bilateral" left-handers, it appears that there is a more diffuse representation of language *within* as well as between hemispheres (Hécaen & Sauguet, 1971). It is conceivable that this allows for greater powers of integration, especially perhaps the integration of verbal with nonverbal information. Thus, in Peterson and Lansky's (1974) study, the task on which the left-handed architectural students were reported to excel was one requiring spatial design according to written instructions. We might note that Leonardo da Vinci, an inventor as well as an artist, was a left-hander. Dimond and Beaumont (1974) found left- and mixed-handed subjects to be better than right-handed subjects at associating digits with nonverbal symbols. They write (p. 277) that "it is of considerable interest to speculate whether the left-handed variant might represent, in evolutionary terms, a superior organization of the brain [Dimond & Beaumont, 1974, p. 77]." As a *general* proposition, this is no doubt an exaggeration, but we would be the last to deny that bilaterality has *some* advantages.

In any event, the record of achievement among left-handers scarcely suggests a people seriously oppressed. Left-handers have been well known to excel in sports such as tennis, baseball, and cricket—every sports enthusiast can supply his own examples.[4] It should also be recalled that the 700 men of the tribe of Benjamin were said to throw with remarkable accuracy. Perhaps the advantage of the left-hander in early warfare and in competitive sport has to do with his unexpectedness — an advantage which depends upon left-handers remaining a minority. Besides Leonardo da Vinci, famous artists who were probably

---

[4]We write shortly after two left-handed tennis players have played in a much publicized match for the title of world champion.

left-handed include Michelangelo and Hans Holbein the Younger. Barsley (1970) lists a great many other left-handers prominent in political, artistic, or public life, modestly omitting himself. There seems to be no reason to believe that the left-hander is an evolutionary throwback, doomed for extinction.

SUMMARY AND PERSPECTIVE

First, a summary. Freely moving animals typically exhibit a striking bilateral symmetry which depends, not on any fundamental biological law, but simply on the fact that the impinging environment is without systematic left–right bias. The advantages of symmetry apply particularly to the locomotory apparatus and the sense organs, and to their associated neural structures. Asymmetries probably emerged in structures involved in *manipulative* behaviors, which represent operations on the environment rather than reactions to it. One example is manual manipulation, which is characterized by handedness. Another is language—clearly manipulative, for is not the pen mightier than the sword? — which is characterized by cerebral lateralization. In man there is reason to believe that vocal speech and its asymmetric representation in the brain evolved from a manual gestural system, which itself exhibited asymmetry due to handedness. Although the origins of cerebral lateralization probably had more to do with *expressive* processes than with *receptive* ones, the hemisphere responsible for initiating speech (and possibly other high-level motor acts) probably evolved a more generalized specialization for language functions, receptive as well as expressive, leaving the other hemisphere specialized for nonverbal perceptual and cognitive functions. This division of labor may have generalized even further to create fundamentally different cognitive styles in the two hemispheres. Functional asymmetries would be further and cumulatively reinforced by the fact that the man-made world exhibits consistent asymmetries, themselves a product of man's asymmetry.

It is easy to exaggerate the extent and importance of lateral asymmetry. Recent research on lateralization of function has been prolific and is apt to make one overlook the underlying symmetry of the brain. Part of the fascination with asymmetry, perhaps, has to do with an age-old desire to convince ourselves that we are fundamentally different from, and of course superior to, the other animals, although now that lateralization of function is being discovered in subhuman species this source of motivation may dwindle. But another source of curiosity about functional asymmetries surely rests on their seemingly poor correlation with structural asymmetries; the brain behaves more asymmetrically than it looks. Thus, von Bonin, summarizing his review of anatomic asymmetries, concludes as follows:

> But all these morphological differences are, after all, quite small. How to
> correlate these with the astonishing differences in function, such as the speech

function on the left side, is an entirely different question, and one that I am unable to answer [von Bonin, 1962, p. 6].

This discrepancy probably has much to do with the precision with which asymmetries are measured. It is worth noting, for example, that perceptual asymmetries in normal human subjects can be detected only with rather refined and subtle psychological techniques, and are not obvious to casual inspection. In auditory perception, lateralization favoring one or other ear typically does not occur if the input is monaural, unless the task is made fairly complicated (e.g., Bakker, 1968; Frankfurter & Honeck, 1973). Most of the evidence on perceptual differences between the ears has come from the so-called dichotic-listening technique, in which different sounds are presented simultaneously to each ear (e.g., Kimura, 1967). Similarly, in visual perception, differences between the left and right hemifields can be detected only under conditions of "minimal" stimulation (White, 1969), as when stimulus exposure is very brief. The structural symmetry of the brain, obvious on casual inspection, may also break down on correspondingly fine-grained analysis. Thus there is recent evidence that the language-mediating area of the superior temporal lobe surface of the brain is typically larger on the left than on the right (Geschwind & Levitsky, 1968). This is true not only of adults, but also of neonates (Witelson & Pallie, 1973). Such observations help establish the correlation which von Bonin found lacking.

In her review of evidence on cerebral lateralization in humans, Brenda Milner adds the following qualification:

. . . the data also indicate that homologous areas in the two hemispheres play somewhat similar behavioural roles, so that both the side and locus of a lesion determine the quality of the deficits seen. This fact helps to bridge the gap between man and lower primates, where numerous studies have shown that bilaterally symmetrical lesions are needed in order to demonstrate the functional importance of a given cortical area. It would be strange if, with the emergence of hemispheric asymmetry, this bilateral cerebral organization were totally superceded in man [Milner, 1971, p. 276].

From one who has done so much to expose and clarify the nature of cerebral asymmetry, this extract sets a final perspective on the relative importance of symmetry and asymmetry.

9
The Inheritance of Symmetry and Asymmetry

For every boy and every gal
That's born into this world alive,
Is either a little Liberal,
Or else a little Conservative!

—Iolanthe
W. S. GILBERT

We now examine the actual biological mechanisms that determine symmetry and asymmetry, and which cause them to be transmitted from one generation to the next. For no very good reason other than the historical, we shall again pay closer attention to asymmetry than to symmetry. Ultimately, in fact, our main focus will be on handedness and cerebral asymmetry of function, although we shall approach these phenomena through a more general discussion of the biological inheritance of symmetry and asymmetry. Handedness, in particular, has long been a source of fascination and speculation, yet opinion is still sharply divided on the question of whether or not it is innately determined, and if it is, whether it is specified by our genes or by some other biological mechanism.

In this chapter, we shall argue that handedness and cerebral lateralization are indeed for the most part predetermined at birth, although there is some degree of plasticity and equipotentiality in the early years of life. However, we shall also maintain that symmetry and asymmetries, including those of hand and brain, are not coded directly in the genes, although they may be subject to indirect genetic influences. Rather, they depend on information that is coded in the cytoplasm of the oocyte, the cell in the mother that undergoes meiosis to form the ovum. This cytoplasmic code is probably expressed in terms of embryonic gradients which govern the growth of spatial form in the developing organism. Following Morgan (1976)[1] we shall develop this theme first from a general biological point of view before we go on to discuss the more

---

[1] We are extremely grateful to M. J. Morgan for making available to us a prepublication draft of his article. Much of the following section is essentially a paraphrase of this article.

hypothetical questions which have to do with handedness and cerebral asymmetry.

THE BIOLOGICAL BACKGROUND

The development of spatial form, the process known as *morphogenesis,* takes place right from the first cleavage of the fertilized ovum. We begin our background discussion with an account of some of the factors which program and control this process with special reference to bilateral symmetry and obvious structural asymmetries.

Morphogenesis of Symmetry and Asymmetry

In the earliest stages of embryonic growth, prior to the stage known as gastrulation, the cells remain functionally undifferentiated as they divide and multiply. The growth is primarily structural. According to evidence reviewed by Davidson (1968) and Gurdon (1969), this early development is not controlled by the genes, but is programmed by information coded in the cytoplasm of the egg. The genes begin to play a role at the time of gastrulation when the cells start to become functionally differentiated. Davidson summarizes:

> The complex processes of predifferentiation morphogenesis appear to be carried out independently of embryo genome control, and, in fact, in the animals we have considered, they show no requirement for embryo genomic function. . . . Since early morphogenesis is evidently programmed through biological information stored in the egg cytoplasm, while the program for subsequent differentiation is synthesized in the embryo genome, the switchover from cytoplasmic to nuclear direction is a fundamental step in early life [Davidson, 1968, pp. 33–34].

Morgan (1976) gives several examples of organisms in which basic symmetries or asymmetries are apparent as early as the first or second cleavage and must therefore depend on a cytoplasmic rather than a genetic code. The direction of coiling of snail shells, for example, can be detected in asymmetries in the earliest cleavages (e.g., Bonner, 1952). By contrast, the embryos of amphibia and higher mammals show a pattern of bilaterally symmetrical cleavages. Indeed, in some anurans and urodeles, the plane of symmetry may be evident even before the first cleavage with the appearance of the so-called "grey crescent," a sickle-shaped area which forms at the margin of the dark and white material in the embryo. Moreover, the eggs develop normal bilateral symmetry when activated artificially by shock or chemical agents, which shows that even fertilization may not be necessary for fixing the median plane (Holtfreter & Hamburger, 1955).

Even when the functional differentiation of cells begins and the genes start to play a major role in development, morphogenesis cannot be exclusively under genetic control. Since the cells carry identical genetic information, there must be some other source of information which serves to differentiate one cell from another. To be sure, there are probably some genes which serve to regulate the expression of other genes, as in the so-called "operon model" of gene regulation developed by Jacob and Monod (1961). However, there must also be a source of what Wolpert (1969) calls "positional information," since the particular functional characteristics a cell will develop must depend in part on its position relative to other cells. In the development of a limb, for example, one cell might become muscle, another cartilage, and so on. Wolpert discusses at some length the formal properties of the positional information code, but notes that its physical basis is unknown. He suggests that it is unlikely to be genetic, however.

Many of the properties of positional information have been inferred from experiments in which tissue is transplanted from one part of the embryo to another. In the chick, for example, the limbs grow from limb buds which are at first undifferentiated, and if a particular bud is grafted onto some new position the final form of the limb will be appropriate for the new position rather than the old (e.g., Zwilling, 1961). This clearly illustrates the role of positional information, since the same limb bud, with the same genetic information, may develop different forms depending on the spatial influence of the surrounding tissue. For an understanding of the coding necessary to produce bilateral symmetry, we may note that if a left-side limb bud, say, is transferred to the right side, it will grow into a right-side limb. This suggests that the positional code makes no reference to left and right in the absolute sense, but simply specifies the position of a cell relative to the midline. There are three major axes: the front–back or anteroposterior, the top–bottom or dorsoventral, and the inward–outward or proximodistal. According to these three dimensions, exactly the same set of instructions could make a left or a right limb, as appropriate. To take a hypothetical and schematized example, the limb bud might be instructed to grow *outward* and make a hand on its outermost part, to construct the muscles and joints of the hand so that it folds inward over the *ventral* surface, to develop the digits so that the *anterior* one is the thumb. These instructions would create a left hand on the left side of the body and a right hand on the right side, but nowhere in the instructions is there any specification of handedness per se.

But if bilateral symmetry is achieved without reference to left and right, the programming of consistent lateral asymmetries must depend upon some absolute left–right gradient. This can be illustrated by the classic work of Spemann and his associates on the development of asymmetries in the heart and internal organs of the newt (Spemann, 1906; Spemann & Falkenberg, 1919). By tying a human child's hair around the developing newt embryo in the plane corresponding to the adult midsagittal plane, Spemann and Falkenberg were able to produce "Siamese twins," joined together on the medial surfaces. The twin that developed on the left side of the embryo was usually normal with respect to the asymmetries of the heart and internal organs, while the twin on the right showed considerable variation: sometimes it was normal, sometimes neither completely normal nor completely reversed, and sometimes it showed complete reversal of the organs—a condition known as *situs inversus*.

Spemann and Falkenberg recognized the fundamental asymmetry of their results and thought that it must be present in the egg from the very beginning. The following quotation has been translated by Morgan (1976):

> By whatever meridian the sperm enters the egg, the cytoplasm must always be different on the left and right sides of entry. If it were otherwise, given the well-known undifferentiation of the spermatozoa, it would be impossible to provide an explanation of the different development of left and right sides following fertilization. This implies that the cytoplasm of the egg possesses a bilaterally asymmetrical structure around the ovular axis, to which one can attribute the overt bilaterally asymmetrical development [Spemann & Falkenberg, 1919, p. 398].

As a result of this cytoplasmic asymmetry, Spemann and Falkenberg suggested there must be a left–right gradient in the rate of development which normally favors the left. However, any constriction in the median plan, such as that which they produced by tying the hair around the embryo, could retard development there. This would only enhance the developmental gradient on the left half of the embryo, but could diminish or even reverse it on the right half. Reversal of the gradient would produce *situs inversus*. As further evidence for this so-called *Defekttheorie* (defect theory) of *situs inversus,* Morgan (1976) cites the more recent work of von Woellwarth (1950) and von Kraft (1968).

Further insight into the nature of the left–right gradient is provided by Lepori (1969), who describes experiments in which he sectioned duck blastoderm, the disclike sheet of cells at one pole of the egg yolk, to produce twins. Unlike the amphibia, very few of the duck twins showed *situs inversus*. In fact, the striking finding was that nearly all of them showed normal positioning of the heart and inner organs *regardless of the orientation of the cut*. This demonstrates that the left–right gradient cannot be a simple linear one. The question as to the nature of this gradient can be reduced to the following: what kind of asymmetrical structure within a disc will produce the same left–right gradient with respect to *any* arbitrarily chosen point on its edge? Although he recognizes that the asymmetry must be ultimately cytoplasmic, Lepori suggests that it is manifest in asymmetrical movements of the cells, which proceed outward from the center in lines curving counterclockwise (see Fig. 9.1). With respect to any location of the so-called "primitive streak" on the edge of the disc, then, the two halves of the blastoderm will always show a consistent left–right asymmetry. During gastrulation, the primitive streak moves into the interior of the embryo, accompanied by converging movements of the cells. With the scheme that Lepori suggests, the movements of the cells on the left

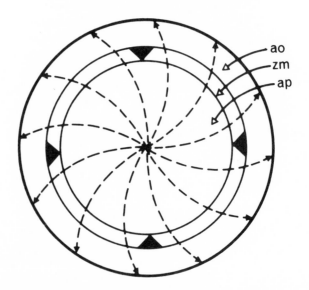

FIGURE 9.1 Schematic representation of the avian blastoderm in which the broken lines represent the directions of cellular movement. The four triangles are hypothetical locations of the primitive streak. In each case, the cellular movements are different on the left and right and converge with the inward movement of the critical streak on the left and diverge from it on the right. ap = area pellucida; ao = area opaca; zm = zone of junction. (After Lepori, 1969.)

side of the embryo would be compatible with this gastrular convergence, while those on the right would be incompatible. Development would therefore be more rapid on the left than on the right.

An asymmetry which conceivably bears on cerebral lateralization in man is that of the habenular nuclei. In vertebrates, these are to be found in the dorsal anterior diencephalon of the brain to either side of the third ventricle. In amphibia, at least, they exhibit a striking asymmetry, as illustrated in Fig. 9.2. The left habenula is larger than the right and actually consists of two nuclei, the lateral and the medial, while the right is a single nucleus only (Braitenberg & Kemali, 1970). Von Woellwarth (1950) has shown that both naturally occurring and induced *situs inversus* in newts produces a reversal of the habenular nuclei along with reversal of the internal organs and that reversal of the habenular nuclei cannot be attributed to reversed blood flow resulting from *situs inversus* of the heart. He therefore attributes both to a common cause, which we may suppose to be the reversal of a generalized left–right gradient in embryonic development.

FIGURE 9.2 Frontal section of the habenular region of the frog showing double form of habenular nuclei on the left. (1. lat. hab. = left habenular nucleus, lateral part; 1. med. hab. = left habenular nucleus, medial part; r. hab. = right habenular nucleus; hab. com. = habenular commissure; sh = shell, and c = core, of the habenular nuclei. (From Braitenberg & Kemali, 1970. Photograph courtesy of M. J. Morgan.)

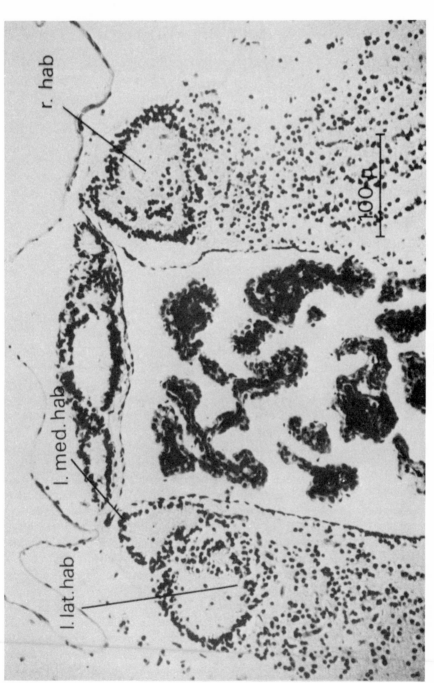

FIGURE 9.2

One cannot but be struck by the high proportion of consistent asymmetries which seem to reflect stronger or more rapid development on the left than on the right. Among those already mentioned are the leftward displacement of the heart, the double structure of the left habenular nuclei in amphibia, the left hypoglossal control of birdsong in chaffinches and canaries (Nottebohm, 1970), the enlargement of the left side of the skull in the mountain gorilla (Groves & Humphrey, 1973), and, of course, left-cerebral dominance with respect to the representation of speech and manual skills in man. Gardner (1967) reminds us that the single tusk of the narwhal, often said to be a prototype for the mythical unicorn, is in fact an enlargement of a tooth on the left side. He also notes that the ovaries and oviducts of most birds develop asymmetrically; the left and right ovaries and their ducts are initially the same size, but as a bird matures, the organs on the right degenerate and become useless. We may observe further that in the echinoderms, the phylum often said to be most closely related to the ancestral vertebrates, there is asymmetrical development of the body cavity favoring the left side (Child, 1941, p. 678).

We do not wish to claim that consistent asymmetries *always* favor the left side. For example, Olsen and Byerly (1935) counted mitoses on the left and right sides of the fowl embryo and found that there were at first more on the left than on the right, but later more on the right than on the left. The change occurred when the embryo turned onto its left side. In some cases, a right-sided advantage can be explained away in terms of some prior left-sided superiority. For example, we have attributed right handedness in man to a left-cerebral dominance of manual control, and the right-hemisphere specialization for nonverbal skills to the prior dominance of the left hemisphere for language functions. One can suppose that the rightward displacement of the stomach is secondary to the leftward asymmetry of the heart. Such arguments can be treacherous, however. For instance, what are we to make of the finding (see Chapter 8) that audiogenic seizures in a strain of inbred mice are induced more rapidly by sound in the left ear than by sound in the right ear (Collins & Ward, 1970)? One might conclude that the left hemisphere of the brain is the less prone to seizure and is therefore the more developed, but the argument is dangerously ad hoc. In any case there are clear examples of consistent asymmetries in some species which are reversed in others. Among flatfish, such as the halibut, both eyes are usually on the right side of the body; the turbot, however, is an example of a left-eyed flatfish (Gardner, 1967). No matter how one interprets this asymmetry, it cannot be concluded that it universally favors the left side.

In spite of the possible exceptions and ambiguities, however, the evidence for a developmental gradient favoring the left is at least fairly general. We have argued that this gradient is probably coded in the cytoplasm rather than in the genes. Morgan (1976) goes further and speculates that it is locked to the fundamental asymmetry of living molecules themselves, but he admits there is no direct evidence for this.

Genetically Influenced Asymmetries

We do not mean to suggest that the genes have no influence in determining phenotypic asymmetries. On the contrary, there are several cases of asymmetries in which the genes can plausibly be supposed to have played some role, although always, we suspect, an indirect one. We illustrate below at least some of the ways this can occur.

One kind of indirect genetic influence has to do with so-called *maternal inheritance*. This is said to occur when some characteristic does not obey the Mendelian laws of segregation, but is always inherited from the mother. Maternal inheritance is usually taken to imply transmission through the cytoplasm rather than through the genes (Srb, Owen, & Edgar, 1965). However, it sometimes happens that the particular characteristic that a mother bestows on her progeny is genetically determined *in the mother*. The genetic influence is thus at a generation removed from the appearance of the characteristic. A pertinent example is provided by the inheritance of the direction of coiling of snail shells. There is evidence that whether the shell will coil clockwise or counterclockwise is imprinted on the embryo during oogenesis by way of the follicle, an asymmetric ring of cells surrounding the egg (Raven, 1967). From the point of view of the progeny, then, inheritance is oocytic. From the point of view of the mother, however, the direction of coiling that she will imprint on the progeny appears to be determined genetically. The distributions of clockwise and counterclockwise coiling in successive generations suggest that the information is carried by a gene with two alleles, the allele causing clockwise rotation being dominant and that causing counterclockwise rotation recessive (Sturtevant, 1923).

Another indirect source of asymmetry has to do with *incomplete penetrance*, which refers to the fact that a particular characteristic represented by a gene may not be manifest in all individuals carrying the gene. Penetrance may be expressed differently on the two sides of the *same* individual if the developmental mechanism that gives expression to the gene on one side is independent of that on the other. This can give rise to asymmetries (Stern, 1955). For example, in a particular strain of the fruitfly *Drosophila*, it sometimes happens that one of the two thoracic dorsocentral bristles on one or other side of the body is missing. It is missing equally often on the left as on the right. That this is a phenomenon of variable penetrance is suggested by the fact that some flies show the defect on both sides and others do not show it at all (Plunkett, 1926).

Variable penetrance need not result in equal proportions of left- and right-handed asymmetries if the developmental mechanism is itself influenced by a left – right asymmetry. For example, harelip and cleft palate in man usually occur asymmetrically and affect the left side about three times as often as they affect the right (Fogh-Andersen, 1943). This unequal penetrance might again be attributed to an overall left – right gradient which favors expression on the left.

It is perhaps questionable whether asymmetries due to incomplete penetrance can properly be called genetic since variations in penetrance appear to have more to do with the embryonic environment in which the gene is expressed than with the gene itself. There is evidence of a more positive genetic effect, however, in the asymmetric expression of polydactylism in fowl. Polydactylism is a genetically determined condition in which the foot has five toes instead of the usual four. It nearly always occurs on both feet among fowl homozygous for the condition, but may occur on one foot only among heterozygotes. It occurs more frequently on the left foot than on the right. What is more important, selective breeding for the sinistral (left-footed) variant significantly increases its incidence, whereas the incidence of the dextral variant is relatively unresponsive to selection (Landauer, 1948). Landauer suggests that these variations are produced by "modifying genes" which can alter the embryonic fields controlling differential growth. It is not possible to tell from the data whether these modifying genes achieve their influence on the embryo itself, or through the mechanism of maternal inheritance.

In any event, Landauer's results and interpretation are not incompatible with the notion that embryonic gradients are coded in the cytoplasm but can perhaps be modified genetically. His findings are also consistent with the view that there is a predominant left–right gradient favoring development on the left. However, he warns against assuming that the left side is favored at all stages of development, citing the evidence of Olsen and Byerly (1935) that mitotic activity in the developing fowl embryo was at first greater on the left, but was later greater on the right (see above). Moreover, although most genetically determined abnormalities are either bilateral or predominantly sinistral, some are biased toward the right. As an example, Landauer cites the work of Taylor and Gunns (1947) on diplopodia, a recessive lethal mutation in fowl in which there is often excessive toe duplication, among other manifestations. In this case, unlike that of polydactylism, the greater abnormality is usually found in the right foot.

Sometimes an asymmetry cannot be attributed to variable penetrance since there are no symmetrically affected or nonaffected individuals alongside the asymmetrical ones. As an example of this, Stern (1955) draws attention to an asymmetrical spotting pattern in the beetle *Bruchus quadrimaculatus*. The normal females have two black spots bilaterally placed on each front wing, but there is a recessive mutant strain in which there are two red spots on one wing and two black spots on the other. The asymmetry is present in all individuals possessing the relevant genotype, but half have the red spots on the left and half have them on the right, regardless of which way round it was in their ancestors. There are no individuals with the red spots on both wings. These observations suggest that the *presence* of the asymmetry is determined by a gene, but its *direction* is arbitrary (Dahlberg, 1943).

Finally, Stern describes what he calls a "unique situation" in which it appears superficially that a specific asymmetry can be attributed to a genetic mutation. In a mutant strain of *Drosophila melanogaster,* the penis appears to be twisted around so that it sometimes protrudes sideways and is sometimes upside down. But the appearance is deceptive, for closer inspection reveals that the genetic influence has actually been to reduce an already existing asymmetry. In the normal male, the external genitalia are rotated clockwise through 360° relative to those in the female. This is not apparent from external appearances, but can be seen internally from the spiral counterclockwise rotation of the sperm duct around the intestine. In the mutant strain, the rotation is partly undone, so the penis is actually *counter*rotated.

In general, there appears to be no evidence that specific directional information can be coded genetically. The example of *Bruchus quadrimaculatus* suggests that a gene may cause the presence of an asymmetry, but not its direction. Where directional asymmetric variations can be linked to genetic variation, we can suppose that the influence occurs through interaction with an underlying cytoplasmic gradient. In most cases, the direction of the asymmetry is such that the genetic expression is more marked on the left than on the right, in line with the prevailing left-to-right growth gradient. Similarly, spiraling asymmetries seem to favor the clockwise over the counterclockwise. Just how genetic influences may interact with underlying gradients is a matter for speculation. The interaction may operate through some mechanism of maternal inheritance, as in the case of the spiral coiling of snail shells; there might be modifying genes which operate directly on the cytoplasm to change the gradients themselves, or there might be regulatory genes which perhaps alter the timing of cell differentiation, thus altering the synchrony between functional and spatial growth.

HANDEDNESS AND CEREBRAL LATERALIZATION

We now turn to a discussion of those asymmetries which have been of most concern to psychologists, namely, handedness and cerebral lateralization. As we shall see, theories about handedness, in particular, have ranged from one extreme to another. We shall discuss some theories, for example, which attribute variations in handedness entirely to genetic variation. The most recent is that of Levy and Nagylaki (1972), who attempt to explain both handedness and cerebral lateralization of language functions in terms of a two-gene model. Yet, in 1946, Abram Blau, in what was probably the most exhaustive review of the evidence up to that time, reached an entirely opposite conclusion:

> Preferred laterality is not an inherited trait. There is absolutely no evidence to support the contention that dominance, either in handedness or any other form, is a congenital, predetermined human capacity. Despite the popularity it has enjoyed with many investigators and the attempts to prove it by various techniques and in relation to different organs of the body, the theory of heredity must be put down as erroneous [Blau, 1946, p. 180].

As we saw in the previous chapter, Blau thought that dextrality was entirely a cultural phenomenon based in the first instance on weapons and tools and now built into the very structure of man's artificial environment. Sinistrality was simply a failure to learn the appropriate convention. It could arise because of a physical defect in a right member, or because of faulty education, or, most commonly, because of emotional negativism — a symptom of infantile psychoneurosis.

Pursuing the theme we have developed so far, we shall argue that genetic and cultural influences on human laterality are secondary to a more fundamental source, which is probably cytoplasmic. We shall organize our discussion around two issues. The first concerns the relative importance of pre- and post-natal influences on handedness and cerebral lateralization. Contrary to Blau, we shall conclude that both of these asymmetries are largely predetermined at birth. The next issue is whether this congenital influence can be attributed to the action of the genes. We shall examine several genetic models which attribute laterality entirely to genetic influences, and conclude that none is satisfactory. The evidence suggests rather that genetic influences are relatively weak and operate through interaction with an underlying left – right gradient.

Human Laterality: Congenital or Learned?

Blau was not the only one to argue that handedness is transmitted culturally. More recently, Collins (1970) has made the same suggestion, although he is less adamant about it than Blau. In the previous chapter, we described his experiments showing that selective breeding for sinistrality failed to alter the distribution of left- and right-pawedness in mice. Paw preference in both rats and mice cannot be predicted from one generation to the next. This is not the case in man; children do tend to resemble their parents in handedness, although the correlation is far from perfect. Collins rejects a genetic explanation for the inheritance of human handedness, however, on the grounds that the distributions of handedness among paired siblings and among twins are very close to what one would expect by chance, and therefore cannot depend on genetic variation. We shall discuss this claim in more detail later in the chapter. Collins (1970, p. 135) concludes that the correlation between generations must result either "from cultural inheritance or from an unknown extrachromosomal biologic predisposition to asymmetry." He seems to prefer the cultural interpretation, mainly on the grounds that it would permit greater plasticity of adaptation, although he does not provide any evidence against the notion that right-handedness and left-cerebral dominance may be expressions of an underlying cytoplasmic gradient which generally favors development on the left side of the embryo.

We have already encountered one difficulty with a purely cultural explanation for right-handedness in the previous chapter. There is a growing evidence to suggest that preference for the right hand is a universal human phenomenon (e.g., Needham, 1973), which suggests that it must have evolved independently among different cultures. As Annett (1972) has pointed out, the origins of right-handedness are therefore likely to be biological rather than cultural. Nevertheless, it is still conceivable that Blau (1946) was correct in suggesting that the original reasons for preferring the right hand have long since become irrelevant and that the preference is now maintained exclusively by cultural transmission.

One way to further assess the relative roles of congenital and environmental influences is to study the postnatal development of laterality, especially over the early years of life. If an asymmetry is present at a very early age, then it is plausible to suppose that it is congenital rather than learned. Asymmetries which emerge later may represent the unfolding of a preprogrammed maturational pattern, or they may depend directly on environmental contingencies. With these points in mind, then, let us consider first the evidence on the development of handedness.

The development of handedness.   The most intensive developmental study of handedness is that of Gesell and Ames (1947). These investigators recorded considerable fluctuations between right- and left-handedness over the early months and years of life. Although individuals differed considerably, some general trends emerged. Among those destined to become right-handed, the earliest observable preference, at about 16 to 20 weeks of age, was usually for the *left* hand. This was followed by a period of ambilaterality, then a preference for the right hand at about 28 weeks. A repetition of the cycle produced a general preference for the left hand at about 36 weeks, then a preference for the right hand at 40 to 44 weeks. Cyclic changes tended to recur, although dominated increasingly by a preference for the right hand, up until about eight years of age, by which time all subjects were consistently right-handed.

If only because the pattern of changes was somewhat complex, yet fairly consistent from child to child, these observations suggest that handedness is governed by maturational rather than environmental asymmetries. This conclusion is further supported by the fact that handedness was partially predicted by the direction of the tonic neck reflex. This reflex may be observed in the fetal infant as early as the 28th week after conception, but has usually disappeared by the age of 20 weeks after birth. It has the following characteristics: the head is turned to the right or left, the arm and leg on the side to which the head is turned are extended, and the opposite arm and leg are flexed. Most children show a right tonic neck reflex, which means they turn their heads to the right. Gesell and Ames found that in 14 of 19 children, the direction of the reflex was consistent with subsequent hand preference, and the handedness of all four left-handers was correctly predicted by a left tonic neck reflex. Handedness therefore seems to be largely predetermined at birth and is not simply an adaption to environmental or cultural asymmetries occurring after birth. Gesell and Ames concluded that handedness is "a product of growth."

It has also been observed that nearly all newborn infants show a spontaneous tendency to lie with their heads turned to the right. Partly as a consequence of this, they are typically more responsive to stimulation on the right than on the left and they turn their heads more often toward a touch on the right than toward a touch on the left (e.g., Turkewitz, Gordon, & Birch, 1965; Turkewitz, Moreau, Birch, & Crystal, 1967). Hammer and Turkewitz (1974) have shown that there is both a sensory and a motor component to these asymmetries. We know of no evidence relating these phenomena to subsequent handedness, but we may note that the right side of the body is not always favored. For instance, Turkewitz et al. (1965) found that 27 of their 36 three-day-old subjects responded with more head movements to a right-side touch than to a left-side touch, five showed no difference, and four showed more movements to the left. These numbers correspond moderately well with the proportions of right-, mixed-, and left-handers one might expect to find in the general adult population (cf. Annett, 1967). Turkewitz and his colleagues also observed their subjects outside of the experimental session and noted that only one was lying with the head turned to the left. This baby was one of the five who had shown no lateral preference in head turning. We suspect that handling practices may influence the proportion of children lying with their heads one way or the other, so the asymmetries in responsiveness may perhaps give the truer picture of innate lateralization.

Of course, experience sometimes does play a role in the determination of handedness. It is well known that children with a natural predisposition to write with their left hands are often forced by parents or teachers to switch to their right hands. To take a more extreme example, it has been recorded that native children in the Dutch Indies often had their left arms completely bound to teach them to use only their right arms (Jacobs, 1892; cited by Hertz, 1909). As we shall see in Chapter 11, some children may suffer some ill effects from the enforced switch, although many undoubtedly adapt without serious impediment. Some level of equipotentiality between the hands must surely be of advantage in case the normally preferred hand is injured. Moreover, such complex bimanual skills as playing the piano illustrate that both hands can be trained to a nearly equal degree of precision and accomplishment. To some limited extent, then, the right shift underlying intermanual differences in skill (Annett, 1972) must be a product of unequal learning. "One of the signs which distinguish a well-brought-up child," wrote Hertz (1960), "is that its left hand has become incapable of any independent action [p. 92]."

Cerebral lateralization and equipotentiality.   In the early years of life, there is considerable equipotentiality between the cerebral hemispheres, at least with respect to the representation of language. According to data tabulated by Basser (1962), lesions to the left hemisphere in the first two years are no more disruptive to the subsequent development of speech than are lesions to the right hemisphere. This must mean that the right hemisphere can take over speech functions without obvious loss of efficiency if the left hemisphere is damaged, providing the damage occurs early enough. Lenneberg (1967) has summarized further data which show that lesions to the left hemisphere between the ages of three and ten years produce only temporary loss of speech functions. The overwhelming majority of children recover full powers of speech, although they may retain some minor impairment of perceptual or cognitive capacities (Teuber, 1950, 1960). There is a marked decrease in equipotentiality after the age of ten years, and by about fifteen years the lateralization of language representation is usually irreversible.

It is sometimes supposed that equipotentiality implies equality, suggesting that cerebral lateralization is primarily a function of experience. Some authors have proposed that handedness is the preemptive factor. For example, Weber (1904) thought that writing was the cause of lateralization of language functions. This idea has superficial plausibility in that reading and writing are the only overtly asymmetrical acts associated with language, although we know of no direct evidence to support it. Gazzaniga (1970) has suggested that handedness may play a more general role. He cites evidence that the corpus callosum is undeveloped in early life so that the infant is functionally "split-brained." Consequently, exploration of the environment with the preferred hand would stimulate and educate only the contralateral hemisphere, which would then, in turn, instigate further exploration. The contralateral hemisphere would therefore be cumulatively enriched and so acquire the complexity necessary to process language. This theory is almost certainly an oversimplification, at best. It does not explain why the majority of left-handers have speech represented primarily in the left hemisphere (e.g., Goodglass & Quadfasel, 1954). Nor does it take into account the fluctuations in handedness described by Gesell and Ames. Moreover, one might expect manual exploration of the environment to enrich the child's spatial knowledge of the world, yet spatial representation appears to be localized primarily in the hemisphere ipsilateral to the preferred hand.

Bever (1971) has argued that experience with language itself might be responsible, at least in part, for cerebral lateralization. He describes evidence to suggest that the dominant hemisphere becomes the locus of a particular strategy for perceiving speech. This strategy involves the immediate labeling of words according to an "actor–action–object" sequence, a strategy which works better with active than with passive sentences. Bever's data do not make it clear whether this strategy is a consequence of lateralization or vice versa. However, he cites Kimura's (1963, 1967) finding that children from a lower middle-class neighborhood developed lateralization later than those from a wealthier neighborhood (see also Geffner & Hochberg, 1971). Both Bever and Kimura take this to be indirect evidence that lateralization is facilitated by an enriched cultural experience.

We do not doubt that experience plays some role in influencing the degree and course of development of cerebral lateralization. However, there is still good reason to suppose that its *direction* is innately specified, at least among the majority of individuals. Bever's account does not explain why it is nearly always the left hemisphere which is the locus for the representation of the speech-processing strategy. Moreover, there is recent evidence to suggest that cerebral lateralization can be detected in infants early in the first year of life, long before they can talk or understand meaningful utterances.

Witelson and Pallie (1973) have shown from postmortem examination that the language-mediating area of the superior temporal lobe surface of the brain tends to be physically larger on the left than on the right, both in neonates and in adults. The asymmetry appears to be functional as well as anatomic. For instance, Molfese, Freeman, and Palermo (1975) found that evoked electrical responses to speech sounds, including meaningless syllables, were generally larger when recorded from an area of scalp over the left temporal lobe than over the right temporal lobe, but that responses to a musical chord or to a noise burst were larger over the right lobe. This was true of a group of infants ranging from one week to 10 months of age as well as of older children and adults. Equally striking is a result obtained by Entus (in press). She presented dichotic pairs of sounds to infants, aged from three to 20 weeks, whenever they sucked on an artificial nipple. When sucking to a particular pair had habituated to a prescribed level, she changed the sound in one ear only and measured the recovery in sucking rate. When the sounds were consonant–vowel syllables distinguished only by the consonant, recovery was greater on the whole when the change occurred in the right ear, but when they were musical sounds (the note A played on different instruments) recovery was generally greater when the change was in the left ear. Molfese *et al.*'s and Entus' results can be taken as evidence that the left hemisphere is already specialized for perception of at least some features of speech sounds and the right hemisphere for the perception of nonspeech sounds early in the first year of life.

The role of maturational gradients.   At first glance, it is difficult to reconcile these findings with the evidence for equipotentiality during the first two years of life. How is it that the left hemisphere is apparently tuned to at least one aspect of language processing shortly after birth, yet the right hemisphere can take over language functions, without detectable loss, if the left hemisphere is lesioned at any time up to two years of age? The answer, or part of it, may be that the two hemispheres are indeed *potentially* equal, but that there is a maturational gradient such that the left hemisphere normally develops slightly *earlier* than the right. This answer is suggested by Nottebohm (1972) in relation to his work on the development of lateralization of vocal control in chaffinches.

We have noted that song in chaffinches is primarily under the control of the left hypoglossal nerve. If this nerve is cut before the song is established, the right hypoglossus takes over. It does not do so if the song is already established. In birds, as in human children, then, there is equipotentiality in the early stages of development. Nottebohm suggests that the left hypoglossus normally assumes control because birdsong develops while maturation is faster and more advanced on the left than on the right. But if the left hypoglossus is sectioned and thus prevented from securing control, the right hypoglossus takes over and proves just as versatile. Notice that this explanation implies that there must be some mechanism which normally prevents the right hypoglossus from subsequently competing with the left hypoglossus once the latter has already secured control; in Nottebohm's (1972) words, the "subordinance of the right hypoglossus is one of acquiescing with [sic] the status quo [p. 48]."

Nottebohm anticipated that this account might have more general application, perhaps to the phenomena of human cerebral lateralization. In the following quotation, he echoes what is in fact the main theme of this chapter:

> This neural lateralization of function could be determined by a bias as simple as different embryonic rates of growth of the left and right hypoglossus. One is led to wonder to what extent many phenomena of neural lateralization of function may not develop out of a left–right differential rate of growth of the whole or part of the embryonic nervous system [Nottebohm, 1972, p. 48].

What, then, are the implications for the development and plasticity of cerebral lateralization in humans? The right hemisphere, we suggest, is potentially just as capable of mediating language functions as the left, but it normally loses the privilege because it develops later. Since language learning is hierarchical, the ability of the right hemisphere to take over control would decline as the left hemisphere gradually assumes dominance. Observe, however, that we must assume that language is paramount in the cognitive growth of the young child, even perhaps in the first weeks of life. It follows that any *right*-hemisphere advantage in early development is associated with stimuli whose main characteristic is that they are not associated with speech. We do not suppose, for example, that Molfese *et al.*'s and Entus' findings necessarily demonstrate any intrinsic specialization of the right hemisphere for the perception of musical sounds. On the other hand, one need not suppose that the right hemisphere is always passively "acquiescing with the status quo"—waiting, as it were, for some mishap to befall the left hemisphere. While the left hemisphere is securing dominance over speech and language functions, the right hemisphere may simultaneously develop its own specialization for nonverbal processing (see Chapter 8).

The maturational advantage does not always lie with the left side, as we have already seen. In the chaffinch, the right hypoglossus exerts control over a few high-frequency song elements, presumably because these are acquired during a later phase of development when the right hypoglossus is undergoing a period of growth (Nottebohm, 1972). The observations of Gesell and Ames (1947) on the development of handedness suggest that in human children, too, maturation may proceed in cycles. Although Gesell and Ames observed an initial preference for the left hand, and thus presumably the right hemisphere, we suspect that the usual maturational pattern is for the left hemisphere to lead, while the right hemisphere periodically catches up. A characteristic or skill which develops during a period of right-hemisphere growth could thus be lateralized to the right rather than to the left.

The idea that congenitally programmed patterns of maturation may serve to delimit and organize the hierarchical acquisition of complex skills is a common one, both in psychology (e.g., Bowlby, 1953) and ethology (e.g., Hinde, 1961). It has been applied specifically to the acquisition of language by Lenneberg (1967). Following Nottebohm (1972), we have suggested that the pattern of growth is spatially as well as temporally organized. An asynchrony between the hemispheres would serve two important functions. It would permit the representation of some complex processes, such as language, to become lateralized in the brain. Second, it would allow a degree of flexibility and plasticity in the representation of lateralized skills. In particular, a right-hemisphere lag would permit this hemisphere to take over control, although perhaps at the expense of other functions, if the left hemisphere is damaged.

We still have much to learn of the detailed interrelations between learning and the spatial and temporal patterns of maturation and we do not wish to claim that our account is in any sense complete. Our main point is that the notion of a left–right gradient in the maturation of the brain can *in principle* help to reconcile the conflict between equipotentiality and the innate predisposition toward a particular direction of lateralization. It would be consistent with the evidence reviewed earlier in this chapter to suppose that this gradient is coded, not in the genes, but in the cytoplasm of the oocyte.

Genetic Influences

We have seen that the more obvious asymmetries of living organisms seem to be little affected by genetic variations. At best, genetic influences appear to be indirect. For instance, we reviewed some evidence to suggest that genetic influences within the mother might alter the prenatal environment she provides for her offspring in such a way that the laterality of the offspring is affected. Again, we saw that genetic influences might alter the degree of an asymmetry, or even its presence or absence, presumably through interaction with nongenetic sources of asymmetry, including a cytoplasmic gradient. However, we found no evidence to suggest that the direction of an asymmetry is ever directly coded in the genes.

These conclusions are borne out by studies of pawedness and cerebral lateralization among subhuman animals, which were reviewed in Chapter 8. We saw from the work of Peterson and of Collins that the distribution of paw preferences among rats and mice is unaltered by selective breeding for the preference of one or other paw. The study of audiogenic seizures in mice by Collins and Ward (1970) revealed a cerebral asymmetry that was present in one inbred strain of mice but not in another. This suggests a genetic influence on the presence of an asymmetry, but not on its direction.

It would be remarkable, therefore, if manual and cerebral asymmetries in man were directionally coded in the genes. Yet it is precisely this assumption which underlies the various genetic models that have been proposed to explain human handedness, and more recently cerebral lateralization as well. These models are critically discussed in the following sections.

Genetic models. There have been persistent attempts to explain variations in handedness in terms of a single, two-allele gene which codes the direction of laterality. For example, Ramaley (1913) thought that right-handedness could be attributed to a dominant allele and left-handedness to a recessive allele carried by about one-sixth of the population. However, if this were true, then left-handed couples should always produce left-handed offspring, which is contrary to fact. Most surveys reveal that only about half the children of left-handed couples are themselves classed as left-handed (see Annett, 1974; also Table 9.1). To explain such departures from a strict Mendelian segregation law, some authors have invoked the concept of variable penetrance. Trankell (1955), for instance, argued that only some of the individuals homozygous for the left-handedness gene will actually be left-handed. More plausibly, perhaps, Rife (1950) has argued that partial penetrance is expressed only in heterozygotes, not in homozygotes.

Rife's theory is pursued by Annett (1964), who suggests as well that the gene responsible for handedness also determines which cerebral hemisphere will be specialized for the representation of speech. According to her model, then, individuals homozygous for the normally dominant allele are always right-handed and have speech represented in the left hemisphere, those homozygous for the normally recessive allele show the reverse pattern, while heterozygotes are inconsistent. Most will develop right-handedness and left-hemisphere representation of speech, but in some the recessive allele will produce some tendency for left-handedness or ambilaterality, and for right-hemispheric representation of speech. If it is supposed that about one quarter of the population of heterozygotes show this reversed pattern and that the proportions of dominant and recessive alleles are about .8 and .2, respectively,

TABLE 9.1
Observed and Predicted Incidence of Right Handedness
as a Function of Parental Handedness

Source	Parental matings		
	R−R	R−L	L−L
Observed proportions (Rife, 1940)[a]	.924	.805	.455
Predicted by Levy–Nagylaki model	.927	.783	.362

[a] Based on 1993 offspring of 620 RXR matings, 174 offspring of 62 RXL matings, and 11 offspring of 5 LXL matings.

then this model gives quite a good fit to the breeding ratios reported by Rife (1940) and shown in Table 9.1.

One difficulty with Annett's model, as Levy and Nagylaki (1972) point out, is that it does not account for the fact that a majority of left-handers, perhaps as many as 70%, have speech represented primarily in the *left* hemisphere (e.g., Goodglass & Quadfasel, 1954; Warrington & Pratt, 1973). Annett did suggest that heterozygotes, but not recessive homozygotes, might switch handedness or cerebral lateralization in the event of injury to the left hemisphere. To account for the data, however, one must suppose that cerebral damage is more likely to cause a switch in handedness than in speech representation (cf. Satz, 1972).

Levy and Nagylaki (1972) propose an alternative, ingenious solution to this problem. They suggest that handedness and cerebral lateralization are controlled by two genes, both with complete penetrance. One gene determines which hemisphere controls both speech and the preferred hand. Left-hemispheric control is represented by the dominant allele. The other gene determines whether the controlling hemisphere controls the contralateral or the ipsilateral hand. Contralateral control is the more common and is represented by the dominant allele. In recessive homozygotes, though, hand control is ipsilateral. Most of these will be left-handers with left-hemispheric control, but there should also be a tiny fraction of right-handers with the right hand under the control of the right hemisphere.

The idea that hand control might be ipsilateral in some persons is a contentious one. It is generally thought that cerebral control of the extremities of the limbs, including hands and fingers, is largely if not exclusively contralateral (e.g., Brinkman & Kuypers, 1973). Levy and Nagylaki cite some evidence to suggest that this may not always be so, at least in humans. For instance, autopsies have revealed that some persons lack decussation of the pyramidal tract (Peele, 1961), and must therefore rely on ipsilateral control.

Morever, it has been shown that commissurotomized patients may develop ipsilateral control within a few months of surgery, even though control was contralateral at first (e.g., Gazzaniga & Sperry, 1967). This shows, according to Levy and Nagylaki, that ipsilateral connections retain some potential functional capacity even among people who normally rely on contralateral ones only. As the reader may recall from the previous chapter, Levy (1971) has maintained that ipsilateral control of the writing hand is responsible for the so-called "hook" or inverted style of writing.

Levy and Nagylaki's two-gene model provides a reasonably good fit to several empirical estimates, including Rife's (1940) data on the segregation of handedness by parentage, shown in Table 9.1, and Goodglass and Quadfasel's (1954) estimate that 53% of left-handers have speech representation primarily in the left hemisphere. Levy and Nagylaki also suggest that individuals heterozygous for the lateralization gene have the capacity to develop language representation in the right hemisphere if the left hemisphere is damaged, but that individuals homozygous for lateralization cannot switch language representation in the event of injury. The model then accounts for the estimated 35% of right-handers and 65% of left-handers who either suffer no speech impediment or else recover completely from it following lesions to the speech areas of the left hemisphere (Zangwill, 1960; after Luria, 1969). To obtain these fits, Levy and Nagylaki estimate that the proportion of genes representing language specialization in the left hemisphere is about .77, while the proportion representing contralateral hand control is about .75.

Critique of genetic models.   Although Levy and Nagylaki's model, in particular, is fairly successful in predicting several characteristics of the distribution of handedness and cerebral lateralization, we suspect that models of this kind continue to misrepresent the nature of lateral asymmetries. We have already argued at length that directional information is probably coded in the cytoplasm of the egg rather than in the genes. More particularly, we found no evidence in our earlier review to suggest that the direction of an asymmetry is ever inherited in direct Mendelian fashion. In fact, we know of no certain instance in which a prevailing asymmetry is actually reversed by a genetic influence except perhaps through maternal inheritance.

Another difficulty with models which attribute variations in laterality to a single gene is that handedness, at least, does not seem to be a truly dichotomous variable. The division into right- and left-handers is often merely arbitrary. For example, Rife (1940) used a questionnaire in which subjects rated themselves right-handed, left-handed, or ambidextrous on ten familiar operations.[2] Only those who claimed to use the right hand for all ten operations were designated right-handed, while all others were designated left-handed. Other authors have used quite different measures, some based on stated preference

[2] Throwing, bowling, marbles, knife, spoon, hammer, saw, sewing, writing, scissors.

and others on differential skill, some relying on questionnaires or batteries of tests and others on single statements or tests (see Clark, 1957). Thus, it is not surprising that estimates of the incidence of left-handedness have ranged from as little as 1% to as much as 30% (Hécaen & Ajuriaguerra, 1964, p. 6). Annett (1967) argued that there are truly three categories: right-, mixed- and left-handers. She reconciled this with her 1964 genetic model by supposing that heterozygotes are really mixed-handers, but that cultural pressures may force the majority to favor the right hand. But more recently still, Annett (1972) seems to have accepted that handedness is a continuous variable. Many years earlier, Woo and Pearson (1927) examined in detail the distributions of interocular differences in visual acuity and intermanual differences in hand grip among 4,948 of the cases recorded by Sir Francis Galton at the Health Exhibition of 1884. They concluded:

> It appears to us that lateralization whether ocular or manual is a continuous variate, and that dextrality and sinistrality are not opposed alternatives, but quantities capable of taking values of continuous intensity and passing one into the other [p. 199].

This is difficult to reconcile with the notion that laterality is determined by a single, two-allele gene.

But the strongest empirical challenge to genetic models of handedness comes from Collins (1970), who reanalyzed published data on the distribution of handedness among sibling pairs and among twins. Table 9.2 shows the proportions of sibling pairs who were both right-handed, of opposite handedness, and both left-handed, in a survey of 687 families conducted by Rife (1940). Collins points out that, if P_R is the overall proportion of right-handers, then the observed proportions of pairs in each category are closely matched by the binomial expectancies P_R^2, $2P_R(1-P_R)$ and $(1-P_R)^2$, respectively, implying that the association is little more than a matter of chance. The

TABLE 9.2
Observed and Predicted Concordance of Handedness
in Paired Siblings

Source	Pairings			Phi coefficient
	R–R	R–L	L–L	
Observed proportions	.856	.133	.071	.075
(Rife, 1940)[a]	.856	.133	.011	.075
Expected by chance	.851	.143	.006	0
Predicted by Levy–Nagylaki model	.828	.130	.042	.319

[a]Based on 3583 pairings among 2178 students.

binomial values are also shown in the table. The data can also be expressed in terms of the fourfold point correlation, phi, which can be computed from the formula

$$\phi = \frac{P_{RR} - P_R^2}{P_R(1 - P_R)},$$

where P_{RR} is the proportion of pairs who are both right-handed. The calculated value is only .075, which is very close to zero.

Nagylaki and Levy (1973) counter that these data do not altogether rule out the possibility of a genetic influence. Although the phi of .075 is indeed small, it can almost certainly be considered reliably greater than zero, implying *some* degree of correlation between siblings. Yet it is clearly lower than one would predict from any simple genetic model. If handedness were controlled by a single gene with two alleles, one completely dominant, the predicted value of phi must lie between .25 and .50. According to our calculations, the two-gene model developed by Levy and Nagylaki (1972) would predict a phi of .318 and the third row of Table 9.2 shows the expected proportions based on this model. These predictions are based on estimated parameters[3] and are therefore at something of a disadvantage compared with the binomial predictions, which depend only on the observed value of P_R. Moreover, one might conceivably argue, as do Nagylaki and Levy (1973), that Rife's data are distorted by the fact that he included all possible pairings among siblings, thereby giving undue weight to large families. Even so, there can be no denying that Levy and Nagylaki's model provides a poor fit to the data.

The discrepancy is more striking when one considers the data on twins, summarized in Table 9.3. Levy and Nagylaki's model predicts that monozygotic twins should be *always* concordant for handedness, *never* discordant, since monozygotic twins carry identical genes. Yet Collins (1970) has shown that the actual distributions lie even closer to binomial expectancies than is the case for paired siblings. The Levy–Nagylaki model predicts a phi coefficient of unity, but the empirical value of .026 does not differ significantly from zero. The proportions among dizygotic twins also follow chance expectancies, yielding a phi of $-.027$, whereas the model predicts a value of .318, as for paired siblings in general. Once again, the predictions from the model are at a technical disadvantage compared with Collins' binomial predictions, but this

---

[3] In the first of two very similar solutions, Levy and Nagylaki (1972) estimated P_R to be .893, and the proportions of dominant alleles to be .769 for left-hemispheric speech representation and .755 for contralateral hand control. We used these parameters to generate the expected proportions of sibling pairs shown in Table 9. 2, and the expected value of phi. It should be noted that Levy and Nagylaki's estimates were also based in part on Rife's (1940) data.

TABLE 9.3
Observed and Predicted Concordance of Handedness
in Monozygotic and Dizygotic Twins

Source	Pairings			Phi coefficient
	R–R	R–L	L–L	
Monozygotic twins				
Observed proportions[a]	.749	.229	.022	.026
Expected by chance	.746	.235	.019	0
Predicted by Levy–Nagylaki model	.893	0	.107	1.0
Dizygotic twins				
Observed proportions[a]	.781	.208	.010	−.027
Expected by chance	.784	.203	.013	0
Predicted by Levy–Nagylaki model	.828	.130	.042	.318

[a]Based on combined samples from Wilson and Jones (1932), Newman, Freeman and Holzinger (1937), and Rife (1950), giving a total of 463 monozygotic and 384 dizygotic twin pairs (after Collins, 1970).

cannot mask the fact that the model does not even come close to predicting the observed values.

Levy and Nagylaki have provided no answer for the failure of their model to predict the data from paired siblings, but they argue that data from twins should not be used to test genetic models of handedness (Nagylaki & Levy, 1973). We discuss this next.

The relevance of twins.   We have just seen that the distributions of concordant and discordant handedness among both monozygotic and dizygotic twins are very closely approximated by binomial expectancies. Handedness might just as well be determined by the flip of a (biased) coin. As Collins (1970) points out, this is strong evidence against *any* genetic model.

Nagylaki and Levy (1973) protest that twins cannot be considered representative of the general population. For one thing, the proportion of left-handedness is higher among twins than among the singly born. Levy and Nagylaki give pooled estimates of .145 for monozygotic twins, .109 for dizygotic twins, but only .067 for the general population. Collins provides similar estimates, but argues that the higher proportion of sinistrality among twins simply imposes an extra burden on genetic explanations. Nagylaki and Levy counter that this is evidence for a spurious, nongenetic influence, related to increased pathology among twins. They cite evidence that twins also show a higher frequency of mental deficiency, brain damage, and infant mortality than the singly born, presumably because of crowding in the uterus. They also note that males are more susceptible than females to prenatal pathology (Weiner, Rider, Oppel, Fisher, & Harper, 1965) and that discordance for handedness is correspondingly higher among males than among females (Gordon, 1920). Because of the high incidence of pathology among twins, Nagylaki and Levy conclude that twins do not provide a fair test of genetic factors operating in the general population.

They also raise the question of special mirror-imaging effects, which may artificially increase the proportion of monozygotic twins who are discordant for handedness. One commonly hears of "mirror twins," in which one twin is said to be the mirror image of the other. Among joined together ("Siamese") twins, in fact, it is usual to find that one twin exhibits *situs inversus,* with reversal of the heart and other visceral organs (Newman, 1940). However, true *situs inversus* is extremely rare among separate monozygotic twins, perhaps as rare as in the general population (Torgerson, 1950). Yet Newman (1940) observes that monozygotic twins do often show reversals in ectodermally derived tissue, which excludes the viscera but includes handprints, hair whorls, handedness, and eye dominance. He suggests that the frequency of mirror-imaged features may depend on how late in development the embryo divides to form twins; in Siamese twins, the division begins so late that it remains uncompleted, and the mirror imaging extends even to the viscera. But Newman also points out that it is difficult to distinguish special mirror-imaging effects peculiar to monozygotic twinning from more general factors which operate in the population at large to produce occasional reversals. He notes that the great majority of twins display no mirror-imaged features. Moreover, as Tables 9.2 and 9.3 make clear, it follows simply from binomial expectancies that if one twin shows reversed handedness, say, the other twin is much more likely not to show it than to show it. The notion of special mirror-imaging effects among twins may therefore be based partly on a superstitious misinterpretation of the evidence.

Newman himself seems to prefer the interpretation that reversals among twins do not depend on twinning per se, but are simply a consequence of prenatal environmental conditions which may also affect the singly born, although perhaps to a lesser extent. However, Rife (1940) notes that environmental pressures among twins, due to crowding in the uterus, may well increase the proportion of cases in which one twin is right-handed and the other left-handed. This would presumably apply to dizygotic as well as to monozygotic twins and could explain why the phi coefficients were lower for both kinds of twins than for paired siblings in general. This influence must have been fairly small, however.

There is an additional point to make about reversals in hair whorling among twins. Nagylaki and Levy refer to data reported by Rife (1933) which show that the frequencies of concordant and discordant hair whorls among monozygotic twins fall very close to binomial expectancies, just as the frequencies of concordant and discordant handedness do. They then cite the often-quoted but seldom-read report by Bernstein (1925), which alleges that the direction of hair whorling is determined by a gene with two alleles, the dominant one being that for clockwise whorling. Quite reasonably, Levy and Nagylaki point out that if the distribution of hair whorls among monozygotic twins is binomial despite the fact that hair whorling is genetically determined, surely the same could be true of handedness. Unfortunately, the argument appears to be without foundation. After consulting Bernstein's article, published in German in a relatively inaccessible journal, Morgan (1976) pronounces it to be nonsense. There is no evidence that the direction of hair whorling is genetically determined.

The fact that twins are more likely than the singly born to be left-handed raises the possibility of an indirect genetic effect. The disposition to give birth to twins might itself be maternally inherited and depend in part on genetic influences in the mother. Newman (1940) suggests that this is more likely to be the case for dizygotic than for monozygotic twins, since dizygotic twinning depends on double ovulation in the mother. He cites evidence that multiple-egg births do tend to run in families, implying a genetic influence, but he states that he knows of no evidence, other than anecdotal, to suggest that monozygotic twinning is inherited. Rife (1940) found that left-handedness was no more frequent among the immediate relatives of dizygotic twins than in nontwin families, and was unaccountably *less* frequent among the immediate relatives of monozygotic twins. These observations suggest that there is no common genetic basis for left-handedness and twinning, but that a tendency to produce twins, perhaps in part genetic, might indirectly increase the proportion of left-handed progeny. Such an influence would presumably be very weak.

The strongest point to emerge from Nagylaki and Levy's critique is simply that twins are more likely to be left-handed than are the singly born, probably because of prenatal environmental stresses. However, this does not prove that the factors which determine handedness in twins are different *in kind* from those which determine handedness in the singly born. Indeed, it has been claimed that left-handedness is *always* due to cerebral anoxia associated with birth stress, on the grounds that left-handed and ambilateral persons are about twice as likely to have suffered known birth stress than are right-handers (Bakan, 1971; Bakan, Dibb, & Reed, 1973). We suspect this claim is exaggerated (see, e.g., Satz, 1973), but the point is that pathological left-handedness is certainly not confined to twins. Overall, Collins' analyses of concordant and discordant handedness suggest continuity rather than discontinuity between twins and nontwin siblings. At most, it might be conceded that a small mirror-imaging effect among both monozygotic and dizygotic twins might have raised the proportion of discordant pairs, dropping the phi coefficient to zero. But the coefficient was very small even for paired siblings. Overall, any genetic influence seems to have been dwarfed by a large random component.

Annett's new theory.   In general, the evidence reviewed so far is consistent with Annett's (1972) most recent analysis of handedness, which we have already briefly discussed in Chapter 8. She proposes that there are two components underlying the distribution of human handedness. One is a bell-shaped component, reflecting random or "accidental" influences. The other is the "right-shift" component, which Annett assumes to be genetic, and which accounts for the fact that most people are right-handed. The random component explains why there is so little consistency between twins and between siblings. If we suppose that the variance of this component is larger among twins than among siblings, perhaps because of a greater variability in intrauterine conditions, then we have a straightforward explanation for the increased incidence of left-handedness among twins. If the *variance* of the right-shift component is small compared with that of the random component, we can understand why the phi values are so small.

It might perhaps be questioned whether there is *any* variation in the right-shift component, since the random component could presumably override the right shift in some small proportion of individuals to produce left-handedness. Annett (1972) suggests, however, that left-handedness might also be attributed partly to a "weak dose" of the right shift. In a later article (Annett, 1974), she suggests that the right shift may sometimes be completely lacking. Among individuals who lack the right shift, an unbiased test of handedness should reveal equal proportions of right- and left-handers. If this condition is inherited,[4] the children of couples who are left-handed should display no overall superiority with either hand. To test this, Annett studied intermanual differences on a peg-moving task among the offspring of 29 left-handed couples. Among these families there were five in which one or both parents reported some history of perinatal difficulty or other early stresses which might have influenced their own handedness. The eight children of these couples were significantly faster on the task with their right hands than with their left. However, the 45 children of the remaining 24 couples showed an average intermanual difference that was essentially zero and were about equally divided between those faster with the right hand (23) and those faster with the left (22). As predicted, these children evidently lacked the right-shift component.

Familial versus nonfamilial left-handedness.   Annett's (1974) experiment suggests that one must distinguish between *familial* and *nonfamilial* left-handers. Familial left-handers do not inherit left-handedness per se; rather, they inherit the absence of any bias toward either left- or right-handedness or toward any consistent cerebral lateralization. The nonfamilial group may be left-handed for reasons associated with birth stress or prenatal pathology. If we suppose that mild damage to the left hemisphere is more likely to cause a child to switch handedness than to switch speech representation (cf. Satz, 1972, 1973), then we can understand why more individuals are left-handed than have speech represented in the right hemisphere (e.g., Goodglass & Quadfasel, 1954).

---

[4]Annett (1972) makes the curious suggestion that right-handedness is inherited, but left-handedness is not. By "inherited," she evidently means "genetically determined."

There is other evidence to support the distinction between familial and nonfamilial left-handers. Zurif and Bryden (1969) defined familial left-handers as those with at least one left-handed parent or sibling, and found that these subjects showed inconsistent cerebral dominance according to tests based on dichotic listening and tachistoscopic visual perception. Nonfamilial left-handers showed the usual left-hemispheric dominance for the processing of verbal items. Similarly, Hécaen and Sauguet (1971), using a somewhat looser definition of familial left-handedness, compared the effects of left- and right-hemisphere lesions on language functions among familial and nonfamilial left-handers. Again, the familial group was equally divided in terms of which hemisphere was dominant for language, while the nonfamilial group was almost exclusively left-hemisphere dominant. Finally, there is evidence that recovery from aphasia is faster and more complete among familial than among nonfamilial left-handers (Luria, 1969), suggesting that familial left-handers show the greater degree of equipotentiality between hemispheres.

Although this analysis suggests that pathological left-handedness is generally nonfamilial, there may be a weak genetic influence transmitted through the mother. Annett (1972) notes that left-handed mothers are more likely to have left-handed children than are left-handed fathers. This tendency can be observed in her own data as well as those of Chamberlain (1928), Ramaley (1913), and Rife (1940). It is probably fairly weak; in Rife's survey, for example, 25.6% of the children of left-handed mothers were left-handed, compared with 21.8% of the children with left-handed fathers. We suspect that this influence, although perhaps weakly genetically determined in the mother, is probably bestowed on her child through the embryonic environment she provides. Torgerson (1950) also argues that *situs inversus* is in part genetically influenced and can be considered a pathological condition, at least insofar as it is associated with such symptoms as defective development of the bronchi and nasal sinuses. However, he gives no indication as to whether or not *situs inversus* is maternally inherited. Although the genetic influence on pathological left-handedness slightly blurs our distinction between familial and nonfamilial left-handedness, we think the distinction is still one that is generally valid and useful. The great majority of pathological left-handers would normally be classified as nonfamilial.

Although there are undoubtedly still some anomalies to be explained, the distinction between familial and nonfamilial left-handers goes a long way toward reconciling conflicting claims. Thus, left-handedness is neither wholly pathological nor wholly genetic. Pathological left-handedness would be largely confined to the nonfamilial group. Its incidence is difficult to assess accurately. Suppose, for example, that we begin with the estimate that about 30% of left-handers have speech represented primarily in the right hemisphere (e.g., Warrington & Pratt, 1973). We may assume that nearly all of these are familial left-handers, although some small proportion may consist of those who have been forced to switch both handedness and speech dominance through damage to the left hemisphere. Zurif and Bryden's data suggest that about the same number of familial left-handers will have speech represented primarily in the left hemisphere. This leaves about 40% who are nonfamilial or pathological left-handers. The estimate may be too high, since the original figure of 30% with which we began is based primarily on lesion studies, and we may suppose that pathological left-handers tend to be overrepresented among neurological patients. Annett's (1974) study of handedness among the families of university undergraduates suggests in fact that the incidence of pathological left-handedness may be considerably less than 40% but again an accurate estimate is not possible from Annett's report.

Conclusions. We conclude that right-handedness and the left-cerebral representation of speech are expressions of a fundamental left–right gradient that is ultimately cytoplasmic rather than genetic. It is because of man's genetic makeup, however, that this gradient is expressed in these particular ways. Variations between individuals can be attributed largely to a random component. Nevertheless, some people inherit a lack of any consistent genetic disposition toward manual or cerebral asymmetry. Among this minority, handedness and cerebral lateralization are determined at random, and possibly independently. Indeed, these persons may possess a cerebral organization that is quite different from the normal, one that is characterized by a more diffuse localization both within and between hemispheres (e.g., Hécaen & Sauguet, 1971). Other people are left-handed for reasons associated with birth stress or prenatal pathology, but may show the normal lateralization of cerebral functions.

We have not found it necessary to suppose that genetic influences actually cause a *reversal* of the usual asymmetries of hand and brain, except perhaps indirectly through maternal inheritance. This is consistent with our earlier conclusion, based on a review of the biological evidence. Left-handedness, except in pathological cases, is due to the cancellation of the usual asymmetry, not to its reversal. Annett's (1974) experiment suggests that this cancellation might be inherited in direct Mendelian fashion and might even depend on a single recessive allele. However, this does not of course mean that left-handedness is inherited in this way. The genetic influence simply removes an overall predisposition to be right-handed, but the ultimate determination of handedness is still essentially random.

SUMMARY

We have argued that the symmetries and asymmetries of organisms are expressions ultimately of positional information that is coded in the cytoplasm of the oocyte rather than in the genes. Genetic influences may interact with positional information, however, to determine the particular forms that these symmetries and asymmetries may take. We emphasize again that lateral asymmetries should be viewed in the wider context of bilateral symmetry. The distinction between left and right depends on the prior establishment of a median plane and an overall symmetrical organization. The underlying symmetry is also illustrated by the phenomenon of *situs inversus,* in which the usual asymmetries are mirror reversed.

Right-handedness and the left-cerebral lateralization of speech functions can be viewed as expressions of the same fundamental left−right gradient which also produces the leftward displacement and asymmetry of the heart, the predominantly leftward manifestation of genetic abnormalities such as polydactylism in fowl or harelip and cleft palate in man, the doubling of the habenular nuclei on the left side of the amphibian brain, or the left-hypoglossal control of song in passerine birds. Annett's (1972) "right shift" is truly a *left* shift, which is manifest in different ways in different species. This left−right gradient probably has to do with a differential *rate* of growth, usually favoring the left side, and not with any difference in absolute *potential.* If the usually predominant left side is damaged or inhibited, the right side can then assume the leading role. The most extreme example is *situs inversus.* As less extreme examples, we have seen how the right hypoglossus can assume control of birdsong if the left is damaged, just as the right hemisphere can assume control of human speech if the left is injured. This growth differential thus makes for equipotentiality and plasticity in the control of those functions which have the highest priority, so that the effects of early damage to one or other side of the brain or nervous system are confined to secondary functions.

Within species, genetic influences are fairly restricted, presumably because they are subject to the constraints of the positional-information code. In particular, we know of no evidence that the genes can influence the *direction* of an asymmetry, except through the mother. Maternal inheritance aside, genetic effects may operate to increase, reduce, or even cancel an existing asymmetry, but not to reverse it. Left-handedness can thus be attributed in part to a genetically determined lack of any cerebral asymmetry, together with random influences which dictate that half of those affected will be right-handed and half left-handed. In other cases, left-handedness can be attributed to birth stress, or to other stresses in the prenatal or early postnatal environment.

This brings us to the end of our discussion of the nature of symmetry and asymmetry in organisms. We can now return to the main theme of our book. We shall be mainly occupied with the ability of humans to tell left from right, and how this can be related to other structural and functional asymmetries.

10

Development of
the Left–Right Sense

Poor little sucker, how will it learn
When it is climbing, which way to turn?
Right — left — what a disgrace!
Or it may go straight up and fall flat on its face!

— Misalliance
MICHAEL FLANDERS[1]

Although young children have great difficulty distinguishing left from right, it does seem, at least superficially, that the problem does not extend much beyond childhood. Some adults continue to experience left – right confusion, particularly under conditions of stress, as when giving or following directions while driving a car, but the overwhelming picture is one of reasonable competence. Few literate adults will inadvertently reverse words or letters when writing and most are quick to spot such reversals in the early efforts of their children.

In this chapter we discuss the development during childhood of the ability to tell left from right. We shall first review the experimental evidence and then turn to more theoretical issues, including a consideration of the nature of the structural asymmetry which must underlie the developing left – right sense. Once again, we shall be mainly concerned with evidence on mirror-image discrimination and left – right differentiation, which we defined in Chapter 2. We urge the reader to review these definitions, for we shall again encounter some studies which purport to test the ability to tell left from right but which do not meet our criteria. For example, some experiments merely require the child to perceive which way round a stimulus is, perhaps to match it to some sample pattern, but do not require him to label it as distinct from its mirror image. Such tasks do not require the ability to tell left from right.

In our review of evidence, we shall also find it convenient to distinguish tests which are modeled on a learning paradigm from those which are not. The learning tests, all concerned with simultaneous or successive mirror-image

[1]Quoted in Gardner (1967, p. 67).

discrimination, are the more comparable to those used in the animal studies reviewed in Chapter 4. In these tests the verbal element is minimized. The child is given brief verbal instructions, but his main task is to learn to select one of two mirror-image stimuli on the basis of simple feedback from the experimenter, who simply informs the child on each trial whether his selection was right or wrong.

By contrast, nonlearning tests are typically made up of multiple items of varying complexity. Each item is presented once only and the child may or may not be told whether his response is correct. The child's success depends in part on his ability or willingness to follow verbal instructions, which may be quite complex. Further ambiguities may arise if the test involves the actual *terms* "left" and "right," as we saw in Chapter 2. For instance, a child might fail to label the sides of another person correctly, not because he does not know his own left and right sides, but because he cannot perform the necessary spatial transformations to map his own body coordinates onto that person's. We do not mean to imply that multiitem nonlearning tests are necessarily inferior to learning tests; they may in fact more accurately reflect the development and range of abilities involved in the correct use of the labels "left" and "right" in the real world. However, these abilities include verbal and spatial abilities as well as the fundamental ability to tell left from right. Learning tests, on the other hand, focus rather more specifically on the ability to tell left from right and depend relatively little on more generalized verbal and spatial abilities.

EXPERIMENTAL EVIDENCE

Nonlearning Tests

Several developmental studies using tests in the nonlearning category have compared the performances of children over various age ranges on their ability to make left – right differentiations of varying complexity. Three of these studies, those of Piaget (1928), Swanson and Benton (1955), and Belmont and Birch (1963), used similar batteries of test items in which the child was required to exhibit left – right response differentiation in relation to his own body parts and to other objects in the environment. These studies showed that by the age of six most children could reliably differentiate between the left and right parts of their own bodies, but that performance on the other items continued to improve up to age ten. This result is not surprising, since we must be able to differentiate the sides of our own bodies before we can respond to other objects in terms of their relation to our left and right sides.

Boone and Prescott (1968) have reported normative developmental data obtained from a nonlearning test of response differentiation. As in the tests just mentioned, the subjects were given verbal instructions, but their responses were made on special stimulus-response panels displaying up to six colored and numbered circles. Of the 40 test items, 17 required left–right differentiation, the other 23 (designated "foil items") requiring up–down, color, or number differentiation, or some combination of these. Of the items requiring left–right differentiation 15 also required color differentiation (for example, "point to the right green circle") or up–down differentiation (for example, "point to the highest left circle"). Analysis performed on errors made on the 17 left–right differentiation items showed a progressive decrease in errors over the entire age range studies (five to ten years). Five-year-olds made an average of 9.32 errors; ten-year-olds made an average of 1.32. The function relating errors to age was essentially a straight line.

Boone and Prescott's analysis shows their 17 left–right items to have excellent discriminative properties. They do constitute a good developmental test of something, but what? It is clear that errors on the left–right items may have been errors of left–right confusion, but only two items did not confound left–right with other types of differentiation. On the remaining 15 items, errors may have been color or up–down confusions rather than, or as well as, left–right confusions. The children may also have been confused simply by the complexity of the items. The various types of error were unfortunately not separated for analysis. The analysis does show that the items that did not involve left–right differentiation were much easier than those that did, but it is also clear that the two simple left–right items were easier than 13 of the 15 items that combined left–right with color or up–down differentiation, indicating that errors on the left–right items were affected by other sources of confusion. Thus we should interpret with caution the developmental trend revealed by Boone and Prescott's "Left–Right Discrimination Test." The developmental function might be radically changed by removal of all but genuine left–right errors.

Boone and Prescott's test is basically concerned with left–right response differentiation. An experiment by Davidson (1935) emphasizes rather the confusion between mirror-image stimuli. She found that confusions between the lateral mirror-image pairs p and q, b and d, were more frequent than those between the up–down mirror-image pairs p and b, q and d. This was so over the age range studied, which was from five to ten years. However, her task was not a true test of mirror-image discrimination. Each child was given a sheet of paper featuring a sample letter on the left side and a box containing four rows of ten letters. The child was instructed to look at the sample letter, then to mark each letter exactly like it in the box. The task was therefore one of matching to sample, with the sample letter continuously available. The child needed only to perceive which way round the stimuli were in order to respond correctly. Yet all children in the lowest mental age group (about four and a half to five years) made errors in which lateral mirror images were treated as equivalent.

Davidson commented as follows:

Sometimes a child would mark the b's as well as the d's, then stop and erase the b's, saying: "This faces this way and that faces that way." Other children would mark all the b's and d's. At the conclusion of the test the writer would point to the 'model' letter then to one after another of the letters marked by the child, asking: "Is this the same as that?" Some children replied in the affirmative to all. One or two said "Yes," then added: "This faces this way and that faces that way." These observations were made on only one or two isolated cases but seemed to indicate that the child noticed the difference in the orientation of the letters but did not consider that this fact made them different. This type of recognition would seem to be similar to that in which the child recognizes a chair no matter which way the seat is facing. A chair turned upside down might possibly be another matter, however [Davidson, 1935, pp. 464–465].

In other words, the children often failed to understand the instructions, which implicitly required them to treat left–right mirror images as "different." Yet this very failure illustrates that the equivalence of left–right mirror images is much more salient than that between up–down mirror images.

The same point emerges from a study by Caldwell and Hall (1969). They showed that children given a matching task like that administered by Davidson made fewer confusions of orientation after prior training on a task in which orientation was relevant. The prior task clearly helped make explicit what was meant by "same" and "different." Unfortunately, however, Caldwell and Hall did not examine the relative frequencies of left–right and up–down errors. Moreover, a misunderstanding of instructions does not explain the confusion of left–right mirror images in learning tasks, which we discuss next.

Learning Tests

Developmental studies of children's ability to learn left–right distinctions have generally been modeled on the discrimination training procedures developed for studying the sensory and learning capabilities of animals. For instance, Rudel and Teuber (1963) performed an experiment in which 93 children, comprising six age groups from three and a half to eight and a half years, had to learn simultaneous discriminations between vertical and horizontal lines, mirror-image obliques, upright and inverted U shapes, and left–right mirror-image U shapes. On each task, the subjects were told to pick which stimulus of each pair was the right one, and that they would be informed on each trial whether or not they had chosen correctly. At first they could only guess. The stimuli to be discriminated were then presented side by side and their relative positions were varied in a quasi-random fashion on successive trials. A maximum of 50 trials were given with each pair of stimuli, but fewer than 50 were given if the child reached a criterion for mastery of the discrimination.

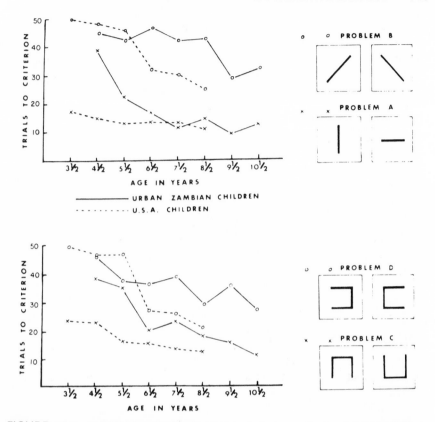

FIGURE 10.1   Trials to master discriminations between vertical and horizontal lines (Problem A), mirror-image oblique lines (Problem B), up–down mirror image U shapes (Problem C), and left–right mirror-image U shapes (Problem D), for children of different ages. The results from Rudel and Teuber's (1963) study with children from the United States are compared with those from Serpell's (1971) study with Zambian children. (From Serpell, 1971. Copyright 1971 by the American Psychological Association. Reprinted by permission.)

The majority of the younger children (three- to four-year-olds) and all the older children mastered the discriminations between vertical and horizontal and between the upright and inverted U's. By contrast, none of the 12 three-year-olds and only one of the 12 four-year-olds learned to discriminate the obliques, and only one of the three-year-olds and two of the four-year-olds mastered the left–right mirror-image U shapes. Performance on the left–right mirror-image problems improved with age, but even in the oldest group performance was still markedly better on the other problems.

The functions relating performance to age (Fig. 10.1) showed that the rate of improvement of performance with age was similar for both types of problem (left–right and other) over all but the middle of the age range studied. Between the ages of five and a half and six and a half, however, the improvement in performance on the left – right problems was markedly greater than at other ages. Since it is likely that the children concerned received their initial instruction in reading and writing between these ages, we may perhaps conclude that the sudden improvement in performance reflects the training in left–right discrimination which must inevitably have been given. This explanation has also been offered by Serpell (1971) and is supported by the results of his replication of the Rudel and Teuber experiment with Zambian children. Serpell's findings generally paralleled those of Rudel and Teuber, save that the greatest rate of improvement in performance on the left – right problems occurred over the range from seven and a half to ten and a half years (see Fig. 10.1). But again, this corresponded to the period during which the children were normally introduced to reading and writing in the school system.

Since the stimuli in both Rudel and Teuber's and Serpell's experiments were presented simultaneously and side by side, there is some ambiguity as to whether the task can be considered a genuine test of mirror-image discrimination, as we pointed out in Chapter 2. If the children responded on the basis of the total configuration represented by each stimulus pair, the task is really one of left–right response differentiation. There is some evidence that children are indeed influenced by configurational cues in this paradigm. Huttenlocher (1967) has reported that five-year-olds found it much more difficult to discriminate left – right mirror-image U shapes than to discriminate up – down mirror-image U shapes when the stimuli were presented side by side, but the difference disappeared when they were placed one above the other.[2] *Overall, the left – right problems were the more difficult, but the way in which the stimuli were aligned evidently affected the discrimination as well.*

We are inclined to think that configurational cues would have had less influence in the Rudel and Teuber experiment than in Huttenlocher's experiment, however, because the stimuli were presented somewhat differently. Rudel and Teuber used a separate card for each stimulus and always presented their two cards two inches apart so that the individual stimuli were separated by 4.5 inches. This distance was large in relation to the size of the stimuli, which were 2.5 inches by 2.5 inches. Huttenlocher, on the other hand, presented two stimuli on a single card, separating by only one inch stimuli that were 4.25 inches by 3.25 inches. We suspect, therefore, that Huttenlocher's stimuli may have emphasized configurational cues rather more than Rudel and Teuber's did.

Two experiments by Over and Over make the important point that the confusion of mirror-image obliques is a problem of labeling and not a problem

[2]Sekuler and Rosenblith (1964) claimed to have found a similar effect, but their task required the children to make judgments of sameness and difference—not a true test of the ability to tell left from right.

of perceiving which way round the stimuli are. They found that young school children and preschool children had extreme difficulty learning a simultaneous discrimination of mirror-image obliques, whether presented visually (Over & Over, 1967a) or tactually (Over & Over, 1967b), but no such difficulty discriminating horizontal from vertical. However, the children in these experiments had no difficulty at all in judging whether two obliques were the same or whether they were mirror images, a task which does not require them to tell left from right. The reader may recall from Chapter 4 a similar experiment by Tee and Riesen (1974) showing that rats have difficulty discriminating mirror-image obliques, but no such difficulty deciding which of two obliques is the same as a sample stimulus. Over (1967) describes the difficulty of discriminating mirror-image obliques as one of "recognition" rather than one of "detection" of the orientation of a line.

The Oblique Effect

At this point we must digress somewhat to reconsider the "oblique effect" (Appelle, 1972), which we also encountered in Chapter 4. Since the experiments of Rudel and Teuber, Serpell, and Over and Over were concerned with the discrimination of mirror-image obliques, it is possible that the difficulty had to do with the fact that the lines were oblique and not with the confusion of left and right. Although Over and Over's results seem to rule out any influence of perceptual or sensory deficits associated with obliques, it is not out of the question that children may find it peculiarly difficult to conceptualize obliqueness at a higher cognitive level or to encode information about a particular oblique line in memory.

Olson (1970) has devoted an entire book to the development of the concept of diagonality, based largely on the fact that children under the age of about seven years find it extremely difficult to fill in a diagonal on a checkerboard array. He argues that the child has no simple way to mentally encode a diagonal. We do not have single word descriptions which differentiate the two diagonals, whereas the terms "horizontal" and "vertical," for example, are in themselves fully explicit. A particular diagonal requires at least two descriptors, such as "*up* to the *right*." Olson does not consider the problem to be fundamentally linguistic, however; rather, the linguistic descriptions reflect properties of deeper cognitive processes. His argument, then, is that the child must encode more information to characterize a given diagonal than to characterize the horizontal or vertical. It should be noted, however, that any descriptive system which distinguishes the two opposite diagonals must make use of the concepts of left and right so that at least part of the difficulty of discriminating them can surely be attributed to left–right confusion. Nevertheless the difficulty may well be compounded by the fact that the terms "left" and "right" are not by themselves sufficient.

Bryant (1969) has also emphasized that the difficulty with oblique lines is one of coding, but he suggests that the problem is not primarily a mirror-image one. He studied the ability of five- and seven-year-olds to match one of two test stimuli to a standard. The test stimuli were either mirror-image obliques, or a horizontal versus a vertical line, or an oblique versus either a horizontal or a vertical. Each pair of test stimuli was presented either simultaneously with the standard or five seconds later. The seven-year-olds had no difficulty with any of the problems and the five-year-olds had difficulty only with mirror-image obliques, and then only when the test pair was delayed. This at least confirms Over's (1967) conclusion that the problem with mirror-image obliques is not primarily perceptual, but reflects a difficulty in encoding the orientation of an oblique line for subsequent recognition.

But Bryant also showed that the five-year-olds continued to have difficulty on the delayed matching task even if the lines were not exact mirror images of one another. In this experiment, the lines were rotated so that one was 22.5° from the vertical, the other 22.5° from the horizontal. More recently, Bryant (1973) has confirmed that children perform as poorly when the stimuli are obliques but are not mirror images as when they are mirror images. In both experiments, however, it appears that the non-mirror-image obliques were still oriented in opposite directions from the vertical and were thus distinguished by left – right orientation as well as by slope. Consequently, the inability of the children to discriminate them could still have been due partly to left – right confusion. It is noteworthy, of course, that the children were also unable to discriminate the lines on the basis of the difference in degree of slope; Bryant (1969) remarked that the children "remember an oblique as an oblique, but they do not remember its slope *or its direction* [p. 1332; our italics]." Although the problem is not exclusively a mirror-image one, therefore, it may still be, at least partly, a problem of left and right.

However, Bryant (1969) went on to propose a totally different interpretation which makes no reference to left – right confusion. He suggested that the discrimination of line orientation in a delayed matching task depends on a "match – mismatch" code. This in turn depends on whether there are lines of like orientation in the stimulus background. Thus when the stimuli are displayed on rectangular cards, horizontal and vertical can be distinguished by the fact that a vertical line is aligned with the sides of the card, a horizontal line with the top and bottom. There are no such matching lines for the obliques. In yet another experiment, Bryant demonstrated that mirror-image obliques proved relatively easy for the five-year-olds to discriminate if an internal, diamond-shaped border was drawn on the cards, its edges parallel to the stimulus lines. However, the top two edges of the diamond were in different colors, one red, one blue, so that the child simply had to code the stimulus line according to whether it was parallel to a red line or parallel to a blue line. The task was no longer one of mirror-image discrimination and the stimuli could be differentially coded without reference to left and right. This, rather than the presence of the border per se, could explain the improved discrimination of the obliques.

An experiment by Fellows and Brooks (1973) suggests in fact that the match–mismatch hypothesis is incorrect. Using the same delayed matching paradigm that Bryant used, Fellows and Brooks compared the discrimination of horizontal versus vertical and of mirror-image obliques, using cards with drawn-in borders that were either square or diamond-shaped. According to Bryant's hypothesis, the horizontal and vertical lines should have been as difficult to discriminate with diamond-shaped borders as the obliques were with square borders. On the contrary, however, the five-year-olds tested by Fellows and Brooks had little difficulty discriminating horizontal from vertical, but were close to chance level in discriminating the obliques, *regardless of the shape of the border*. Moreover, discrimination of the obliques was just about as poor when the two top edges of the diamond-shaped border were different colors as when they were both the same color. These results therefore fail even to replicate Bryant's findings, probably because Bryant gave his subjects pretraining designed to draw their attention to the borders around the stimuli, while Fellows and Brooks did not. Fellows and Brooks' experiment nevertheless demonstrates that the presence or absence of matching lines is of little importance, except perhaps in the very special circumstances of Bryant's experiment with the colored borders.

We are left with the strong impression that left–right confusion is a major factor underlying the five-year-old's inability to discriminate mirror-image obliques. It would be surprising if this were not so, since the five-year-old also has extreme difficulty with left–right response differentiation and with the discrimination of lateral mirror images which contain no obliques. Figure 10. 1 shows in fact that the development of the ability to discriminate mirror-image obliques is paralleled by the development of the ability to discriminate mirror-image U shapes, suggesting a common mechanism. This is not to deny that the difficulty with mirror-image obliques may be compounded by sensory or perceptual factors, or by an added complexity in the code required to characterize one oblique as distinct from its opposite, or by difficulties in coding the degree of slope of a line.

Procedures That Improve Left–Right Discrimination

We have seen that children seem to be able to make the simplest kind of response differentiation by about the age of six years, when they can identify the left and right sides of their own bodies on request. Thereafter, their ability to make the same differentiation with respect to other bodies or objects gradually develops and is usually mastered by about the age of ten. Mirror-image discrimination also gradually improves from the age of about four to about ten years, the most rapid improvement coinciding with the first year of instruction in reading and writing. Up–down discrimination shows a more constant, more gradual rate of improvement, remaining always superior to left–right discrimination.

Our account so far suggests that instruction in reading and writing may play an important role in the development of left–right discrimination. It is also possible, however, that both the development of left–right discrimination and readiness for reading and writing depend on some underlying maturational development. In order to assess more accurately the role of instruction, therefore, it seems most appropriate to examine studies in which the instructional procedures are more specifically geared to left–right discrimination than to reading and writing, and are therefore more amenable to analysis.

Training procedures have usually been directed toward teaching the child to make some nonverbal, overt response to mirror-image forms. Jeffrey (1958) reported an experiment in which four-year-olds were required to attach different verbal labels to two stick figures, one pointing left and the other pointing right. The figures were presented successively and a learning paradigm was followed. Most of the children were unable to learn the task. Half of the children, designated the experimental group, were then given instructions to push a button located in the direction to which the stick figure pointed. The children were trained on this task to a criterion of ten successive correct responses and then returned to the labeling task where their performance was found to have markedly improved compared with their original performance or the performance of a control group that had continued on the original task. Jeffrey's discussion provides some insight into the effect of the response training with the buttons:

> A number of the children, however, obviously used the button-pressing response or fractional parts of it in learning to apply the names. In one case, a child who had to be told twice to discontinue the button pressing started lifting the appropriate shoulder for each stimulus before applying labels. Other children would look at the appropriate button before supplying the name of the figure [Jeffrey, 1958, pp. 273–274].

How are we to interpret these observations? The button responses are easily made because they do not require a left–right distinction; they simply copy the left–right asymmetries in the stick figures. The facilitative effect of this training on performance of the labeling task suggests that the children found it easier to discriminate between their own left–right responses than the left–right asymmetries that these responses copied. We should not find this surprising, since we have already noted that left–right distinctions about our own bodies are mastered before those about other objects. Empirical considerations aside, this much is evident from the fact that the left–right dimension has meaning only in relation to our own laterality.

It seems, then, that one function of the response training was to draw attention to the relation between the laterality of the stick figures and that of the child's own body. Thus, the response training is seen as a formalization of an essential step in the discriminative process. This analysis is borne out by the results of a second experiment by Jeffrey (1966) which replicated Rudel and Teuber's (1963) finding that four-year-old children had great difficulty discriminating mirror-image obliques. Jeffrey also demonstrated that certain changes in stimuli and procedure significantly increased the number of children able to master the discrimination. Furthermore, following pretraining with these facilitative procedures, a significantly greater proportion of children could differentiate oblique lines under the conditions used by Rudel and Teuber. The stimulus changes consisted of adding arrowheads to the lower end of the oblique lines. The procedural difference was to train the children to press a different button for each stimulus. For one group of children the buttons were placed to the left and right of the stimulus card and the child was required to press the button indicated by the arrowhead. For the other group of children the buttons were aligned one in front of the other, perpendicular to the stimulus cards, and the child was required to press the nearer button for one stimulus and the further button for the other. The arrowheads were omitted from the stimuli for this group. The first procedure was learned more easily than the second and had a much greater facilitative effect on performance in the Rudel and Teuber task. This result is consistent with our above interpretation of the facilitative function of the button-pressing training in Jeffrey's (1958) earlier experiment. Responses to near and far buttons would not be expected to facilitate discrimination, since they did not involve a left–right response. In fact, we would expect the near–far button task to be as difficult as the verbal labeling task in Jeffrey's earlier experiment, since both involve genuine mirror-image discrimination; the results suggest that this was the case.

Clarke and Whitehurst (1974) trained kindergarten children on successive discrimination tasks with either left–right or up–down mirror-image stimuli. Learning was faster on the up–down stimuli, but the rate of learning on the left–right stimuli depended on the spatial relation between the stimuli and the response made to them. When the children were instructed to touch a particular side of the stimuli before applying a verbal label, they learned more rapidly than in other conditions in which they did not touch the stimuli, touched the center, or touched both sides. Transfer tests revealed that children who touched only one side of the stimuli learned to distinguish the stimuli on the basis of only those parts of the stimuli that were touched. The asymmetric touching of the stimuli effectively converted the problem from a mirror-image discrimination into a simple color discrimination. Children who initially failed to discriminate the left–right mirror images were able to master the problem when they were instructed to touch one side of the stimuli before labeling them.

A study by Hill, McCullum, and Sceau (1967) showed that the performance of mentally retarded children on the Belmont and Birch (1965) test of left–right differentiation was facilitated by practice in motor activities featuring asymmetrical responses. These activities included games in which a ball was thrown and caught with the left hand, for example. In another activity the children were required to imitate the asymmetrical pose of a model illustrated in a picture— for instance, a boy holding a ball in his right hand. Perhaps this training served to make more salient the relation between the laterality of the child and that of objects in the environment. The training may also have afforded an opportunity for the child to experience differences in the feedback from his own left or right responses, so making his left and right movements more discriminable.

Fernald (1943) has advocated a tracing technique to improve discrimination of mirror-image letters. Using his preferred hand, the child traces over the letters to be discriminated. So long as the same hand is always used and tracing is begun on the same side of each letter (say, the side opposite the hand used), the tracing would produce different non-mirror-image kinesthetic feedback from the mirror-image forms. If "internalization" of this tracing activity were possible, the child might have access to discriminable kinesthetic cues generated by the letters without having to perform the overt tracing.

A different explanation, based on the notion of cross-modal transfer from haptic to visual perception (e.g., Piaget & Inhelder, 1956) has been proposed by Fellows (1968) as follows:

> If it is the case that a child fixates where he points, then tracing a figure with the finger will carry along with it a scanning of its contours by the eyes. After a little practice we would expect some stimulus generalization to occur. Operationally this means that the mere exposure of the figure will tend to produce some scanning of its contours, even in the absence of the overt tracing movements. [p. 134].

Fellows implied that visual scanning would somehow facilitate discrimination, but he did not elaborate the point. At the least, it is clear that left-to-right scanning creates a consistent asymmetry which is all that is necessary for the child to be able to perform a mirror-image discrimination. It is easy to be misled about how this asymmetry influences the discrimination, however, and we shall return to this issue in the later discussion.

Whether the effective response asymmetry is manual or ocular, this analysis helps to explain why improvement in left–right discrimination often appears to coincide with regular instruction in reading and writing. For example, children learn to copy a sentence written by the teacher by beginning at the left of the page and working toward the right. In learning to read, they are told to follow the words from left to right, perhaps pointing to each word with a finger. Thus, asymmetrical (left-to-right) responses, both manual and ocular, are acquired as a result of initial instruction in both reading and writing.

The effectiveness of Fernald's tracing technique or of instruction in reading and writing need not derive solely from the development of response asymmetries. It is well established from experiments on both humans and subhuman animals that spatial contiguity between stimulus and response is an important factor promoting ease of discrimination learning. The usual explanation for this is that animals attend selectively to those parts of the environment that they manipulate when making a reinforced response (e.g., Stollnitz, 1965). In the case of Fernald's young patients, for example, improvement in discriminating the letters may have resulted partly because touching the letters made them more likely to be noticed.

Nevertheless, we suspect that response asymmetry is an important and possibly even a necessary ingredient in the learning of mirror-image discriminations. We saw in Chapter 4 how pigeons may solve mirror-image problems by cocking their heads to one side or by consistently pecking on one side of the key displaying the stimuli. We also observed that most species learn simple response asymmetries much more readily than they learn mirror-image discriminations. As Ernst Mach (1897) long ago observed, the mirror-image patterns we are most likely to confuse are those with "no motor interest."

We cannot conclude our discussion of facilitative procedures without mentioning the successful technique developed by Bijou (1968) for teaching left–right distinctions to retarded children. Bijou's technique differed from those already described in that it involved variation of the stimuli rather than of the response made to them. It is unfortunate, however, that the technique was applied only to a matching task, so its applicability to genuine mirror-image discrimination is unknown. It is essentially an application of the stimulus fading procedures developed earlier by Terrace (1963). The learning paradigm used was simultaneous matching-to-sample, the sample being displayed above a row of five alternatives made up of one matching stimulus and four distracters. Numerous trials were given in which the stimuli were changed in a carefully graded sequence, the mirror image of the sample being gradually faded in as one of the distracters. Fading in was achieved by presenting a distracter that was basically the lateral mirror image of the sample, but also differed from it in some detail of form. The form difference was gradually reduced over a long series of trials until the sample and mirror-image distracter did not differ in other than their left–right orientations.

This description does not begin to do justice to Bijou's elegant procedure and is not intended to provide more than an appreciation of the basic plan for introducing the mirror-image relation. Under Bijou's fading technique, discriminative responding to near mirror images was initially controlled by form differences. As these differences were faded out, control apparently shifted from form to left–right orientation. How might this have occurred? Bijou was careful to locate the form differences on a part of the stimulus that also determined its left–right orientation. Thus the fading procedure would have drawn attention to the left–right orientation of the stimulus and its relevance to the matching operation.

Whether Bijou's procedure would prove effective in a genuine mirror-image discrimination is a matter for empirical investigation. At the very least, it seems to provide an effective method for drawing a child's attention to the relevance of left–right orientation and it might have potential application in, say, teaching children the left – right discriminations involved in learning the letters of the alphabet.

THEORETICAL DISCUSSION

We should note first of all that the evidence reviewed here provides further documentation of the confusion of left and right and thus supplements the evidence reviewed in Chapter 4. For theoretical discussion we refer the reader back to Chapters 5 and 6. For our present purposes, our main interest lies not in left–right confusion per se, but rather in the manner in which it is overcome, in the roles of maturation and learning, and in the progression of left – right skills.

Asymmetry and the Left–Right Sense

We saw in Chapter 3 that the ability to tell left from right requires some structural asymmetry. The question is, then, what is the nature of the asymmetry which underlies the development of the left–right sense in children?

We have already suggested, both from our review of the animal evidence in Chapter 4 and from the evidence on children reviewed in this chapter, that asymmetries emerge more readily in response systems than in sensory or perceptual systems. This is perhaps not surprising. We argued in Chapter 8 in an evolutionary context that it is generally more adaptive, at least in the natural world where parity is by and large preserved, to maintain symmetry with respect to the cognitive representation of the perceptual world than with respect to the manipulation of the world. Thus, asymmetries appear to have evolved first in response systems—particularly those concerned with manual manipulation and with speech. It is understandable that the same trend should emerge in ontogenetic development.

There can be little doubt that handedness is a powerful mnemonic for the distinction between left and right in the young child. We quote from Boone and Prescott (1968) who observe

> . . . that for "up–down" and "front–back" the child has a perceptual bias, that is, the child has a bias for "down" because of gravity and a bias for "front" because he lacks posterior visual receptors. For "left" and "right," however, the child has a freedom to go in either direction until the emergence of handedness. After handedness is developed, the child has a bias for one side which may well aid in the learning of left–right discrimination [p. 268].

It is quite common to observe a six-year-old going through the motions of writing to determine which is his right hand—or, in Roman Catholic cultures, making the sign of the cross. In both examples, the response element is clear.

Benton (1959, p. 38) reports data showing that performance on a test of left–right differentiation is positively correlated with the strength of unilateral hand preference. He also claims (Benton, 1959, p. 141) that children with unilateral motor disabilities are relatively good discriminators of left and right, while otherwise normal adults who profess to experience frequent left–right confusions tend to be ambidextrous.

The acquisition of asymmetrical eye movements probably also plays a role in the development of the left – right sense. However, the influence of eye movements on mirror-image discrimination is easily misinterpreted. Consider, for example, the following extract from Blau (1946):

> In reading, the left–right image has become mandatory by convention. The right –left movement is not only incorrect, but is known as regressive and may result in a reversed mirror-image of the letter or word symbol. It is eye movement that discriminates in the sensory image of such converse letters as p and q, b and d, and others. For example the capital letter E when viewed in the conventional left–right direction registers correctly, when the direction is reversed it is seen as Ǝ, a reversed or mirror form. Each child must thus learn the left–right direction in eye movement for correct sensing and this must become habitual as a preferred direction of eye-gaze. In most normal children, this habit is well established after the first few grades, and the first fundamental step in eye movement for reading is correctly set [p. 134].

Although he was undoubtedly correct in stressing the importance of left-to-right eye movements in reading and in mirror-image discrimination, Blau was surely wrong in asserting that a pattern is seen as reversed if scanned in the opposite direction. An E looks like an E regardless of how we scan it. It is indeed a remarkable characteristic of visual perception that the world appears stable no matter how we move our eyes over it. Blau has made the common error of supposing that mirror-image confusion is a confusion about the way things look, whereas we have been at pains to emphasize that it is rather a confusion of labeling. Eye movements are important in determining the order in which we extract information from the world, and the child must of course learn to scan the printed page from left to right if he is to extract the intended message from it. But this is a matter of interpretation rather than of perception.

We suspect therefore that eye movements play an interpretive or mnemonic role in the discrimination of mirror images rather than a perceptual one. The child may learn, for example, that the symbol he calls a "dee" is the one with the straight edge on the side *toward* which he moves his eyes. If he scans it the wrong way, he may therefore make the mistake of *calling* it a "bee," but he does not *see* it any differently. Thus eye movements may play a role in labeling, but not in the perception of which way round things are. With extended practice in scanning from left to right, we may perhaps associate a temporal gradient with the left–right dimension so that objects or patterns in the left visual field may be seen as more prominent or "immediate" than those in the right — a phenomenon known to painters and stage directors. Once again, however, we emphasize that although this gradient may be established during the acquisition of left-to-right eye movements, it does not depend on eye movements during the act of perception itself. We are aware of a left–right gradient and can tell a b from a d even while maintaining stable fixation.

Although the left–right gradient may have its origins in motor asymmetries, it undoubtedly acquires some sensory or perceptual component so that it is indeed meaningful to speak of a "left–right sense." Benton (1959) wrote as follows:

> The idea may be advanced that during the fifth and sixth years of life there is a further differentiation of the body schema in the form of a right–left gradient on a conscious level, the two sides of the body are felt as different from each other, although it is impossible, at least for most people, to specify the nature of the difference in verbal terms. The sensory components of the right–left gradient are both somesthetic (i.e., tactual and proprioceptive) and visual. . . . The verbal concepts of right and left do *not* enter into the gradient which is essentially sensory-postural in nature [p. 141; Benton's italics].

Presumably, proprioceptively experienced asymmetry is the direct result and tactually and visually experienced asymmetry the indirect result of prior motor asymmetries.

In Chapter 3, we expressed doubt that the asymmetries of the internal organs would contribute significantly to the left–right sense. Nevertheless we may draw attention here to a mnemonic used by actors on the French stage. One side of the stage traditionally leads off to the *cour,* or courtyard, while the other side leads off to the *jardin,* or garden. From the viewpoint of the actor facing the audience, the *cour* is on the left, and his mnemonic for remembering this is that the word "cour" resembles "coeur," which is French for "heart."[3] Should he become confused as to which is which, then, he may perhaps be reminded by the anxious beating of his heart.

Finally, it is possible that the left–right sense depends on the development of cerebral lateralization. The most powerful advocate of this view was undoubtedly Samuel T. Orton, whose theory of interhemispheric mirror-image reversal we discussed in Chapter 5. Although we were critical of Orton's account of the mechanisms producing mirror-image reversal, it is nonetheless a plausible notion that cerebral lateralization could underlie the ability to tell left from right, if only because it provides the necessary structural asymmetry. Our own theory of interhemispheric mirror-image reversal, presented in Chapter 5, suggested that memory traces might tend to become "symmetrized" by the transfer from one cerebral hemisphere to the other. This tendency would of course be attenuated by the predisposition of the hemispheres to process information in different ways or to store different kinds of memories (see

---

[3]The audience of course requires a reverse mnemonic. The pious among them may think of Jesus Christ, whose initials, read from left to right, provide the necessary information.

Chapter 8). To the extent that a given memory trace is confined within a single hemisphere, one would expect no left–right confusion, since each hemisphere alone is manifestly asymmetrical.

Empirical evidence on the relation between cerebral lateralization and the left–right sense comes mainly from studies of reading disability or from neuropathology and will be discussed in the following chapters.

The Roles of of Maturation and Learning

We have suggested that the left – right sense may be related to handedness, cerebral lateralization, and perhaps to other internal asymmetries. In the previous chapter, we argued that these asymmetries depend primarily on preprogrammed maturational gradients rather than on learning or experience. It is not surprising therefore that the period of development of left–right skills coincides at least approximately with the maturation of handedness and cerebral lateralization. We have seen that children develop and refine the ability to tell left from right between the ages of about four and ten years. In the previous chapter, we described the work of Gesell and Ames (1947) showing that right-handedness gradually predominates over cyclic changes in handedness over the early years of life and stabilizes at about the age of eight years. Although cerebral lateralization can be detected shortly after birth, we also saw that there is considerable flexibility and equipotentiality, at least with respect to the representation of language, in the early years. However, equipotentiality gradually declines between the ages of about three and ten years. Several studies have suggested that a right-ear superiority in the recall of dichotically presented words — implying a left-hemisphere advantage for verbal processing — emerges somewhere within the age range of four to seven years (e.g., Geffner & Hochberg, 1971; Kimura, 1967; Knox & Kimura, 1970), although we remind the reader of Entus' (in press) study showing a right-ear advantage in the processing of elementray speech sounds among infants only a few months old. Evidence on the development of laterality in visual perception is also somewhat conflicting. Miller and Turner (1973) found a right-field advantage in the recognition of words among children in the fourth grade but not among second graders; however, Marcel, Katz, and Smith (1974) found a reliable right-field superiority among seven- and eight-year-olds. The left-to-right pattern of eye movements appears to be present in six-year-olds (Elkind & Weiss, 1967; Gottschalk, Bryden, & Rabinovitch, 1964).

The ability to tell left from right cannot be attributed entirely to the maturation of asymmetries. At the very least, we require experience to teach us the *relevance* of the distinction between left and right. Our review of evidence also suggested that the period of most rapid improvement in left–right discrimination often appears to coincide with early instruction in reading and writing, which in Western culture includes the teaching of response asymmetries. Although this association might be attributed partly to a spurt in the growth of lateralization, creating a readiness for both reading and other left–right skills, we reviewed other evidence which showed that specific learning procedures could facilitate the ability to perform left–right discriminations. In the main, these procedures seemed to achieve their effect by drawing the child's attention to the relevance of his own laterality. He might learn to use his own handedness, say, to code the particular left–right orientation of a stimulus. Moreover, as we saw in the previous chapter, handedness itself may be influenced by training. Obviously, so is left-to-right visual scanning. Even cerebral lateralization can apparently be influenced by the quality of verbal experience a child receives, as we saw in the previous chapter.

We may conclude therefore that maturation sets limits on the growth of the left–right sense, but does not rigidly determine it. Educational influences are of roughly two kinds. First, there are those influences which develop the child's own laterality. These include the teaching of unimanual skills, instruction in reading and writing, and general exposure to verbal culture. To be effective, however, these influences must be preceded or accompanied by maturation of a left–right gradient. Second, to exploit his left–right sense and to apply it to the world about him, the child must be taught the relevance of left and right and the relation between his own laterality and that of other bodies and objects.

The Progression of Left–Right Skills

We have seen that children first learn to tell left from right in relation to their own bodies before they go on to discriminate left and right with respect to external objects or patterns. Benton (1959) suggested in fact that the ultimate development of left–right skills requires more than just a left–right sense; an additional conceptual component is involved as well.

We remind the reader of the important distinction between telling left from right and knowing how to apply the labels "left" and "right" to objects in the world; we discussed this in Chapter 2. For example, since people normally meet and converse face to face, the child may well reverse the labels "left" and "right" when describing the body parts of someone questioning him. He does not realize that the questioner's *left*-hand side is aligned with his own *right*-hand side. So long as the child is consistent in this reversal, however, he demonstrates the ability to tell left from right. In order to apply the labels "left" and "right" correctly, though, he requires the additional ability to map his own body coordinates onto those of the person facing him. To label the "left" and "right" of objects or geographic features may require the even more complex ability to mentally transform one's own body coordinates into some *imagined* location.

Piaget (1928) has discussed the problem of assigning the labels "left" and "right" in terms of the development of "socialization of thought." The child is at first egocentric, then is able to take the point of view of another, and is finally able to coordinate many points of view. With respect to left and right, therefore, the child first learns his own left and right sides, then those of another person, and finally the relative left–right relations among objects in space. Of course, this analysis deals only with the progression of left–right skills and does not tell us anything of the left–right problem per se—of why, for example, children solve left–right discriminations later than they solve up–down ones. Piaget's approach was rather the converse; he chose left–right discrimination as a vehicle for studying the more general process, the socialization of thought. It is possible, however, that the peculiar difficulty of left–right discrimination detracts from the generality of his conclusions. For example, with respect to judgments other than those to do with left and right, children may lose their egocentricity at an earlier age than Piaget's analysis would suggest.

SUMMARY

The evidence reviewed in this chapter further documents the psychological *equivalence* of lateral mirror images and of left and right responses. We have argued again that this equivalence is not perceptual. For example, a child may interpret left–right mirror images as basically the same pattern, although at some level he can tell that the actual percepts are different. Nevertheless, we saw that in some experiments relying on verbal instructions, the equivalence can be so compelling as to influence performance on perceptual tasks such as the matching of one of two mirror-image patterns to a sample. Presumably, the children sometimes responded on the basis of what they interpreted the patterns to be rather than on the actual perceptual information. As much of our earlier discussion testifies, we have enough difficulty explaining this distinction even to adults!

Although left–right equivalence may be reinforced by experience, we suspect that it is more fundamentally a product of evolution in a world where parity is largely conserved. Our built-in disposition to treat mirror-image patterns as equivalent helps us understand that the same faces may appear in opposite profiles or that a two-dimensional pattern appears reversed if viewed from the other side. However, for humans in particular, the problem is to learn that in certain specific situations, largely created by man, left and right are not equivalent. We have argued that children learn this in relation to their own developing laterality, including handedness and cerebral lateralization. Functional asymmetries appear first in response systems and provide strategies or mnemonics enabling the child to discriminate mirror-image stimuli. Subsequently, asymmetries become internalized and invade perceptual as well as response systems so that we may speak of a "left–right sense."

11

Left–Right Confusion, Laterality, and Reading Disability

> . . . I struggled through the alphabet as if it had been a bramble-bush, getting considerably worried and scratched by every letter. After that, I fell among those thieves, the nine figures, who seemed every evening to do something new to disguise themselves and baffle recognition. But at last I began, in a purblind groping way, to read, write, and cipher, on the very smallest scale.
>
> —*Great Expectations*
> CHARLES DICKENS

In the previous chapter we saw that the ability to tell left from right usually improves markedly during the first year of reading instruction. There can be little doubt that this ability is an important component of the ability to read, at least in countries where the script maintains a consistent left–right orientation and direction. The child must learn mirror-image discriminations in order to label a b as distinct from a d, or a p as distinct from a q, or any other letter as distinct from its mirrored form; he must also learn a left – right response differentiation in order to scan script consistently in the appropriate direction and to write it correctly. In this chapter we document more fully the evidence relating the ability to tell left from right, cerebral lateralization, and reading. Following the main trend of the literature, however, we shall emphasize reading disability rather than reading ability. More particularly, we shall examine Orton's proposition that reading disability is often a result of left–right confusion, which in turn is a symptom of incomplete cerebral lateralization (e.g., Orton, 1937).

In Western countries especially, reading failure is widespread and is a cause for great concern among educators and parents. Symptoms vary widely, and no doubt there are many causes. As one recent authority puts it:

> Reading is a very complex psychological process, the ingredients of which may differ in amounts from one individual to the next. One child may have slight central nervous system visual defects, while another may have equally slight auditory defects; one child may find decoding to be a particular problem while another may have difficulty in remembering sound–symbol associations. Still others may lack the necessary motivation to speak or read their native language [Bannatyne, 1971, p. 6].

It is clear then that left–right confusion is unlikely to be the sole cause of reading disability.

The more specific term "dyslexia" is now in common use to refer to reading and spelling disabilities that are not associated with other disturbances, such as mental retardation, sensory impairment, speech impairment, or emotional problems.[1] Sometimes a distinction is drawn between developmental dyslexia, implying a developmental or maturational anomaly, and acquired dyslexia, implying brain damage. Estimates of the incidence of dyslexia vary widely, owing largely to the lack of agreed criteria as to the degree of impairment that distinguishes the dyslexic from the child who is merely a slow reader. Bannatyne (1971) puts the figure for Western countries at a conservative 2%, but Critchley (1970) believes it to be much higher:

> Without doubt, dyslexia is commoner than generally imagined. Cases are constantly being overlooked by teachers, and misinterpreted by educational psychologists, and sometimes even by child psychiatrists. Hermann's figure of 10 percent among Danish schoolchildren tallies exactly with Sinclair's survey of primary schools in Edinburgh. Until recently I would have imagined this figure too high for England. . . . Today I am less confident, suspecting that the percentage is higher [p. 96].

Critchley goes on to plead for official recognition of the problem and for better facilities to diagnose and deal with it.

As if to highlight the specificity of the problem, the literature often depicts the dyslexic as one who may be in all other respects highly talented. Certainly the affliction is more noticeable among otherwise gifted people. Critchley (1964) remarked that the reading faults exhibited by the dyslexic "are unlike those met with in the case of a dullard, or a poorly educated person [p. 111]." Thompson (1971) chronicles the case histories of several exceptional men who may have been dyslexic, among them the inventor Thomas A. Edison, the surgeon Harvey Cushing, the sculptor Auguste Rodin, and President Woodrow Wilson. On somewhat surer grounds, it has been said that Hans Christian Andersen was also a dyslexic (Critchley, 1970).

---

[1]We cannot do full justice to the wealth of research and controversy on the nature and treatment of dyslexia. The reader who wishes to pursue the matter beyond its relevance to the left–right problem should consult the recent monographs by Bannatyne (1971) or Critchley (1970).

However, Zangwill (1960, p. 15) has expressed doubt that dyslexia is ever quite so circumscribed as this somewhat idealized characterization would suggest. He notes that there is at least some evidence, which we review more fully below, to support Orton's view that dyslexics have particular difficulty in telling left from right. They may also suffer a more generalized spatial deficit. Zangwill himself presents summarized case records of 20 backward readers, of whom all but one exhibited some associated disability or pathology. Thirteen of them showed some manifestation of a left–right confusion, either in the form of letter reversals, sinistrad scanning, or confusion over the left and right sides of the body. Other disabilities included poor spatial ability, deficits of learning or memory, and backwardness in arithmetic. A few children had experienced mild epileptic seizures or showed abnormalities in electroencephalographic recordings. Of course, not all of these children would be classed as truly or purely dyslexic, but they do illustrate the multifaceted nature of reading disability, surely reflecting the complexity of the reading process itself. They also raise doubts as to whether dyslexia can be considered so pure a category as much of the literature suggests.

If we include left – right confusion as at least one of the additional characteristics of the dyslexic, then the subject studied by Zangwill and Blakemore (1972) may be as close to a typical case as one is likely to find. We may also note that this subject fits the idealized picture in that he appears to be otherwise somewhat gifted. Zangwill and Blakemore describe him thus:

> The subject, D.A., was a 23-year-old postgraduate student who had always regarded himself as an exceptionally slow reader and writer as well as a poor speller. He had achieved a bachelor's degree in biology largely on the basis of good intelligence combined with an excellent memory for lectures and demonstrations, and confessed that he had done very little reading in the course of his undergraduate career. He was right-handed for writing, tennis and throwing, but a left-handed batsman. He was left-footed and left-eye dominant, and had always found exceptional difficulty in distinguishing left from right. His mother and maternal first cousin were likewise partly left-handed. [p. 371].

Note that he seems to fit into that category of individuals, discussed in Chapter 9, who appear to inherit a *lack* of any consistent lateralization (cf. Annett, 1972). Analysis of his reading disability suggested that it was characterized primarily by an inability to scan correctly from left to right. Recordings of his eye movements during his attempts to read revealed an excessive number of regressive movements when he would look back at words he had already read. Oddly enough, he appeared to be able to scan from right to left more rapidly and naturally than from left to right, although Zangwill and Blakemore did not test his ability to read mirror writing. His problem was apparently a failure to learn an asymmetrical habit rather than a simple motor disability, since his saccadic eye movements to flashing lights were normal. He seemed to have no difficulty identifying letters, digits, or words exposed very briefly, for 40 msec or less.

It has been suggested that dylexia might be specific, not merely to reading, but to the reading of specific language groups, notably those of Western culture. There is evidence that reading problems are comparatively rare among Japanese children (Makita, 1968). In Japan, children are usually taught two different scripts — first, the *Kana*, in which the symbols correspond more or less to syllables and are combined to form words, and later the *Kanji* script, in which the symbols are based on Chinese ideographs and stand for whole words. In neither case is there any confusion created by reversing a symbol, since no two symbols are mirror images of each other. There can be no mirror-image confusion in *reading* the symbols. Makita states that children frequently reverse a symbol in *writing*, but the error is regarded as relatively unimportant and is usually transient. It is also relevant to note, perhaps, that Japanese is traditionally written in vertical columns and read from top to bottom, although the left-to-right arrangement is also used, borrowed from Western culture. It is therefore reasonable to conclude that any child suffering acute left–right confusion would have less difficulty learning to read Japanese than learning to read English.

Yet this is surely not the only reason why reading disability is less common among Japanese than among Western children. Rozin, Poritsky, and Sotsky (1971) have reported that slum children who were apparently unable to learn to read English script could nonetheless be readily taught to read English represented by Chinese characters, and even to write their own stories in Chinese script. The characters were presented left-to-right in the English rather than the Chinese manner, so it is perhaps unlikely that the original difficulty with English had much to do with left-to-right scanning. Rozin *et al.* (1971) admit that improved motivation could partly explain the success of their subjects, but they suggest that the main difference lay in the level at which the language was represented by the symbols. English script is difficult to learn to read because it is phonemic; the elements represented by the letters are phonemes and are in many cases unpronounceable by themselves. Scripts in which the symbols correspond to syllables, as in Kana, or to words, as in Kanji or Chinese script, are easier to learn because each symbol can be pronounced; the relation between symbol and sound is more obvious.

Before we turn to a more detailed examination of the experimental evidence on the reading disability, left–right confusion, and laterality, let us briefly recapitulate our discussions of Chapter 6, where we examined Orton's theory in some detail. Orton, it will be recalled, argued that spatial information is recorded correctly in the dominant hemisphere and in mirror-reversed fashion in the nondominant hemisphere. If a child failed to establish cerebral dominance, therefore, the reversed memory traces in the nondominant hemisphere could intrude to create left–right confusion and thus hinder the child in his attempts to read and write. We pointed out that Orton's argument is irrational, and suggested that if there is any truth at all to the notion of interhemispheric mirror-image reversal it would apply to the *transfer* of memory traces from one hemisphere to the other and not to the way in which traces are *directly* laid down in the hemispheres. This led us to the somewhat complex formulation depicted schematically in Fig. 6. 6.

Even if our theory of interhemispheric mirror-image reversal is correct, which is by no means proven, the role of cerebral dominance is now potentially more complicated. For one thing, we saw in Chapter 8 that one hemisphere is not uniformly "dominant" over the other. Rather, each hemisphere is to some extent specialized, the left normally more so for verbal processing and the right more so for nonverbal or spatial analysis. To some extent this specialization implies an attenuation in the transfer of learning from one hemisphere to the other, and consequently a reduction in the mechanism of mirror-image equivalence. Consequently, Orton may have been correct in supposing that left–right confusion and reading disability arise from poorly developed lateralization, even though the details of his theory were wrong.

But there is of course an even more basic reason for relating left – right confusion to lack of dominance or lateralization, which is simply that in order to tell left from right we require some structural asymmetry (see Chapter 3). Quite apart from any speculations about interhemispheric mirror-image reversal, it is reasonable to seek this asymmetry in the structure of the brain itself.

In reviewing the experimental evidence, we consider first the relation between reading disability and left–right confusion, then the relation between reading disability and laterality.

EXPERIMENTAL EVIDENCE ON THE ROLE
OF LEFT–RIGHT CONFUSION

As we have seen, the strongest advocate of the view that dyslexia is at least partly the result of left–right confusion—or "strephosymbolia"—was Samuel T. Orton. Although much of the evidence he cited was based on observations of individual patients, he also referred to evidence of a more experimental nature:

> That the mirror-image reversals play a significant role in strephosymbolia is adequately supported by our earlier studies in Iowa. The errors made by a group of reading disability cases were tabulated and compared with those made by a carefully selected control group of normal readers of the same grade and intelligence, and the errors of reversal were found to be significant statistically for the reading disability cases at each of the first four reading grades which were studied. Not only was this so, but the frequency with which errors by reversal appeared in the work of a given case proved to correlate with the amount of his retardation in reading, that is, with the severity of his disorder [Orton, 1937, p. 151].

Several other studies have similarly shown that poor readers make more errors involving left – right reversals of letters and words than do normal readers, although poor readers also make more errors of other kinds (e.g., Bennett, 1942; Monroe, 1928; Schonell, 1942). Schonell also found that reversals persisted longer in poor readers than in normals, but nonetheless became much less frequent with age.

Although these early studies show that poor readers as a group show more left–right reversals than do normal readers, they certainly do not prove that left –right confusion is the source of reading difficulty; neither do they show that all children with reading disability suffer from left–right confusion. A more recent study by Liberman, Shankweiler, Orlando, Harris, and Berti (1971) suggests a much more moderate conclusion. They studied errors in reading isolated words or nonsense syllables among 54 second-grade pupils, all of whom had been screened for sensory impairment and were of normal intelligence. Reversals of letter sequence or of letter orientation were restricted to the 18 worst readers, confirming the studies mentioned above, but even among these 18 children reversals of sequence accounted for only 10% and reversals of orientation only 15% of the total number of errors. Moreover, the two types of reversal error were uncorrelated, suggesting that they did not derive from a single common source, such as a *general* inability to tell left from right. Liberman *et al.* (1971) also found that the pattern of reversals among the letters b, d, p, and g (sic) depended on the context in which they were presented— that is, on whether they were presented in words or in nonsense syllables. There were few confusions when the letters were presented tachistoscopically by themselves, and up–down reversals were just as frequent as left–right ones. The authors concluded as follows:

> Although we have stressed that reversals of either type [sequence or orientation] do not account for a large proportion of the total error in most of the children we have studied, it may be that reversals loom larger in importance in certain children with particularly severe and persisting reading difficulty. Our clinical experience suggests this may be so . . . [Liberman *et al.*, 1971, p. 138].

In short, few if any of their "poor readers" would be classed as genuine dyslexics.

Other studies have in fact confirmed this suggestion that left–right confusion is restricted to those with the most severe reading disability. Ginsberg and Hartwick (1971) have maintained that the incidence of true dyslexia is about 2.5%, or about one quarter of the 10% of elementary-school pupils usually found to have clinically significant reading problems. In a study of all second-grade pupils in five elementary schools, they found only 10 out of 429 children showing both left–right confusion and a tendency to make reading errors in all categories measured, even though 43 of the children were considered by their teachers to be very poor readers. The authors noted that the 10 subjects in the lowest performance category were almost exactly the predicted 2.5% of the total group studied, and they recommended that a test of left–right confusion be used as a screen for potential reading disability in young children.

In another large-scale study, Belmont and Birch (1965) reached similar conclusions. They drew a sample of 150 nine- and ten-year-old boys from among the lowest 10% in reading ability in the city of Aberdeen, Scotland, with the restriction that none had IQ's below 80 on the Wechsler Intelligence Scale for Children (WISC; see Wechsler, 1949). This sample was matched for age and school class placement by a control group of 50 boys from the remaining levels of reading ability. Twenty-nine of the poor readers failed to achieve a perfect score on seven items requiring left – right differentiation of their own body parts (e.g., "Touch your left ear"), compared with only one of the control group. These 29 poor readers were generally poorer on tests of reading skill than the remaining 121 who showed no left – right confusion with respect to their own body parts. However, nine of the 29 boys scored zero on the left–right differentiation items, which means that they *systematically reversed* "left" and "right." This subgroup was considerably worse on the tests of reading skill than the 121 who showed no left – right confusion. The poor readers also scored significantly lower than the control group on the differentiation of the left and right sides of the examiner facing them and on tests of the left – right relations among objects. However, these more complex items did not discriminate levels of reading ability *within* the group of poor readers. Belmont and Birch concluded that "right – left awareness of parts of one's own body bear a more significant relation to reading performance than do later acquired . . . and more complex features of right – left orientation [p. 69].''

It is of interest that among the poorest readers of all were the subjects showing systematic reversal of "left" and "right." Earlier, Benton and Kemble (1960) and Coleman and Deutsch (1964) had reported that backward and normal readers did not differ in basic left – right differentiation, but that backward readers did show a tendency to reverse the labels "left" and "right," both in relation to their own bodies and to that of a confronting person. We pointed out in Chapter 2 that systematic reversal can be considered strictly a valid demonstration of the ability to tell left from right. Systematic reversal with respect to a confronting person may be due to a spatial deficit, whereby the subject is unable to map his own body coordinates onto the other person's, but this does not explain reversal with respect to his *own* body. Benton and Kemble thought that the deficit might be verbal, but this is not borne out by Belmont and Birch's data. Neither the 29 poor readers who failed at least one of the items on differentiation of their own body sides nor the subgroup of nine who showed systematic reversal showed any deficit on the verbal subscale of the WISC compared with the 121 poor readers who passed all of the items. The reversal subgroup was significantly lower on the performance subscale, however. Our own interpretation is that the subjects who showed systematic reversal probably *were* confused about left and right, but made some arbitrary decision as to which was which and maintained this choice for all items. For example, a child might decide his left hand is his "right" hand, and clench the fist of that hand so that all responses will be consistent with the decision. If this interpretation is correct, we must suppose that there were an approximately equal number of subjects who were equally confused, but who happened upon the correct choice and so passed all of the items. This suggests that about 38 of the 150 poor readers may have suffered some degree of left–right confusion—or almost exactly a quarter of the 10% sample!

Two recent studies of mirror-image discrimination in children with severe reading problems show clearly that the problem is not a general confusion of orientation but is specific to *left–right* mirror images. Newland (1972) presented a small asymmetric stimulus on a screen every second and had her subjects call out which way the stimulus faced (left, right, up or down) each time it appeared. Children referred to clinics for remedial reading made more left–right errors than did normal readers of the same age, but the two groups did not differ on up–down errors. Newland found no evidence for systematic left–right reversal. Sidman and Kirk (1974) studied 15 children referred to a reading clinic who still reversed letters and words at ages ranging from seven years nine months to 14 years seven months. The children were required to match letters, which could be left – right reversed, up – down reversed, or normal, to a sample letter. They made frequent left–right errors when matching lower-case letters to an upper-case sample. Left – right errors were relatively few when both the matching letters and the sample were in lower case and were simultaneously available. They increased, however, when a delay was imposed between showing the sample and allowing the matching response. Up–down errors were comparatively rare under all conditions. It is noteworthy that the conditions which resulted in significant numbers of left–right errors were those requiring correct labeling or delayed recognition rather than simultaneous perceptual matching.

Some investigators have not explicitly studied the ability to tell left from right, but have reported data which nonetheless suggests that poor readers may be prone to spontaneous reversals. These studies may be said to demonstrate left–right equivalence rather than left–right confusion, although we suspect that both depend on the same mechanism. For example, Monroe (1928) found that poor readers were more likely than normals to name rows of pictures in right-to-left order. They also made more left – right errors in reproducing pictures from memory. Similarly, Galifret-Granjon (1951) observed a tendency among poor readers to make mirror reversals when reconstructing matchstick figures. There is even evidence that boys who read normal printing poorly do better than a normal control group when the printing is mirror-reversed (Wolfe, 1939). Orton (1937, p. 151) also claimed that dyslexics were better at mirror reading than normals, but that skill in mirror reading declined as a child progressed in normal reading.

Left–right equivalence may also be demonstrated by the tendency of many dyslexics to make regressive eye movements; we have seen, for example, that this was a characteristic of the subject studied by Zangwill and Blakemore (1972). Bannatyne (1971) has suggested that dyslexics are less able than average readers to inhibit a natural tendency to scan the environment in either direction. He cites an experiment by Lesevre (1966) to support this. Lesevre found that in normal readers the ability to scan to the right increases with age after the commencement of reading instruction. At the same time, there is a decrease in the number of irregular movements and fixations during a scan to the right. Compared to the normal reader, most dyslexics studied by Lesevre showed poorly lateralized scanning in either direction, making more short pauses and showing a generally greater oculomotor instability. It should be noted, however, that Lesevre did observe a few dyslexics with a normal pattern of eye movements as well as a few normal readers with poorly lateralized scanning. Other studies have also shown that poor reading is characterized by more frequent regressions of eye movement and more fixations than is usual in normal reading (e.g., Rubino & Minden, 1973; Taylor, 1966). The difficulty with studies of regressive eye movements and reading disability, however, is to determine which is the cause and which the effect. Vernon (1960) effectively reverses Bannatyne's interpretation: ". . . there is ample evidence," she writes, "to show that irregular eye movements and frequent regressions are caused by inability to read and confusion in reading, rather than causing them [p. 106]." We do not know of the "ample evidence," but the point is at least potentially valid.

To summarize up to this point, the evidence is fairly compelling that at least some children with reading problems also suffer a confusion of left and right. This seems to be especially true of those who might be described as truly dyslexic and who comprise the lowest 2 or 3% in reading ability — barring neuropathological cases. Thus, left–right confusion emerges as a significant factor in reading disability only in large-scale studies or in the studies of severe cases referred for treatment.

The next question is whether children with reading disability show reduced or incomplete cerebral lateralization.

READING DISABILITY AND LATERALITY

Handedness and Eyedness

The early studies on reading disability and laterality were concerned with handedness or eyedness rather than with cerebral lateralization per se, presumably because no simple ways of directly measuring cerebral lateralization had been developed. These studies might be considered only indirectly relevant to the theory that reading disabililty is associated with incomplete cerebral lateralization since the correlation between handedness or eyedness and cerebral lateralization is far from perfect (e.g., Zangwill, 1960). Even so, Orton (1937) claimed that 69 of his 102 cases were of opposite handedness and eye dominance and that many were also ambidextrous or came from families with some history of mixed- or left-handedness. Harris (1956), using an extensive test for lateral preference, also found that a high proportion of young disabled readers showed mixed preferences, and similar findings have also been reported by Eames (1934), Monroe (1932), and Schonell (1940, 1941). However, there are several other studies which reveal no such difference between normal and poor readers (e.g., Smith, 1950; Wolfe, 1941). Witty and Kopel (1936) argued that poor reading may result, not from mixed laterality per se, but rather from an enforced switch from on hand to the other.

Some authors have reported a high incidence of left handedness among disabled readers (e.g., Dearborn, 1933; Wall, 1945, 1946). This finding may also be taken as evidence for the role of incomplete cerebral lateralization, since left-handers exhibit less pronounced lateralization than do right-handers (see Chapter 9). Once again, however, there are several studies which fail to confirm the association between left-handedness and reading disability (e.g., Gates & Bond, 1936; Jackson, 1944). After a thorough review of the available evidence, Vernon (1960) was unable to conclude that there was any clear association between reading disability and handedness. Unfortunately, studies of the relation between reading backwardness and handedness are complicated by difficulties and inadequacies in the measurement of handedness, a point already discussed in Chapter 9.

In the large-scale study by Belmont and Birch (1965), discussed in some detail in the previous section, there was little evidence for differences in hand preference or eye dominance between the samples of normal and retarded readers. If anything, there was a tendency for the retarded readers to show a higher incidence of mixed or left-eye dominance and a higher incidence of crossed hand and eye preference, but these differences were not statistically significant. Unfortunately, Belmont and Birch did not provide information about the handedness or eye dominance of the 29 poor readers who showed left – right confusion about their own bodies, or of the subgroup of nine who showed systematic left – right reversal. They did observe, however, that the relation between reading disability and weak or inconsistent laterality typically emerges more strongly from studies of subjects drawn from clinical settings than from community samples. Once again, this implies that laterality problems might be largely restricted to the most severe cases of reading disability.

Clay (1974) has reported some observations which bear on the role of handedness in the reading process itself. She tabulated the responses of children to the command "read it with your finger," during their first year at school when they received their first instruction in reading. Among one small and unusual sample, consisting of four supposedly identical quadruplet girls, she observed three developmental stages in the choice of hand the girls used for pointing. At first, they were guided principally by whether they were reading from a left-hand or a right-hand page, and chose the left or the right hand, accordingly. After a few weeks they had learned consistently to use the preferred hand, regardless of the page. (One of the girls was left-handed, the other three right-handed.) At this stage, handedness evidently served as a mnemonic to guide the direction of reading. Finally, at intervals ranging from 12 to 46 weeks, and when reading had become fairly accomplished, the girls reverted to the use of either hand, but in a more indiscriminate way than in the initial stage. The directionality of the script was now "internalized," so that handedness was no longer required as a mnemonic.

In less detailed analysis of 100 children observed over the first year of reading instruction, Clay also observed that those below average in reading progress were still predominantly in the first stage, while those above average had progressed to the third stage. It is not clear whether the poorer readers suffered from poorly established handedness, or whether the relevance of handedness as a mnemonic had eluded them.

In recent years, there has been less emphasis on handedness than on the more direct measures of cerebral lateralization which have been developed. These include measures of the difference between visual hemifields in the report of tachistoscopically presented information, and of the difference between ears in the report of material presented dichotically.

Hemifield Differences

We have already seen in Chapter 8 that alphabetic material is usually identified more readily and accurately when presented tachistoscopically in the right visual hemifield than in the left hemifield. This is usually taken to reflect, at least partly, the dominant role of the left cerebral hemisphere in processing verbal information (e.g., Bryden, 1965; Kimura, 1966). Consequently, the difference between hemifields might be considered an index of the degree of cerebral lateralization.

However, there is a difficulty with this technique that is particularly critical if one seeks to relate hemifield differences to reading disability. Heron (1957) suggested that the right-field superiority might be due, not to cerebral lateralization, but to the fact that English is read from left to right. It will clearly be more difficult to scan information in the left field than in the right field, since attention must first be directed to the left of the array. Of course, with tachistoscopic presentation, a person does not have time to move his eyes over the actual array. However, brief presentation of a pattern is thought to leave behind a decaying iconic image (Sperling, 1960), and there is evidence that subjects do in fact move their eyes over the image as though it were actually a percept (Hall, 1974). Moreover, even to the extent that scanning may be "internalized" and partially independent of overt eye movements, one would still expect its spatiotemporal characteristics to resemble those of eye scanning. There is evidence that left-to-right scanning does indeed contribute to hemifield differences. Harcum and Finkel (1963) showed that although normal words are better identified in the right visual hemifield, mirror-imaged words are better identified in the left. Although one may be tempted to interpret this as evidence for Orton's theory of interhemispheric mirror-image reversal, the more likely explanation is that mirror-imaged words are scanned from right to left, which favors the left hemifield. Mishkin and Forgays (1952) found that English – Hebrew bilinguals identified English words more accurately in the right hemifield, but Hebrew words more accurately in the left, which is also consistent with the scanning interpretation because Hebrew is read from right to left.

This is not to say that cerebral lateralization makes no contribution to hemifield differences. Single letters are identified more accurately in the right visual hemifield, whether mirror-imaged or not (Bryden, 1966). More recent studies with Israeli subjects have shown that, under some conditions at least, a right-field superiority can be obtained in the recognition of Hebrew letters, digits, and even Hebrew words (Barton, Goodglass, & Shai, 1965; Carmon & Nachshon, 1973; Carmon, Nachshon, Isseroff, & Kleiner, 1972; Orbach, 1967). Chinese subjects recognize Chinese ideographs more accurately in the right visual hemifield than in the left, even though they are normally scanned vertically (Kerschner & Gwan-Rong Jeng, 1972). More generally, White (1969) has reviewed the evidence and concluded that cerebral lateralization plays a greater role the more "minimal" the stimulation; for example, the briefer the exposure, or the fewer the elements, and so on. Yet in any given study, there is always the problem of separating the role of scanning from that of cerebral lateralization. This is particularly crucial in studies of reading disability because poor scanning might be considered the result of reading disability, while incomplete lateralization might be considered its cause.

In spite of this difficulty, there has been at least one study in which it was claimed that poor readers exhibit a smaller hemifield difference than good readers and that this was due to a less pronounced cerebral lateralization. Marcel, Katz, and Smith (1974) compared the 20 best with the 20 poorest readers from 74 seven- and eight-year-olds on the identification of five-letter words, exposed tachistoscopically to the right or left of fixation. The children were encouraged to report as many of the letters as possible if they could not identify the words. Both groups reported more whole words and more letters correctly when the words were exposed in the right hemifield than when they were exposed in the left, but the difference was greater for the good readers than for the poor readers. The results are shown in Fig. 11.1, plotted

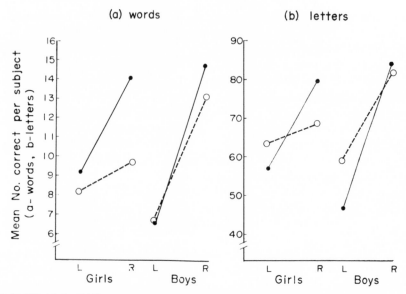

FIGURE 11.1   Difference between left and right visual fields in report of (a) words and (b) letters for good readers (solid lines) and poor readers (broken lines). From Marcel *et al.*, 1974; with the permission of Pergamon Press Ltd. and A. J. Marcel.)

separately for girls and boys (who were equally represented in each group). It is clear that this result cannot be attributed to a "floor effect" among the poor readers, since their report of letters in the left field was actually better than that of the good readers. Marcel *et al.* (1974) also rule out interpretation in terms of left-to-right scanning, since an internal analysis of serial-position effects among the letters suggested that the good readers scanned no more efficiently than poor readers. They therefore interpret their result to mean that cerebral lateralization for language is more pronounced among good readers than among poor readers.

Ear Differences in Dichotic Listening

In so-called "dichotic" listening, different auditory messages are presented simultaneously to each ear of the listener. As we have already noted, it is now fairly well established that more accurate perception or recall of the information presented to one ear than of that presented to the other can be attributed, at least in part, to hemispheric lateralization; in most people, for example, verbal material is reported more accurately when presented to the right ear, reflecting the specialization of the left hemisphere for verbal processing (e.g., Kimura, 1961; Milner, Taylor, & Sperry, 1968). In one respect, ear differences in dichotic listening might appear to be a more satisfactory index of hemispheric lateralization than hemifield differences in visual perception, since there is no confounding influence of left-to-right scanning or other peripheral adjustments. On the other hand, there is some evidence that the two measures may reflect different components of hemispheric specialization. For example, both Bryden (1965) and Zurif and Bryden (1969) found no correlation between ear differences and hemifield differences for verbal material, although Hines and Satz (1974) found a moderate positive correlation among right-handers but no correlation among left-handers. Moreover, although some 99% of right-handers appear to have speech represented primarily in the left hemisphere (Rossi & Rosadini, 1967),[2] only about 85% of normal right-handed adults show a right-ear superiority for verbal material in dichotic listening (Bryden, 1973). These observations raise doubts, first, about the reliability of ear differences as a measure of hemispheric specialization, and second, about the unitary nature of lateralization for verbal processes. If ear differences and hemifield differences do measure different aspects of lateralization, then it is presumably the latter which are the more directly relevant to the reading process (cf. Marcel *et al.*, 1974). Consequently, there might be some doubt as to whether the measurement of ear differences can provide strong evidence on the relation between cerebral lateralization and reading disability.

Even so, there is some support from dichotic listening studies for the proposition that poor readers show less pronounced laterality than do normal readers in the processing of verbal material. Zurif and Carson (1970) compared 14 poor readers with 14 normal readers, matched for intelligence, ability in arithmetic, and handedness, and selected from boys in Grade 4. The normal readers showed a right-ear superiority, the poor readers a slight left-ear superiority. Bryden (1970) tested children in Grades 2, 4, and 6, and found that boys who were poor readers were more likely to exhibit crossed ear – hand dominance (e.g., left-ear superiority and right-handedness) than were boys who were normal at reading. This effect was less pronounced among the girls. Satz, Rardin, and Ross (1971) found that dyslexics showed less of a difference between ears than normal readers, but the effect was much more pronounced among an older group, consisting of eleven- and twelve-year-olds, than among seven- and eight-year-olds. Similarly, Bakker, Smink, and Reitsma (1973) reported a positive relation between the degree of ear dominance and reading ability among children between nine and eleven years old, but the relation was *negative* for seven-year-olds. Like Satz and his colleagues, these authors suggest that cerebral lateralization may not become important until about the age of ten years. They also go so far as to suggest that lateralization might be a *disadvantage* at an earlier age:

> A too advanced lateralization seems to hamper rather than promote efficiency in early reading. This may be due to the fact that in early reading, a great deal of non-lingual as well as lingual information must be processed, which may be facilitated by bilateral hemispheric processes [Bakker *et al.*, 1973, p. 309].

[2]Milner, Branch, and Rasmussen (1964) found a somewhat lower proportion—about 92%—but suggest that their sample was probably biased.

A far cry from Orton!

This conclusion may well be too strong, however, since Satz and his colleagues found no such reversal in their younger group. Research in this area is especially prone to methodological difficulties and artifact, particularly with respect to the uncritical use of difference scores to measure laterality. Not only are difference scores notoriously unreliable, but floor and ceiling effects may artificially reduce differences where real laterality effects exist. Nevertheless, the experiments we have described lend further support to the notion that cerebral lateralization is less pronounced among poor readers than among normal readers, and suggest further that that aspect of laterality which is measured by ear differences in dichotic listening may reach maximum importance somewhat late in the development of reading skills.

CONCLUSIONS

Taken as a whole, the evidence we have reviewed is at least consistent with the proposition that there is a syndrome characterized by left – right confusion, poorly established lateralization, and reading disability. In some cases this syndrome may simply represent a maturational lag; a child may be somewhat behind his peers in development of the structures and skills necessary for reading, but later catches up. In other cases, the problem may be more severe and more lasting.

We were frequently reminded, however, that there are many disabled readers who do not appear to exhibit left – right confusion or anomalies of cerebral lateralization, just as there are many poorly lateralized individuals who suffer no reading disability. Given the complexity of the reading process, the unreliability and superficiality of many of the tests used, and the ingenuity with which people compensate—often overcompensate—for their deficiencies, one should not be surprised that such cases exist. We can agree with Clark (1957), for example, who protests that Orton overstated his case, for there are undoubtedly many different reasons for reading disability. At the same time, however, we can also accept the following comment by Critchley (1970):

> The role of reversals in the attempt to read has often been played down by those who are sceptical as to the existence of dyslexia, asserting that many children perpetrate reversals at some time or other during their reading apprenticeship. But, as Money [1962] rightly asserted, the dyslexic individual is not unique in making reversals and translocations, but he is conspicuous in making so many of them and for so long a time [p. 31].

Large-scale studies suggested that those disabled readers who do suffer left–right confusion are among the most severe cases, and comprise perhaps a quarter of the some 10% of children who need remedial help in reading. This helps explain why the evidence for a relation between reading disability and left–right problems emerges more strongly from studies of children drawn from a clinical setting than from normal classrooms. At the same time, it should be noted that clinical records are likely to be biased, since referrals are more likely to be made on the basis of reading disability combined with left – right confusion and anomalies of lateralization than on the basis of reading disability alone. Nevertheless, this should not detract from the conclusion that these symptoms constitute an identifiable syndrome, even if it is not the only one which bears on the problem of reading disability. We might also note that the estimate of the incidence of this syndrome, about 2.5%, is close to the more conservative of the estimates of the incidence of true dyslexia (e.g., Bannatyne, 1971).

Even in those studies where there seemed to be a clear relation between reading disability and left–right confusion or anomalies of lateralization, there was often doubt as to the direction of causality. For example, there was some question as to whether poorly lateralized scanning was the cause or the effect of reading disability. In general, it is consistent with the evidence reviewed in the previous chapter to suppose that the maturation of structural asymmetry is a necessary prerequisite for the development of asymmetrical skills, but does not rigidly determine them. Within the limits set by maturation, different learned manifestations of asymmetry may mutually interact. Therefore, questions about causality may often be misplaced. The development of handedness, for instance, may both assist and be assisted by learning to read and write. Even the manifestation of cerebral lateralization may depend partly on experience, and thus may both influence and be influenced by the acquisition of reading skills.

There was some suggestion from the evidence that different manifestations of laterality become relevant at different stages in the development of reading. It is probably his handedness which first informs the child about the difference between left and right, and which serves to orient him with respect to the directionality of script. Further progress may then depend on his ability to learn to scan left to right (or right to left in some cultures) with his eyes. Gradually, this asymmetry may become less motoric, more perceptual, so that hemifield differences in tachistoscopic perception are predictive of reading ability at around eight years of age. Although the lateralization of auditory processing appears to be manifest somewhat earlier than that of visual processing, its relevance to reading may occur later, perhaps not until the age of about ten years. Relative reading ability may then depend on general verbal skills rather than on visual perceptual ones.

We conclude in a more speculative vein. In Chapter 9 we suggested that there is a category of individuals who inherit the lack of any consistent predisposition to be lateralized one way or the other. In the absence of so-called "right shift" (Annett, 1972), the direction and degree of different manifestations of laterality may be largely a matter of chance. Annett's (1974) study suggested that these individuals are divided about equally into left- and right-handers. However, they would comprise a much larger proportion of *total* left-handers than of *total* right-handers, and here we may recall that Hines and Satz (1974) found no correlation between visual and auditory lateralization among left-handers, but a moderate correlation among right-handers. These observations are consistent with the more general proposition that, in individuals lacking the right-shift factor, the different manifestations of laterality are determined at random and more or less independently of one another. If different aspects of laterality contribute to the development of reading at different stages, such a person might find himself hampered at any one of these stages. Moreover, persons in this category would be especially prone to the confusing influence of crossed lateralization, perhaps between hand and eye, perhaps between visual and auditory lateralization in perceptual processing. However, many individuals would suffer no disability, particularly if chance bestows on them asymmetries of sufficient degree and consistency. Our estimate of 2.5% for dyslexics with associated left – right problems would certainly lie within any estimate of the number of persons lacking the right shift (see Chapter 9).

It seems reasonable to speculate, therefore, that these unusually symmetrical individuals might comprise a high proportion of dyslexics, particularly in those cases where the disability is highly specific and is not accompanied by evidence of brain damage, birth trauma, and the like. Because chance is assumed to play a major role in determining the actual pattern of asymmetries, this hypothesis could help further to explain why the experimental evidence generally reveals rather weak associations between reading disability and particular measures of lateralization. To test the hypothesis adequately, however, would require a reversal of research strategy. Rather than select subjects for reading disability and test for lateralization, it would seem more appropriate to screen subjects on the basis of tests of lateralization, including tests carried out on immediate relatives, and study their progress in reading.

If our hypothesis is correct, it suggests that dyslexia may be not so much a pathological condition as a manifestation of a particular organization of the brain. As Critchley (1970) notes, many dyslexics do learn to read, but they may develop their own special strategies for doing so. Moreover, they may compensate for their disability in other ways; throughout this book we have emphasized the trade off between the advantages of symmetry and those of asymmetry. If a child has a specific reading problem, but is otherwise intelligent and aware, the prognosis may be excellent; he may be another Leonardo da Vinci.

12

The Pathology of Left and Right: Some Further Twists

> Where left handedness is present, the character pertaining to the opposite sex seems more pronounced. This sentence is not only invariably correct, but its converse is also true: Where a woman resembles a man, or a man resembles a woman, we find the emphasis on the left side of the body. Once we know this we have the diviner's rod for the discovery of left handedness. This diagnosis is always correct.[1]
>
> —*Der Ablauf des Lebens*
> WILHELM FLIESS

The link between sexuality and the left and right sides of the body is one that has permeated many different cultures through the ages (see, e.g., Hertz, 1960; Needham, 1973). Generally, the right side is associated with masculinity, the left side with femininity. No doubt these associations are largely a matter of superstition, based perhaps on the inferior status bestowed both on women in relation to men and on the left hand in relation to the right. According to Fisher (1970), men who have problems in heterosexual adjustment are more likely to focus their attention on the *right* sides of their bodies than on the left. This appears contrary to the myth, although it might perhaps be argued that it represents an attempt to compensate for a right-sided deficiency.

Fliess' dogmatic theory about the association between bilateralism and bisexuality was never accepted by his close friend Sigmund Freud, and actually led to an estrangement between the two men. Indeed, in an analysis of Leonardo da Vinci, Freud (1948) discussed Leonardo's homosexuality but

---

[1] Quoted in English by Fritsch (1968, p. 133).

evidently did not consider it particularly relevant that Leonardo was left-handed. He mentioned it but once, in passing. However, he wrote to Fliess that "Leonardo, of whom no love affair is recorded, was perhaps the most famous case of left-handedness. Can you use him?" (Freud, 1954, p. 268).

Perhaps Freud's reluctance to pursue Fliess's theory was due to his suspicion that he may himself have been somewhat "bilateral." As he confessed to Fliess: "I am not aware of any preference for the left hand, or that I had any such preference in childhood: I should rather say that in my early years I had two left hands" (Freud, 1954, p. 243). Freud then went on to recall the difficulty he had had in telling left from right, as we saw in Chapter 1. Here it may have been Fliess' son, Robert, who took special note. Robert Fliess became a psychoanalyst and attached some significance to the theory, apparently originated by Abraham (1927), that left–right confusion was symptomatic of a more profound confusion between anal and genital impulses (Fliess, 1956).

Since this theory seems to us more predictive of a back–front than of a left–right confusion, this is perhaps an appropriate place to end our brief digression into psychoanalysis. In general, we suspect that disorders of personality or psychosexual development, if related at all to laterality, are the products rather than the causes of left-handedness or left–right confusion. Besides, some of our best friends are left-handers. In the rest of this chapter, we shall focus on disorders of left–right discrimination or left–right orientation which can be related more explicitly to neurological or constitutional factors.

We begin with a discussion of a bizarre but fairly common manifestation of left–right disorientation—mirror writing.

MIRROR WRITING

Leonardo da Vinci was not only left-handed, he was also a mirror writer; he wrote from right to left instead of from left to right (see Fig. 12.1). For most of us, mirror writing is virtually illegible, and we can read it with ease only by holding it up to a mirror. It is sometimes said that Leonardo wrote backward in order to conceal his heretical writings from the Church, although it is perhaps difficult to believe that so inventive a man would have resorted to so obvious a subterfuge. An alternative theory, consistent with neurological evidence from other cases, is that Leonardo's mirror writing and his left-handedness were the outcome of injury to his left cerebral hemisphere (Critchley, 1928). Cardinal Luis of Aragon observed that Leonardo, when an old man of 65, was afflicted with a paralysis of the right arm. Yet one may wonder why this was not

FIGURE 12.1 Leonardo da Vinci's *The Proportions of the human figure, after Vitruvius,* showing mirror writing. (Reproduced from L. Goldscheider, Leonardo da Vinci, an Artist. London: Phaidon Press Ltd., Publishers, with permission from the publishers.)

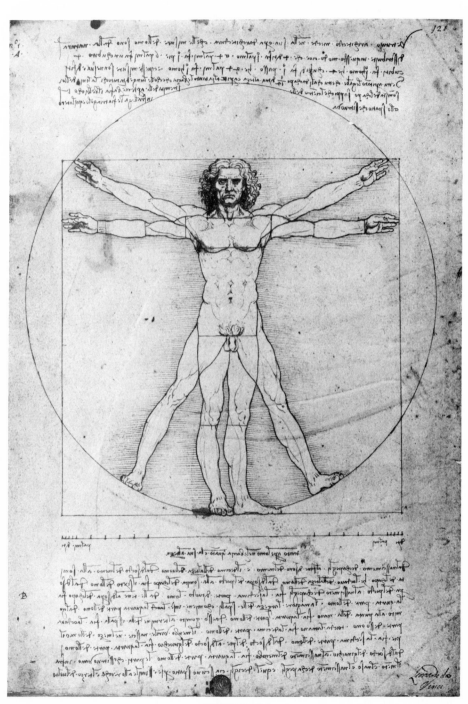

FIGURE 12.1

mentioned by others, since Leonardo had probably always been left-handed and wrote backward at least from the age of 20 (Burt, 1957). Another occasional mirror writer was Lewis Carroll. He apparently did it for fun, to amuse his young lady friends. There may have been more to it than this, however: Burt (1957) has suggested that Carroll was a changed left-hander, on the grounds that he stammered.

In pathological cases, mirror writing is easier or more natural than normal writing, even though the subject himself may be unable to read what he has written. Orton (1937) described several cases of children with reading disability who preferred to write backward although Hécaen and Ajuriaguerra (1964, p. 87) refer to a study which shows that mirror writing, like normal writing, is in general very poor among dyslexics. It is fairly well established that mirror writing is sometimes included among the symptoms of left-cerebral damage, including aphasia, right hemiplegia, and apraxia (Critchley, 1928); the reader may recall the case described by Ireland (1881), whom we quoted in Chapter 6. According to Critchley, however, the first adequate neurological description was a report by Fox and Holmes in 1926 of a mirror writer with a glioma in the posterosuperior angle of the left parietal lobe, which destroyed the angular gyrus. Critchley also noted that mirror writing sometimes occurs spontaneously in states of "dissociation," including postconcussion state, light anesthesia, intoxication, hypnosis, trance, hysteria, and mental abstraction or "daydreaming."

Mirror writing often accompanies a switch from one hand to the other. Rosinus Lentilus, at the beginning of the eighteenth century, observed a soldier who lost his right arm and then wrote backward with his left hand (Critchley, 1928). A more remarkable case was described by Pierocinni in 1903 (cited by Hécaen & Ajuriaguerra, 1964). The subject was a twelve-year-old girl who was born with only a stump in place of the right arm and had great difficulty learning to write with the left hand. When she wrote rapidly for herself, she wrote backward. She was then taught to write with a pen fixed to her right stump, and at once wrote normally.

The difficulties which may result from an enforced switch in handedness have been well described by a person who wrote to us in 1971 of his personal experiences. This remarkable man is a senior research chemist with a doctorate degree in chemistry, and speaks eight languages. Yet he appears to have a serious laterality problem, and would probably have been classed as dyslexic as a child. Here are some extracts from his letter:

> I am left handed. At the age of four my orthodox Jewish parents began to teach me Hebrew, a language written . . . from right to left. . . . At the age of six I went to school and learned to read and write German. Early in the first grade my lady teacher caught me writing with my left hand, stood me out in front of the class and painted a big cross on my right hand so that I would remember what hand to use. For a while she watched me if I would revert back, and eventually I yielded.

He goes on to describe his reading problems and his otherwise excellent progress in school. Later, he turned to psychoanalysis for help:

> For many years I have been envious of people who write with their left hand, but I never thought I could do anything about it. As a student I went through a Freudian psychoanalysis which lasted for nearly four years with four weakly [sic] sessions. This gave me an insight into many traumatic experiences during my early childhood, etc., but unfortunately, conflicts of laterality are not in the books of Freud's teachings, and this somewhat became glossed over.

It is as well, perhaps, that he never encountered Wilhelm Fliess' views on laterality! In fact, he states that it was Hécaen and Ajuriaguerra's (1964) book which helped most to resolve his difficulties. He taught himself, at the age of 48, to write with his left hand, and has been doing so ever since. At the same time, he discovered he could write backward with his left hand. His comments are insightful:

> [My left-handed mirror-image writing] in its style resembles my right-hand writing but of a somewhat earlier period in life. My mirror-image writing when using my right hand resembles my left-hand straight writing. This, then, looks to me like a proof for a double cross-over, where the right-hand skill is projected in mirror-image to the left hand, and the left-hand skill in its mirror-image to the right hand.

> I can write mirror-image writing with my left hand at a rapid speed, but the curious thing about it is, that I can't read it back unless I reverse the paper and hold it against the light. This then indicates to me that the reading and writing skills use completely different pathways.

This man's experiences and observations are not only informative, they also convey a moral: if a child wants to write with his left hand, let him!

Most normal people can fairly readily write backward with the nonpreferred hand. Hécaen and Ajuriaguerra (1964) report that right-handers can write backward with the left hand more easily as they grow older, and that 86% of right-handed adults can do it without difficulty. Interestingly enough, the same is true of left-handers; that is, 80% of left-handed adults can easily write backward with the *left* hand. One can write backwards with the nonpreferred hand more easily, it appears, if one simultaneously writes forward with the preferred hand. Clark (1957) tested eleven- and twelve-year-old children on a test requiring them to write down digits rapidly with both hands, and over half of them spontaneously wrote normally with the preferred hand and backward with the nonpreferred hand. This was true both of right- and left-handers.

Yet pathological mirror writing does not seem to be associated exclusively with one or other hand. It may be recalled that Ireland's (1881) hemiplegic patient, discussed in Chapter 6, continued to write backward even after she had regained control of her right hand. Even normal right-handers will usually mirror write with their right hands if instructed to write on their own foreheads or on the underside of a board. This suggests that writing is not primarily a motor skill, but is rather a spatial one. Hécaen and Ajuriaguerra (1964) refer to a survey of mirror writing among school children by Bloede, whom they quote as saying that "only the frustrated left-handed child [spontaneously] performs mirror writing, and the hand which guides the pen is of little importance [p. 87]."

In general, these observations support the notion of mirror-image generalization. Although we have just seen that the mirror-image relation is not always associated with opposite hands, it is probably fairly generally true to say that one hand vicariously learns the mirror image of what the other hand has been taught. Once again, it should be noted that mirror-image generalization could serve an adaptive purpose in a natural environment where there is no overall bias favoring one or other side; the monkey who learns to reach and break off a banana with one hand might find it more convenient to use the other hand next time. Moreover, many skills, such as flying or swimming, involve bilaterally symmetrical movements, and coordination would be assisted by symmetrization of the learning process.

It is of interest to inquire whether the mirror-image generalization implied by the phenomenon of mirror writing can be attributed to the interhemispheric mirror-image reversal of memory traces, as we proposed in Chapter 6. If a person learns to write with his right hand, for example, we may suppose that the learning would be directly registered primarily in the left hemisphere — although not exclusively, perhaps, since kinesthetic information from a single hand appears to be relayed ipsilaterally as well as contralaterally (Levy, Nebes, & Sperry, 1971). Homotopic mapping between hemispheres would then tend to produce mirror writing if the person tried to write with the left hand, assuming that the left hand is controlled by the right hemisphere. However, there is some conflicting evidence as to whether the learned engram is itself mapped homotopically onto the right hemisphere or whether the information is simply relayed homotopically from the left to the right hemisphere during the act of writing itself. The fact that mirror writing often occurs as a result of damage to the left hemisphere suggests that the actual learning may have been transferred to the right hemisphere, which can then control the left-handed writing without communicating at all with the left hemisphere. Yet, if this were so, one might expect commissurotomized patients also to mirror write with their left hands. Levy, Nebes, and Sperry (1971) tested two right-handed commissurotomized patients who apparently showed no tendency to mirror write with their left hands even when they were obstructed from seeing what they wrote. Of course, the observations of Levy and her colleagues are not definitive; the patients were not *asked* to mirror write, and their left-handed efforts were in any case very clumsy and hesitant. Moreover, their attempts to write with the left hand may have been at least partially under ipsilateral, left-hemispheric control. As we saw in Chapter 9, there is evidence that commissurotomized patients can achieve ipsilateral control of either hand as soon as three months after surgery (Gazzaniga, Bogen, & Sperry, 1967; Gazzaniga & Sperry, 1967).

It is possible that interhemispheric mirror-image reversal of the actual learned engrams for writing is most pronounced among those symmetrical, if still hypothetical individuals who lack consistent lateralization (cf. Annett, 1972, 1974; see also Chapter 9). This could explain why left-handers, "frustrated" left-handers, and ambidextrous persons are especially prone to mirror writing.

SPATIAL REVERSAL

We have seen that damage to the left cerebral cortex, particularly in the parietal lobe, often results in mirror writing. We tentatively interpret this to mean that a mirror-image engram for writing is laid down in the right hemisphere and may control the writing process if the normally dominant left hemisphere is damaged. According to this reasoning one might expect to find a converse phenomenon with respect to *spatial* engrams. Since the right hemisphere is presumed to be dominant for the recording of spatial information in most persons (see Chapter 8), one might suppose that damage to this hemisphere would "release" reversed information from the left hemisphere.

Luria (1966) has confirmed that spatial confusions and reversals do sometimes result from lesions to the right occipitoparietal regions. An excellent example is described, together with an illustration, in Luria's (1970) article in *Scientific American*. A patient who had suffered a war injury to his right parietal lobe drew a reversed map of Russia—see Fig. 12.2. His verbal labels were written normally, however, and as the figure shows he was somewhat

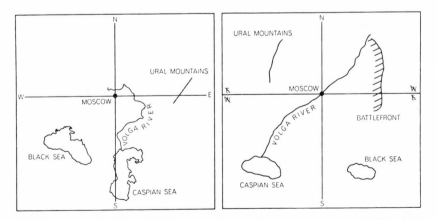

FIGURE 12.2   Reversal in map drawing by patient with injury to right parietal lobe. Left panel shows correct map, right panel shows patient's drawing. (Labels redrawn in English; from Luria, A. R. *The Functional organization of the brain.* Copyright 1970 by Scientific American, Inc. All rights reserved.)

confused as to which side to label "east" and which side "west." Presumably his verbal knowledge conflicted with his disoriented spatial engram. This patient's confusion and reversal provide further evidence, not only for the idea that there may be some mirror-image exchange between the hemispheres, but also for the dissociation in the brain between verbal and spatial representations.

GERSTMANN'S SYNDROME

Sometimes it is claimed that a brain injury causes an inability to tell left from right. Perhaps the best known syndrome involving left–right confusion is that described by Gerstmann (1940) in which the other symptoms are finger agnosia, agraphia, and acalculia. Gerstmann's syndrome is said to result from a unilateral lesion in a discrete area of the left parietal lobe (Critchley, 1953).

The notion that a unilateral lesion could produce a bilateral deficit in telling left from right is somewhat controversial. It appears to run counter to our general theme that left – right confusion is a fundamental consequence of structural bilateral symmetry, since unilateral lesions should decrease rather than increase symmetry — although we should also remember that to begin with, the human brain is not perfectly symmetrical. It is therefore worth investigating more closely what is typically meant, in cases of Gerstmann's syndrome and other neurological disorders, by the inability to tell left from right.

The tests used to determine a patient's ability to tell left from right vary somewhat, but usually require the patient to identify his own or a confronting person's lateral body parts (for example, right hand, left knee). These are tests of left – right response differentiation; we have seen, however, that they may also require abilities other than the basic capacity to tell left from right, including an understanding of the meaning of the *words* "left" and "right," and an ability to make mental transformations of bodily coordinates in space. Benton has described the variety of impairment as follows:

A patient's failure may be absolute or relative, i.e., he may make an incorrect response or show excessive slowness in making correct discriminations. There are patients who fail at the simplest level of left–right orientation, i.e., they cannot show their right hand or point to their right eye. When such a patient is manifestly dysphasic, it is reasonable to ascribe this failure to the language deficit and to conclude that he has lost the symbolic meaning of the terms "left" and "right." Indeed, he will often express his profound language impairment by failing even to point to the appropriate body part, e.g., he will point to his eye instead of his ear. . . . However, failure on the higher levels of right–left orientation with preservation of the capacity to make simple "own body" localizations is more frequently seen. The patient may become confused when instructed to perform double crossed commands, he may fail to make the required 180-degree transformation in identifying the lateral body parts of the confronting examiner, or he may fail completely on tasks requiring simultaneous operation of the "own body" and "other person" orientation systems [Benton, 1968, p. 754].

One fairly commonly accepted explanation for why lesions of the left hemisphere may cause left–right disorientation has been proposed by Bonhoeffer (1923). He suggested that knowledge of which is the right hand is critical to the left–right sense. Damage to the left hemisphere could lead to defective sensory representation of the right hand, and so deprive the individual of critical information which normally guides his decisions about left and right. Certainly it is true that deficits in verbal tests of left–right differentiation are produced by lesions to the hemisphere opposite the dominant hand, but not by lesions to the ipsilateral hemisphere. For example, McFie and Zangwill (1960) found that five of eight patients with lesions in the dominant hemisphere suffered impairment of left–right differentiation, but none of 21 patients with comparable lesions in the nondominant hemisphere did so. Yet we do not find Bonhoeffer's explanation convincing. Loss of sensory information from the right hand is not the same as loss of knowledge as to which *is* the right hand; indeed, if one were to lose the sensation from the right hand, one might be all the better informed as to which hand was which, since the difference between the hands would be if anything enhanced!

There are some cases where the left–right disorientation does appear to be unilateral rather than bilateral (Benton, 1959). A patient with a unilateral lesion may lose awareness of the opposite side of his body. In these cases, all reactions to verbal commands tend to be directed to the unaffected side, so the patient may lift his right arm, say, in response to both "left" and "right" commands. This may be spuriously represented as a left–right confusion, but is in fact a more fundamental disability involving neglect of one side of the body.

Benton (1959, 1968) has also pointed out that hemiplegics — patients with one-sided paralysis due to contralateral brain damage — usually have little difficulty telling left from right. For example, mentally retarded individuals are generally even poorer on tests of left–right differentiation than their mental ages would predict, but if they are also hemiplegic this particular disability disappears. A revealing example, originally reported by Rosenberg, is described by Benton as follows:

> . . . an imbecile [hemiplegic] patient . . . with a mental age of about four years showed excellent right–left discrimination with respect to his lateral body parts. When asked to show his right hand, he might show his right or his left; however, having made his initial response, he was consistent in his subsequent responses, including reactions to double crossed commands (e.g., "put your right hand on your left ear"). This he performed either consistently correctly or consistently incorrectly (i.e., he showed systematic reversal of response). He did not show the inconsistent performance one sees in most four-year-old children [Benton, 1968, p. 752].

In cases of more genuinely bilateral confusion about left and right, as in Gerstmann's syndrome, Benton (1959) has proposed that the impairment is one of understanding the actual concepts of "left" and "right." "This is tantamount," he observes, "to saying that right–left disorientation of this type is an expression of aphasia [p. 153]." Bonhoeffer (1923) did not think the problem could be attributed to aphasia, at least in the patient that he observed, because there did not seem to be any deficit in the comprehension of oral language. Yet aphasic disturbances can be selective. Benton points out that the verbal concepts of "left" and "right" are acquired relatively late in the developmental history of the child, and may therefore be especially vulnerable to the influence of a general language impairment. Another of the symptoms of Gerstmann's syndrome, finger agnosia, can be similarly explained. In finger agnosia, the patient is unable to identify his fingers in response to oral command or to tactual stimulation. Benton (1959, p. 159) states that verbal functions play an important role in the typical clinical test for finger agnosia; the patient is effectively required to be able to *name* his fingers. Benton observes that the names of the inner fingers of the hand are acquired relatively late in the development of vocabulary, and like the labels "left" and "right," may therefore be particularly sensitive to language impairment.

The ability to write and the ability to calculate are also fairly late acquisitions which could explain why agraphia and acalculia are also included in Gerstmann's syndrome. However, Benton (1959) reviews evidence to suggest that this constellation of symptoms is not invariant. Deficits of reading, speech, and constructional praxis are also often associated with finger agnosia and left–right confusion. Moreover, these different symptoms may be identified with localized lesions in different cortical areas—for example, finger agnosia with the angular gyrus, and left–right disorientation with the supramarginal gyrus. These observations raise doubts as to whether any particular constellation of symptoms, including those described by Gerstmann, can be properly termed a "syndrome" at all. Nevertheless it seems reasonable to conclude that all of these symptoms reflect some deficit in symbolic understanding, and that those symbolic skills that are acquired relatively late are the more likely to be affected by brain lesions.

If Benton's interpretation is correct, then the deficit in left–right differentiation has little to do with the left–right sense or with telling left from right as we defined it in Chapter 2. The deficit is symbolic, not directional. We suspect, in fact, that it may not be restricted to the verbal concepts of "left" and "right," but may also be enhanced by a general inability to understand complex verbal instructions. Instructions like "touch my right shoulder with your left hand" are complicated, especially for a patient with left-hemisphere lesions, quite apart from references to sidedness.

TURNER'S SYNDROME

Another syndrome said to be characterized by some degree of left – right confusion is that described by Turner (1938). Turner's syndrome, also known as gonadal aplasia, ovarian agenesis, or gonadal dysgenesis, results from a chromosomal abnormality. In about 80% of cases the sex chromatin is negative and the chromosome count is only 45 (44 plus XO) instead of the usual 46 (44 plus XX). In other cases the sex chromatin is positive but there are other irregularities. The victim is characterized by short stature and the body morphology of a sexually immature girl. Other physical stigmata may include webbed neck, webbed fingers and toes, small receding chin, defects of heart, kidney, and ureter, and hearing loss.

The main cognitive symptom is a deficit in spatial ability (Money, 1963), including an alleged "right–left disorientation" (Alexander & Money, 1966). Unlike Gerstmann's syndrome, Turner's syndrome does not seem to involve any language deficit, and there is no evidence for either dyslexia (Alexander & Money, 1965) or dysgraphia (Alexander & Money, 1966). The fact that these patients can read normally suggests that they can tell left from right, at least according to our criteria. In fact, their so-called "right – left disorientation" appears to be of a rather specific sort. Alexander and Money (1966) found that their patients had no difficulty identifying the left or right sides of their own bodies or in drawing a line to the left or right according to verbal instructions. It was on more complex tasks that the difficulty emerged. Seven of the 18 patients could not identify the left and right sides of a confronting person, and most of them were much worse than normal controls on the Standardized Road-Map Test of Direction Sense (Money, Alexander, & Walker, 1965). The road-map test requires the subject to say whether the various turns on a path drawn on a road map are to the left or right, and she must not turn the map around to make her decisions.

It seems clear that the deficit the patients suffered was not one of telling left from right, but was rather one of imagining their own bodies in different locations in space. Those who failed to label the sides of a confronting person appropriately may have failed to mentally rotate their own body coordinates through 180°, and those who could perform this task may have simply learned to reverse their own left and right—a verbal rather than a spatial solution. The road-map test requires more varied mental transformations, since the route takes many turns, not all at right angles; to solve the task, the testee must imagine herself variously proceeding north, south, east, or west, or occasionally at intermediate compass points, and she must then judge the left or right turn relative to this imagined direction. Once again, the patients evidently failed to make the appropriate mental transformations.

SUMMARY AND CONCLUSIONS

In this chapter, we have collected some of the evidence on left–right reversals and left–right confusion as symptoms of some underlying disorder. Although somewhat heterogeneous, this evidence does relate to various themes we have developed in earlier chapters.

The evidence on left–right confusion reveals a lack of precision, both in the actual tests of so-called "left–right discrimination" and in the interpretation of results. The typical clinical test goes well beyond the basic ability to tell left from right as we defined it in Chapter 2. Usually, the patient is required to follow verbal instructions, often quite complex, and to *verbally* comprehend the meanings of "left" and "right." Consequently, failure to perform the test might result from a failure of verbal or symbolic comprehension rather than from any fundamental deficit in the left–right sense. In addition, the patient may be required to imagine himself or herself in different spatial locations in order to judge the left and right sides of others, perhaps, or to make left–right decisions about map locations. Failure to accomplish the test might also occur because of an inability to make mental transformations, and may have nothing to do with left and right per se.

We suggested that the so-called left–right deficit in Gerstmann's syndrome is fundamentally a verbal deficit, while that in Turner's syndrome is a spatial one. If so, it is in both cases misleading to refer to left–right confusion or left–right disorientation. Even if our analysis is incorrect or oversimplified, we urge that clinical testing procedures should be refined somewhat in order to specify more precisely the nature of the deficit. For example, it is possible to test the ability to tell left from right by nonverbal means, as we saw in Chapter 2 and illustrated in Chapters 4 and 10. Tests of mirror-image discrimination and of left–right differentiation could be fairly easily contrived without use of verbal labels. Again, tests of the ability to make mental transformations of one's own body coordinates need not involve decisions about left and right.

The evidence on left–right reversals was more positively related to the problem of telling left from right, and in particular to the notion of interhemispheric mirror-image reversal, which we discussed at length in Chapter 6. It is of interest to note that both mirror writing and the more isolated instance of reversed map drawing seem, at least superficially, to be consistent with Orton's theory, since the reversal in each case appears to emanate from the nondominant hemisphere. Thus mirror writing is often a consequence of left-hemisphere damage or of a switch from right to left hands, suggesting that when the nondominant right-hemisphere controls writing it produces mirror writing. Conversely, Luria's patient who drew the map of Russia backward had suffered right-hemisphere damage, suggesting that the left hemisphere, which is normally nondominant for spatial processing, had recorded the reversed engram.

It is possible, then, that Orton was correct in asserting that engrams tend to be laid down normally in the dominant hemisphere and in mirror-reversed fashion in the nondominant hemisphere, but for the wrong reasons. He thought that this symmetrical arrangement was simply a consequence of the symmetry of the brain, which, as we pointed out in Chapter 6, does not follow. Our own view is that if there is any truth at all to the notion of interhemispheric mirror-image reversal, the reversal would result from homotopic *transfer* from one hemisphere to the other. The mechanisms which establish cerebral lateralization may restrict the primary memory processing to one or other hemisphere, depending on the nature of the information that is being processed. But although the engram is laid down primarily in one hemisphere, homotopic connections between hemispheres might serve to establish a weaker, reversed engram in the other hemisphere.

This account suggests how Fig. 6.6, which illustrates schematically our theory of interhemispheric mirror-image reversal, could be modified to accommodate the phenomenon of cerebral lateralization. We suspect that lateralization occurs primarily at the level of access to memory and the formation of memory traces. Thus, the engram for the word CAT, for example, would be established primarily in one hemisphere (presumably the left in most people), so that the reversed engram TAƆ would then be established secondarily in the other hemisphere. The reader should appreciate, however, that this analysis is highly speculative.

13

Man, Nature, and the Conservation of Parity

Why is nature so nearly symmetrical? No one has any idea why. The only thing we might suggest is something like this: There is a gate in Japan, a gate in Neiko, which is sometimes called by the Japanese the most beautiful gate in all Japan; it was built at a time when there was great influence from Chinese art. This gate is very elaborate, with lots of gables and beautiful carving and lots of columns and dragon heads and princes carved into the pillars, and so on. But when one looks closely he sees that in the elaborate and complex design along one of the pillars, one of the small design elements is carved upside down; otherwise the thing is completely symmetrical. If one asks why this is, the story is that it was carved upside down so that the gods will not be jealous of the perfection of man. So they purposely put the error in there, so that the gods would not be jealous and get angry with human beings.

We might like to turn the idea around and think that the true explanation of the near symmetry of nature is this: that God made the laws only nearly summetrical so that we should not be jealous of His perfection!

—*The Feynman Lectures on Physics*
R. P. FEYNMAN, R. B. LEIGHTON,
AND M. SANDS

This final chapter is intended partly as a summary and partly as an extension of the themes developed in earlier chapters. We shall try to place the psychological problem of telling left from right in a broader scientific and cultural perspective, touching on related issues in anthropology, molecular biology, and theoretical physics. The common thread that unites our discussion is the conservation or nonconservation of parity. The question is whether the laws or phenomena within some given domain are altered by mirror reflection. If they are not, we may say that parity is conserved. But if reflection produces a different set of phenomena or laws, then parity is not conserved.

Throughout this book we have argued that the confusion or equivalence of left and right is not primarily a matter of perception, at least in the most immediate sense of the term. Neither animals nor people seem to have any serious difficulty in seeing which way round an object is, for example. The problem occurs at the higher level of analysis at which patterns or objects are identified according to *what* they are, rather than according to where they are located or which way they are oriented. Thus there is a strong tendency to treat left – right mirror images as equivalent. They may be perceived as different simply because they are facing opposite ways, but they may be labeled and recognized as the same.

These phenomena presumably have their origins in the characteristics of the natural environment. By the "natural" environment, we mean the everyday environment as it impinges on the sense organs and confines the movements of animals, but we exclude certain man-made artifacts. In the *particulars* of this world parity is not conserved, that is, any particular scene would in general look different if viewed through a mirror. It is therefore necessary for an animal to be able to correctly *perceive* the left–right orientation of an object or event; it must know which side it is being attacked from, or which way its prey is facing. But in the *generalities* of the natural world parity is very largely conserved. At the molar level at which they affect animals, the laws of nature are unaltered by mirror reflection; attacks may occur from either side, prey may face in either direction, and so on. It is for this reason that animals have evolved mechanisms for *mirror-image generalization.* One such mechanism is simply the bilateral symmetry of the sensory and motor apparatus of the body, for it enables an animal to be equally sensitive to stimulation on either side, or equally capable of response in either direction. We have also suggested that a mechanism of mirror-image generalization may apply to the products of experience so that learning based on any particular experience is generalized to the left–right mirror image of that experience. Mirror-image generalization, if total, means that an animal would be as well adapted to the reflected world as to the original world.

We have seen, however, that parity is not conserved in the man-made world, either in the particulars or in the generalities. This was illustrated by Fig. 1.3 in Chapter 1. Given a picture of a city street, say, one can usually tell whether or not it has been mirror-reversed, even if the street is not one we are familiar with — although we may have difficulty if the scene is of a totally foreign culture. The most obvious clues come from the printed word, from street signs, shop signs, or car license plates. There are more subtle clues in the way jackets are buttoned, where front door knobs are placed, and so on.

The asymmetry of the man-made world derives fairly obviously from our own asymmetry, and especially from the general preference for the right hand. Man himself does not obey the conservation of parity. But since we are in other respects highly symmetrical and have evolved to expect symmetry in the phenomena of nature, the discovery of our own handedness has had a profound impact, not only on the things man has built, but on our culture and modes of thought. In virtually all cultures, *left* and *right* convey a symbolic significance well beyond the mere reference to sidedness. In the Pythagorean tradition among the ancient Greeks, for example, the right is associated with the odd numbers, the one, the male, the light, the straight, the good, while the left is linked to the even numbers, the many, the female, the dark, the crooked, the evil (Fritsch, 1968). Similar and often extended associations are to be found in many other cultures, both ancient and modern, including the Polynesians, various African tribes, the Arabs, and the Indians (Needham, 1973). Chinese culture is somewhat exceptional in that the left is accorded the more honorable status, even though the Chinese themselves are predominantly right-handed (see Granet, 1973). Generally, however, the right is associated with the more positive attributes. We can discover this in our very language by contrasting the *adroit* and *dexterous* with the *gauche* and *sinister*.

It has even been suggested that differences in status associated with left and right may be manifest in the profiles artists paint in their portraits. Humphrey and McManus (1973) examined 1474 portraits produced in western Europe over the last 600 years and found that 60% of them were predominantly in left profile or displayed more of the left cheek than of the right. It is commonly believed that the preponderance of left-profile portraits is due to the fact that the right-hander finds it easier to draw left profiles than right profiles. But Humphrey and McManus uncovered some additional facts which suggest that there is more to it than this. For one thing, there was a significant disparity between portraits of men and women; 68% of the women were portrayed as displaying more of the left cheek than of the right, compared with only 56% of the men. In a more detailed analysis of Rembrandt's portraits, they found that self portraits nearly always displayed more of the *right* cheek; the percentage of left profiles increased from 15.8% among self-portraits, to 17.6% among portraits of Rembrandt's own male kin, to 39.1% among male nonkin, to 56.2% among female kin, to 78.8% among female nonkin. Humphrey and McManus suggest that this progression is a function of the social distance between artist and subject; the closer the artist feels to his subject in status, the more likely he is to portray the subject in right profile.[1] They also observe that Van Gogh tended to portray male peasants in right profile more often than he did the bourgeoisie, suggesting that he was "more at home" among the peasants.

---

[1] Humphrey and McManus have overlooked another factor which may partly explain the difference between portraits of men and women. It is common practice for portraits to be hung in pairs, the male on the left, the female on the right. They look toward each other, and therefore display opposite cheeks. This tradition is carried over even to portraits hung singly, and almost certainly applied to the portraits painted by Rembrandt. We are grateful to Professor Anthony Green of the University of Auckland for pointing this out to us.

In an essay first published in 1909, the French social anthropologist Robert Hertz argued that the right and left hands have become general symbols for polar opposites—for example, male and female, light and dark, life and death (see Hertz, 1960). He documented his thesis primarily with reference to left–right symbolism in Maori culture, but his conclusions appear to have remarkable cross-cultural generality (Needham, 1973) — although there is some dissenting opinion (e.g., Beattie, 1968). Why should the hands be such potent symbols? Presumably, it is because they are at once alike and different, the paradox of left–right mirror images. "What resemblance more perfect than that between our two hands!" wrote Hertz (1960, p. 89). "And yet what a striking inequality there is!"

With the discovery of cerebral lateralization of function, we are perhaps again witnessing the growth of a left – right symbolism, the spread of a metaphor. As we saw in Chapter 8, the empirical evidence suggests that the functional distinction between hemispheres may be little more than that between verbal and nonverbal processing. Yet many authors have speculated well beyond the facts, linking hemispheric asymmetry to fundamental dichotomies in philosophy and culture. The left hemisphere is rational, propositional, analytic, Yang; the right hemisphere is intuitive, appositional, gestalt, Yin. Perhaps this speculation again owes something to the fascination of left and right. Like the hands, the two sides of the brain are alike and yet different.

It is no doubt because we expect symmetry in the general laws of nature that the discovery of fundamental asymmetries seems so momentous and full of cosmic significance. This is again illustrated in the discovery in the nineteenth century that living molecules are asymmetrical. Louis Pasteur found that the molecules of tartaric acid could assume either of two mirror-image forms, called *enantiomers,* and that a certain plant mold acted upon one but not the other. This implied a fundamental asymmetry in the molecular structure of the plant mold itself. Pasteur at once saw in asymmetry, or the difference between left and right, the key to life itself: "This important criterion [of molecular asymmetry]," he wrote, "constitutes perhaps the only sharply defined difference which can be drawn at the present time between the chemistry of dead or living matter." But he then went further and sought the origins of asymmetry in the forces of the universe: "Life is dominated by asymmetrical actions. I can even imagine that all living species are primordially, in their structure, in their external forms, functions of cosmic asymmetry [quoted by Dubos, 1960, p. 36]." These were extravagant, but oddly prophetic words.

Given the fundamental asymmetry of our molecular make-up, one might predict that mirror-image discrimination would pose no problem to the so-called "chemical" senses, taste and smell, that is, one would expect enantiomers to taste and smell different. Bentley (1969, pp. 284–286)) summarizes evidence that there is often a difference in taste between enantiomeric pairs. For example, Piutti noted as long ago as 1886 that L-asparagine was tasteless while its enantiomer, D-asparagine, was slightly sweet. There is also evidence that amino acids are sweet in the D form but flat or bitter in the L form, while glutamic acid is almost tasteless in the D form but has a meaty taste in the L form. The question of odor differences is more controversial. According to Bentley, it is complicated by the problem of obtaining pure enantiomers and by the lack of an adequate theory of smell. Nevertheless, he maintains that there is no case in which one enantiomer is odorous and the other not (Bentley, 1969, p. 286). Wright (1963) concluded from this that smelling must depend on a physical rather than a chemical interaction. However, this conclusion has been disputed by Russell and Hills (1971), who report distinct odor differences between the enantiomeric pairs of four highly purified compounds.[2]

To return to the question of the conservation of parity, the asymmetry of organic molecules perhaps does not challenge our deepest instincts about symmetry, since the particular asymmetry that characterizes life on our planet may have simply been a matter of chance. The asymmetry *could,* perhaps, have gone the other way. More compelling would be a violation of parity in the fundamental laws of physics. Ernst Mach thought there was an example of the nonconservation of parity in the deflection of a magnetic needle in an electrical field. Characteristically, he was aware of the psychological implications:

> Even instinctive knowledge of so great logical force as the principle of symmetry employed by Archimedes, may lead us astray. Many of my readers will call to mind, perhaps, the intellectual shock they experienced when they heard for the first time that a needle lying in the magnetic meridian is deflected in a definite direction away from the meridian by a wire conducting a current being carried along in a parallel direction above it. The instinctive is just as fallible as the distinctly conscious [Mach, 1893, p. 27].

Mach's shock was actually premature since on deeper analysis the deflection of the needle does not violate the conservation of parity. The designations "north" and "south," applied to the poles of the needle, are essentially arbitrary. If magnetized one way, the needle swings counterclockwise, but if magnetized the other way it swings clockwise. Overall, therefore, parity is conserved.

It is now generally accepted that the principle of conservation of parity holds for all electromagnetic and so-called "strong" physical interactions, which include the interactions involved in gravitational force and the nuclear force

---

[2]In an earlier article (Corballis & Beale, 1970a), we cited Fritsch (1968, p. 97) as stating that "geraniol gives off a scent of roses [while] its optical isomer smells like fresh oil." Professor Ronald Bentley of the University of Pittsburgh kindly wrote to us to tell us that these two isomers do not fit the enantiomeric relationship. He added that both are generally thought to smell like roses. Dr. R. Boch of the Canadian Department of Agriculture also wrote that he personally finds it very hard to tell geraniol from its isomer, nerol, but that bees can very easily distinguish them. He claimed to be unable to locate an isomer of geraniol that smells like fresh oil.

which holds the nucleus of the atom together (Salam, 1958). In 1956, however, two physicists of Chinese extraction, T. D. Lee and C. N. Yang, suggested that parity might not be conserved in the so-called "weak" interactions involved in spontaneous nuclear decay (Lee & Yang, 1956). To many observers, the idea seemed most improbable. In a letter to a friend, the physicist Wolfgang Pauli wrote: "I do *not* believe that the Lord is a weak left-hander, and I am ready to bet a very high sum that the experiments will give symmetric results [quoted by Salam, 1958, p. 103; the *not* was heavily underscored in the original letter]." He wrote just two days before the fall of parity.

The experiments were conducted by Madame Chien-Shiung Wu early in 1957, and showed in effect that the nucleus of the cobalt-60 atom is more likely to emit electrons from one end than from the other. As we have seen, the labels

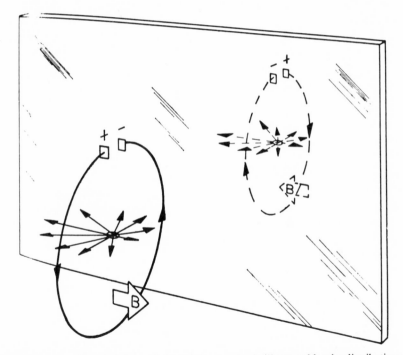

FIGURE 13.1   The violation of left–right symmetry is illustrated by the distribution of electrons emitted by the cobalt-60 nucleus in a magnetic field and its mirror image. The wire loop perpendicular to the mirror produces a magnetic field B parallel to the mirror. The lengths of the arrows illustrate the intensity distribution of electrons in a plane perpendicular to both the mirror and the wire loop. Note that the distributions are not mirror images of one another, as one would expect if parity was to be conserved. (From Sachs, 1972. Copyright 1972 by the American Association for the Advancement of Science.)

"north" and "south" to designate the poles of a magnetic field are assigned purely arbitrarily, and until Madame Wu's experiments there was thought to be nothing in principle to distinguish one from the other. But now a fundamental polarity emerges, and the "south" pole of the nucleus may be defined as that which emits the more electrons. As illustrated in Fig. 13.1, the conservation of parity is violated.

The profound impact of this result is now a matter of history. The Lord, after all, *is* a weak left-hander; or, as Salam (1958) prefers to put it, "space is a weak left-eyed giant [p. 103]," and perhaps a southpaw to boot. Yang and Lee both received the Nobel Prize for their remarkable insight. It is noteworthy that the architects of the fall of parity, including Madame Wu as well as Yang and Lee, should have been of Chinese extraction, for we have seen that the left hand is held in special esteem in Chinese culture.

From our own point of view, the psychological implications are the most interesting. Clearly, the expectation of symmetry had been very strong. Salam (1958) has pointed out that the evidence for the nonconservation of parity had actually been available some ten years earlier, but had passed unnoticed. What was needed was not so much the evidence as the idea. No doubt the "shock" of the violation of parity was derived partly from the fact that parity is still conserved in other physical domains. After the results were announced, Pauli wrote:

> I am shocked not so much by the fact that the Lord prefers the left-hand but by the fact that he still appears to be left – right symmetric when he expresses himself strongly. In short, the actual problem now seems to be the question why are strong interactions right and left symmetric? [quoted by Salam, 1958, p. 103].

Yet the desire for symmetry remains, and there are those who seek to restore the conservation of parity by appealing once more to deeper principles. For example, Yang has noted that parity is still conserved if mirror reflection can be said to reverse *charge* (that is, positive and negative) as well as left and right (see Gardner, 1967).

We suspect that the expectation of symmetry depends on more than the knowledge that other physical forces obey the conservation of parity; it has been shaped throughout evolutionary history by adaptation to these forces and is embedded in the very symmetry of the nervous system. In other words, it is the "strong" interactions which have shaped our own structural symmetry and are thus responsible for the shock of the discovery that parity may be violated. There is therefore a sense in which it is not surprising that the nonconservation of parity should be discovered only in forces outside normal experience.

In this book, we have witnessed a fundamental duality between symmetry and asymmetry. This was expressed in many ways: we often confuse left and right, yet we can tell them apart; artists use symmetry as an organizing principle, but deviate from it to create special effects; the growth of organisms is governed by a symmetrical plan, but there are asymmetrical deviations; the two hands are alike, yet different; parity in physical interactions is seen to be conserved, then seen not to be. The duality is also to be understood in terms of the conflict between man's symmetrical brain and its evolving asymmetry. In separating the enantiomorphic crystals of tartaric acid, Pasteur demonstrated his own ability to tell left from right, and thus his own asymmetry. A perfectly symmetrical physicist could have neither discovered nor even suggested the nonconservation of parity.

If the evolution of symmetry can be understood in terms of the conservation of parity in the strong interactions and observable laws of nature, is there a common thread underlying the emergence of consistent asymmetry? Could there be a link between the asymmetry of nuclear decay, the asymmetry of living molecules, and the left – right gradient which seems to underlie the morphological asymmetries of animals and men, including cerebral asymmetries in the human brain? We have no idea.

References

Abraham, K. *Selected papers on psychoanalysis.* London: Hogarth Press, 1927.

Alajouanine, T. Aphasia and artistic realization. *Brain,* 1948, **71,** 229–241.

Alexander, D., & Money, J. Reading ability, object constancy, and Turner's syndrome. *Perceptual & Motor Skills,* 1965, **20,** 981–984.

Alexander, D., & Money, J. Turner's syndrome and Gerstmann's syndrome: Neuropsychologic comparisons. *Neuropsychologia,* 1966, **4,** 265–273.

Anderson, A. L. The effect of laterality localization of focal brain lesions on the Wechsler-Bellevue subtests. *Journal of Clinical Psychology,* 1951, **7,** 149–153.

Annett, M. A model of the inheritance of handedness and cerebral dominance. *Nature,* 1964, **204,** 59–60.

Annett, M. The binomial distribution of right, mixed and left handedness. *Quarterly Journal of Experimental Psychology,* 1967, **19,** 327–333.

Annett, M. The growth of manual preference and speed. *British Journal of Psychology,* 1970, **61,** 545–558.

Annett, M. The distribution of manual asymmetry. *British Journal of Psychology,* 1972, **63,** 343–358.

Annett, M. Handedness in the children of two left-handed parents. *British Journal of Psychology,* 1974, **65,** 129–131.

Appelle, S. Perception and discrimination as a function of stimulus orientation: The "oblique effect" in man and animals. *Psychological Bulletin,* 1972, **78,** 266–278.

Bakan, P. Hypnotizability, laterality of eye-movements and functional brain asymmetry. *Perceptual & Motor Skills,* 1969, **28,** 927–932.

Bakan, P. Birth order and handedness. *Nature,* 1971, **229,** 195.

Bakan, P., Dibb, G., & Reed, P. Handedness and birth stress. *Neuropsychologia,* 1973, **11,** 363–366.

Bakker, D. J. Ear asymmetry with monaural stimulation. *Psychonomic Science,* 1968, **12,** 62.

Bakker, D. J., Smink, T., & Reitsma, P. Ear dominance and reading ability. *Cortex,* 1973, **9,** 301–312.

Bannatyne, A. *Language, reading and learning disabilities.* Springfield, Ill: Charles C Thomas, 1971.

Barnsley, R. H., & Rabinovitch, M. S. Handedness: Proficiency versus stated preference. *Perceptual & Motor Skills,* 1970, **30,** 343–362.

Barron, F. The psychology of imagination. *Scientific American,* 1958, **199** (3), 151–166.

Barron, F. The psychology of creativity. In T. M. Newcombe (Ed.), *New directions in psychology II.* New York: Holt, Rinehart & Winston, 1965.

Barsley, M. *Left-handed man in a right-handed world.* London: Pitman, 1970.

Bartlett, F. C. *Remembering: A study in experimental and social psychology.* Cambridge, England: Cambridge University Press, 1932.

Barton, M. I., Goodglass, H., & Shai, A. Differential recognition of tachistoscopically presented English and Hebrew words in right and left visual fields. *Perceptual & Motor Skills,* 1965, **21,** 431–437.

Basser, L. S. Hemiplegia of early onset and the faculty of speech with special reference to the effects of hemispherectomy. *Brain,* 1962, **85,** 427–460.

Beale, I. L., & Corballis, M. C. Laterally displaced pecking in monocularly viewing pigeons: A possible factor in interhemispheric mirror-image reversal. *Psychonomic Science,* 1967, **9,** 603–604.

Beale, I. L., & Corballis, M. C. Beak shift: An explanation for interocular mirror-image reversal in pigeons. *Nature,* 1968, **220,** 82–83.

Beale, I. L., & Williams, R. J. Experimental evidence of beak shift during tests for interocular transfer of a lateral mirror-image discrimination. *Psychonomic Science,* 1971, **24,** 7–8.

Beale, I. L., Williams, R. J., Webster, D. M., & Corballis, M. C. Confusion of mirror-images by pigeons and interhemispheric commissures. *Nature,* 1972, **238,** 348 –349.

Beattie, J. Aspects of Nyoro symbolism. *Africa,* 1968, **38,** 413–442.

Belmont, L., & Birch, H. G. Lateral dominance and right-left awareness in normal children. *Child Development,* 1963, **34,** 257–270.

Belmont, L., & Birch, H. G. Lateral dominance, lateral awareness, and reading disability. *Child Development,* 1965, **36,** 57–71.

Bennett, A. An analysis of errors in word recognition made by retarded readers. *Journal of Educational Psychology,* 1942, **33,** 25–38.

Bennett, J. The difference between right and left. *American Philosophical Quarterly,* 1970, **7,** 175–191.

Bentley, R. *Molecular asymmetry in biology.* Vol. I. New York: Academic Press, 1969.

Benton, A. L. Significance of systematic reversal in right-left discrimination. *Acta Psychiatrica et Neurologica (Kopenhagen),* 1958, **33,** 129–137.

Benton, A. L. *Right–left discrimination and finger localization: development and pathology.* New York: Hoeber-Harper, 1959.

Benton, A. L. Right–left discrimination. *Pediatric Clinics of North America,* 1968, **34,** 747–758.

Benton, A. L., & Kemble, J. D. Right–left orientation and reading disability. *Psychiatria et Neurologia* (Basel), 1960, **139,** 49–60.

Berlucchi, G., & Marzi, C. A. Veridical interocular transfer of lateral mirror-image discriminations in split-chiasm cats. *Journal of Comparative & Physiological Psychology,* 1970, **72,** 1–7.

Berlucchi, G., & Rizzolatti, G. Binocularly driven neurons in visual cortex of split-chiasm cats. *Science,* 1968, **159,** 308–310.

Bernstein, F. Beiträge zur mendelistischen Anthropologie. II. Quantitative Rassen-analyse auf Grund von Statistischen Beobachtungen über den Drehsinn des Kopf-haarwirbels. *Sitzungsberichte Physikalische-mathematische Klasse der Preussische Akademie der Wissenschaffen,* 1925. (Cited by Rife, 1933)

Bever, T. G. The nature of cerebral dominance in speech behavior of the child and adult. In R. Huxley & E. Ingram (Eds.), *Language acquisition: Models and methods.* London: Academic Press, 1971.

Bever, T. G., & Chiarello, R. J. Cerebral dominance in musicians and nonmusicians. *Science,* 1974, **185,** 537–539.

Bijou, S. W. Studies in the experimental development of left-right concepts in retarded children using fading techniques. In N. R. Ellis (Ed.), *International review of research in mental retardation.* Vol. 3. New York: Academic Press, 1968.

Blake, W. The Tiger. In J. Sampson (Ed.), *The poetical works of William Blake.* London: Oxford University Press, 1913. P. 85.

Blakemore, C. B. Binocular depth discrimination and the nasotemporal division. *Journal of Physiology,* 1969, **205,** 471–497.

Blau, A. *The master hand.* Research Monograph No. 5. New York: American Orthopsychiatric Association, 1946.

Bogen, J. E. The other side of the brain I: Dysgraphia and dyscopia following cerebral commissurotomy. *Bulletin of the Los Angeles Neurological Society,* 1969, **34,** 73–105. (a)

Bogen, J. E. The other side of the brain II: An appositional mind. *Bulletin of the Los Angeles Neurological Society,* 1969, **34,** 135–162. (b)

Bogen, J. E., & Bogen, G. M. The other side of the brain III: The corpus callosum and creativity. *Bulletin of the Los Angeles Neurological Society,* 1969, **34,** 191–220.

Bogen, J. E., DeZure, R., Tenhouten, W. D., & Marsh, J. F. The other side of the brain IV: The A/P ratio. *Bulletin of the Los Angeles Neurological Society,* 1972, **37,** 49–61.

Bogen, J. E., & Gazzaniga, M. S. Cerebral commissurotomy in man: Minor hemisphere dominance for certain visuospatial functions. *Journal of Neurosurgery,* 1965, **23,** 394–399.

Bonhoeffer, K. Zur Klinik und Lokalisation des Agrammatismus und der Rechts-Links-Desorientierung. *Monatsschrift für Psychiatrie und Neurologie,* 1923, **54,** 11–42.

Bonner, J. T. *Morphogenesis.* Princeton, New Jersey: Princeton University Press, 1952.

Boone, D. R., & Prescott, T. E. Development of left-right discrimination in normal children. *Perceptual & Motor Skills,* 1968, **26,** 267–274.

Bowlby, J. Critical phases in the development of social responses in man and other animals. In J. M. Tanner (Ed.), *Prospects in psychiatric research: The proceedings of the Oxford Conference of the Mental Health Fund.* Oxford: Blackwell, 1953.

Brain, R. Speech and handedness. *Lancet,* 1945, **249,** 837–841.

Braitenberg, V., & Kemali, N. Exceptions to bilateral symmetry in the epithalamus of lower vertebrates. *Journal of Comparative Neurology,* 1970, **138,** 137–146.

Branch, C., Milner, B., & Rasmussen, T. Intracarotid sodium amytal for the lateralization of cerebral speech dominance. Observations in 123 patients. *Journal of Neurosurgery,* 1964, **21,** 399–405.

Brindley, G. S., & Lewin, W. S. The sensations produced by electrical stimulation of the visual cortex. *Journal of Physiology (London),* 1968, **196,** 479–493.

Brinkman, J., & Kuypers, H. G. J. M. Cerebral control of contralateral and ipsilateral arm, hand and finger movements in the split-brain rhesus monkey. *Brain,* 1973, **96,** 653–674.

Brown, F. *Nightmares and geezenstacks.* New York: Bantam Books, 1961.

Bruner, J. S. *On knowing: Essays for the left hand.* New York: Atheneum, 1965.

Bruner, J. S. *Processes of cognitive growth: Infancy.* Vol. III. Heinz Werner Memorial Lecture Series. Worcester, Massachusetts: Clark University Press, 1968.

Bryan, W. L. On the development of voluntary motor ability. *American Journal of Psychology,* 1892, **5,** 125–205.

Bryant, P. E. Perception and memory of the orientation of visually presented lines by children. *Nature,* 1969, **224,** 1331–1332.

Bryant, P. E. Discrimination of mirror images by young children. *Journal of Comparative & Physiological Psychology,* 1973, **82,** 415–425.

Bryden, M. P. Tachistoscopic recognition, handedness, and cerebral dominance. *Neuropsychologia,* 1965, **3,** 1–8.

Bryden, M. P. Left-right differences in tachistoscopic recognition: directional scanning or cerebral dominance? *Perceptual & Motor Skills*, 1966, **23**, 1127–1134.

Bryden, M. P. Laterality effects in dichotic listening: Relations with handedness and reading ability in children. *Neuropsychologia*, 1970, **8**, 443–451.

Bryden, M. P. Perceptual asymmetry in vision: Relation to handedness, eyedness, and speech lateralization. *Cortex*, 1973, **9**, 418–432.

Burt, C. L. *The backward child*. London: University of London Press, 1957.

Burton, M., & Burton, R. *The international wildlife encyclopedia*. London: B.P.C. Publishing Co., 1969.

Butler, C. R. A memory-record for visual discrimination habits produced in both cerebral hemispheres of monkey when only one hemisphere has received direct visual information. *Brain Research*, 1968, **10**, 152–167.

Butler, J. Visual discrimination of shape by humans. *Quarterly Journal of Experimental Psychology*, 1964, **16**, 272–276.

Caldwell, E. C., & Hall, V. C. The influence of concept training on letter discrimination. *Child Development*, 1969, **40**, 63–71.

Campbell, A. Interocular transfer of mirror-images by goldfish. *Brain Research*, 1971, **33**, 486–490.

Carmon, A., & Nachshon, I. Hemifield differences in binocular fusion. *Perceptual & Motor Skills*, 1973, **36**, 175–184.

Carmon, A., Nachshon, I., Isseroff, A., & Kleiner, M. Visual field differences in reaction times to Hebrew letters. *Psychonomic Science*, 1972, **28**, 222–224.

Carroll, Lewis. *The works of Lewis Carroll*. London: Spring Books, 1965. P. 120.

Chamberlain, H. D. The inheritance of left handedness. *Journal of Heredity*, 1928, **19**, 557–559.

Chaney, R. B., & Webster, J. C. Information in certain multidimensional sounds. *Journal of the Acoustical Society of America*, 1966, **40**, 449–455.

Child, C. M. *Patterns and problems of development*. Chicago, Illinois: University of Chicago Press, 1941.

Clark, K. *Civilisation: A personal view*. London: British Broadcasting Corporation & John Murray, 1969. P. 202.

Clark, M. M. *Left-handedness: Laterality characteristics and their educational implications*. London: University of London Press, 1957.

Clarke, J. C., & Beale, I. L. Selective stimulus control in discrimination of lateral mirror images by pigeons. *Animal Behavior*, 1972, **20**, 656–661.

Clarke, J. C., & Whitehurst, G. J. Asymmetrical stimulus control and the mirror-image problem. *Journal of Experimental Child Psychology*, 1974, **17**, 147–166.

Clay, M. M. Research in brief: Orientation to the spatial characteristics of the open book. *Visible Language*, 1974, **8**, 275–282.

Clowes, M. B. Perception, picture processing and computers. In N. L. Collins, & D. Michie (Eds.), *Machine intelligence, I*. Edinburgh: Oliver & Boyd, 1967.

Cole, J. Paw preference in cats related to hand preference in animals and man. *Journal of Comparative & Physiological Psychology*, 1955, **48**, 137–140.

Cole, J. Laterality in the use of the hand, foot, and eye in monkeys. *Journal of Comparative & Physiological Psychology*, 1957, **50**, 296–299.

Coleman, R. I., & Deutsch, C. P. Lateral dominance and right-left discrimination: A comparison of normal and retarded readers. *Perceptual & Motor Skills*, 1964, **19**, 43–50.

Collins, R. L. On the inheritance of handedness: II. Selection for sinistrality in mice. *Journal of Heredity*, 1969, **60**, 117–119.

Collins, R. L. The sound of one paw clapping: An inquiry into the origin of left-handedness. In G. Lindzey & D. D. Thiessen (Eds.), *Contributions to behavior-genetic analysis—The mouse as a prototype.* New York: Meredith Corporation, 1970.

Collins, R. L., & Ward, R. Evidence for an asymmetry of cerebral function in mice tested for audiogenic seizures. *Nature,* 1970, **226,** 1062–1063.

Cooper, F. S. How is language conveyed by speech? In J. F. Kavanagh & I. G. Mattingly (Eds.), *Language by ear and by eye.* Cambridge, Massachusetts: M.I.T. Press, 1972.

Cooper, L. A., & Shepard, R. N. Chronometric studies of the rotation of mental images. In W. G. Chase (Ed.), *Visual information processing.* New York: Academic Press, 1973.

Corballis, M. C. Binocular interactions in letter recognition. *Australian Journal of Psychology,* 1964, **16,** 38–47.

Corballis, M. C. The left-right problem in psychology. *Canadian Psychologist,* 1974, **15,** 16–33.

Corballis, M. C., & Beale, I. L. Bilateral symmetry and behavior. *Psychological Review,* 1970, **77,** 451–464.   (a)

Corballis, M. C., & Beale, I. L. Monocular discrimination of mirror-image obliques by pigeons: Evidence for lateralized stimulus control. *Animal Behavior,* 1970, **18,** 563–566.   (b)

Corballis, M. C., & Beale, I. L. On telling left from right. *Scientific American,* 1971, **228** (3), 96–104.

Corballis, M. C., Miller, A., & Morgan, M. J. The role of left-right orientation in interhemispheric matching of visual information. *Perception & Psychophysics,* 1971, **10,** 385–388.

Corballis, M. C., & Roldan, C. E. On the perception of symmetrical and repeated patterns. *Perception & Psychophysics,* 1974, **16,** 136–142.

Corballis, M. C., & Roldan, C. E. Detection of symmetry as a function of angular orientation. *Journal of Experimental Psychology: Human Perception & Performance,* 1975, **1,** 221–230.

Critchley, M. *Mirror-writing.* Psyche Miniatures Medical Series. London: Kegan Paul, Trench, Trubner & Co. Ltd., 1928.

Critchley, M. *The parietal lobes.* London: Arnold, 1953.

Critchley, M. *Developmental dyslexia.* London: Heinemann, 1964.

Critchley, M. *The dyslexic child.* London: Heinemann, 1970.

Cumming, W. J. K. An anatomical review of the corpus callosum. *Cortex,* 1970, **6,** 1–18.

Dahlberg, G. Genotypic asymmetries. *Proceedings of the Royal Society of Edinburgh,* 1943, **63,** 20–31.

Davidson, E. H. *Gene activity in early development.* New York: Academic Press, 1968.

Davidson, H. P. A study of the confusing letters *b, d, p, q. Journal of Genetic Psychology,* 1935, **47,** 458–468.

Day, H. I. Evaluations of subjective complexity, pleasingness and interestingness for a series of random polygons varying in complexity. *Perception & Psychophysics,* 1967, **2,** 281–286.

Day, H. I. The importance of symmetry and complexity in the evaluation of complexity, interest and pleasingness. *Psychonomic Science,* 1968, **10,** 339–340.

Dearborn, W. F. Structural factors which condition special disability in reading. *Proceedings of the 57th Annual Session of the American Association for Mental Deficiency,* 1933, **38,** 266–283.

Deregowski, J. B. Symmetry, gestalt, and information theory. *Quarterly Journal of*

Experimental Psychology, 1971, **23,** 381–385.

DeSante, D. F. An analysis of the fall occurrences and nocturnal orientations of vagrant wood warblers (Parulidae) in California. Unpublished doctoral dissertation, Stanford University, 1973.

Deutsch, J. A. A theory of shape recognition. *British Journal of Psychology,* 1955, **46,** 30–37.

Deutsch, J. A. A system for shape recognition. *Psychological Review,* 1962, **69,** 492–500.

Dickens, C. *Great Expectations.* London: J. M. Dent & Sons, Ltd., 1907. P. 40.

Dimond, S. *The double brain.* London: Churchill Livingstone, 1972.

Dimond, S., & Beaumont, G. Hemispheric function and paired-associate learning. *British Journal of Psychology,* 1974, **65,** 275–278.

Dodwell, P. C. Shape recognition in rats. *British Journal of Psychology,* 1957, **48,** 221–229.

Dodwell, P. C. A coupled system for coding and learning in shape discrimination. *Psychological Review,* 1964, **71,** 148–159.

Dodwell, P. C. *Visual pattern recognition.* New York: Holt, Rinehart Winston, 1970.

Douglas, R. J. Cues for spontaneous alternation. *Journal of Comparative & Physiological Psychology,* 1966, **62,** 171–183.

Dubos, R. *Pasteur and modern science.* London: Heinemann, 1960.

Dunn, L. M. *The Peabody picture vocabulary test.* Minnesota: American Guidance Service Inc., 1959.

Durnford, M., & Kimura, D. Right hemisphere specialization for depth perception reflected in visual field differences. *Nature,* 1971, **231,** 394–395.

Eames, T. H. The anatomical basis of lateral dominance anomalies. *American Journal of Orthopsychiatry,* 1934, **4,** 524–528.

Ehrlichman, H., Weiner, S. L., & Baker, A. H. Effects of verbal and spatial questions on initial gaze shifts. *Neuropsychologia,* 1974, **12,** 265–277.

Eisenman, R. Complexity – simplicity: I. Preference for symmetry and rejection of complexity. *Psychonomic Science,* 1967, **8,** 169–170.

Elkind, D., & Weiss, J. Studies in perceptual development, III: Perceptual explorations. *Child Development,* 1967, **38,** 553–563.

Elze, K. Rechtslinksempfinden und Rechtslinksblindheit. *Zeitschrift für angewandte Psychologie,* 1924, **24,** 129–135.

Entus, A. K. Hemispheric asymmetry in processing of dichotically presented speech and nonspeech stimuli by infants. Paper presented at the Biennial Meeting of the Society for Research in Child Development, Denver, Colorado, 1975. Also to appear in S. J. Segalowitz & F. Gruber (Eds.), *Language development and neurological theory.* New York: Academic Press, in press.

Ettlinger, G., Blakemore, C. B., & Milner, A. D. Opposite hand preferences in two sense-modalities. *Nature,* 1968, **218,** 1276.

Fellows, B. J. *The discrimination process and development.* Oxford: Pergamon Press, 1968.

Fellows, B. J., & Brooks, B. An investigation of the role of matching and mismatching frameworks upon the discrimination of differently oriented line stimuli in young children. *Journal of Child Psychology & Psychiatry,* 1973, **14,** 293–299.

Fernald, G. M. *Remedial techniques in basic school subjects.* New York: McGraw Hill, 1943.

Feynman, R. P., Leighton, R. B., & Sands, M. *The Feynman lectures on physics, Vol. 1.* New York: Addison-Wesley, 1963. P. 52-12.

Finch, G. Chimpanzees' handedness. *Science,* 1941, **94,** 117–118.

Fisher, S. *Body experience in fantasy and behavior.* New York: Appleton-Century-Crofts, 1970.

Fitts, P. M., Weinstein, M., Rappaport, M., Anderson, N., & Leonard, J. A. Stimulus correlates of visual pattern recognition: A probability approach. *Journal of Experimental Psychology,* 1956, **51,** 1–11.

Fliess, R. *Erogeneity and libido.* New York: International Universities Press, Inc., 1956.

Fliess, W. *Der Ablauf des Lebens.* Vienna: Deuticke, 1923.

Fogh-Andersen, P. Inheritance of harelip and cleft palate. *Opera ex Domo biologiae hereditariae humanae Universitatis hafniensis,* 1943, **4,** 266 pp. (Cited by Stern, 1955).

Frankfurter, A., & Honeck, R. P. Ear differences in the recall of monaurally presented sentences. *Quarterly Journal of Experimental Psychology,* 1973, **25,** 138–146.

Freud, S. *Leonardo da Vinci: A psychological study of an infantile reminiscence.* London: Routledge, 1948.

Freud, S. *The origins of psychoanalysis. Letters to Wilhelm Fliess, drafts and notes: 1887–1902.* London: Imago Publishing Co. Ltd., 1954.

Frey, D. Zum Problem der Symmetrie in der bildenden Kunst. *Studium Generale* (Berlin), 1949, **2,** 268–278.

Fritsch, V. *Left and right in science and life.* London: Barrie & Rockliff, 1968.

Galifret-Granjon, N. Le probleme de l'organisation spatiale dans les dyslexics d'évolution. *Enfance,* 1951, **5,** 445.

Gardner, B., & Gardner, R. A. Two-way communication with an infant chimpanzee. In A. Schrier & F. Stollnitz (Eds.), *Behavior of nonhuman primates.* New York: Academic Press, 1971.

Gardner, M. *The annotated Alice.* New York: Charles N. Potter, 1960.

Gardner, M. *The ambidextrous universe.* London: Allen Lane, The Penguin Press, 1967.

Gardner, R. A., & Gardner, B. Teaching sign language to a chimpanzee. *Science,* 1969, **165,** 664–672.

Gates, A. I., & Bond, G. L. Reading readiness. A study of factors determining success and failure in beginning reading. *Teacher's College Record,* 1936, **37,** 679–685.

Gautrin, D., & Ettlinger, G. Lateral preferences in the monkey. *Cortex,* 1970, **6,** 287–292.

Gazzaniga, M. S. Effects of commissurotomy on a preoperatively learnt visual discrimination. *Experimental Neurology,* 1963, **8,** 14–19.

Gazzaniga, M. S. *The bisected brain.* New York: Appleton-Century-Crofts, 1970.

Gazzaniga, M. S., Bogen, J. E., & Sperry, R. W. Dyspraxia following division of the cerebral commissures. *Archives of Neurology,* 1967, **16,** 606–612.

Gazzaniga, M. S., & Sperry, R. W. Language after section of the cerebral commissures. *Brain,* 1967, **90,** 131–148.

Geffen, G., Bradshaw, J. L., & Wallace, G. Interhemispheric effects on reaction time to verbal and non-verbal stimuli. *Journal of Experimental Psychology,* 1971, **87,** 415–422.

Geffner, D. S., & Hochberg, I. Ear laterality performance of children from low and middle socioeconomic levels on a verbal dichotic listening task. *Cortex,* 1971, **7,** 193–203.

Gerstmann, J. Syndrome of finger agnosia, disorientation for right and left, agraphia and acalculia. *Archives of Neurology & Psychiatry,* 1940, **44,** 398–408.

Geschwind, N. The apraxias. In E. W. Straus & R. M. Griffith (Eds.),

Phenomenology of will and action. Pittsburgh: Duquesne University Press, 1967.

Geschwind, N., & Levitsky, W. Human brain: Left-right asymmetries in temporal speech region. *Science*, 1968, **161**, 186–187.

Gesell, A., & Ames, L. B. The development of handedness. *Journal of Genetic Psychology*, 1947, **70**, 155–175.

Gilbert, C., & Bakan, P. Visual asymmetry in the perception of faces. *Neuropsychologia*, 1973, **11**, 355–362.

Gilbert, W. S. *The Savoy Operas*. London: Macmillan, 1959. P. 234.

Ginsberg, G. P., & Hartwick, A. Directional confusion as a sign of dyslexia. *Perceptual & Motor Skills*, 1971, **32**, 535–543.

Goldmeier, E. Über Ähnlichkeit bei gesehenen Figuren. *Psychologische Forschung*, 1935, **21**, 146–208.

Goldmeier, E. Similarity in visually perceived forms. *Psychological Issues*, Monograph 29, 1972, **8**, 1–136.

Goodglass, H., & Quadfasel, F. A. Language laterality in left-handed aphasics. *Brain*, 1954, **77**, 521–548.

Gordon, H. Left-handedness and mirror-writing, especially among defective children. *Brain*, 1920, **43**, 313–368.

Gordon, H. W. Hemispheric asymmetries in the perception of musical chords. *Cortex*, 1970, **6**, 387–398.

Gottschalk, J., Bryden, M. P., & Rabinovitch, M. S. Spatial organization of children's responses to a pictorial display. *Child Development*, 1964, **35**, 811–815.

Granet, M. Right and left in China. In R. Needham (Ed.), *Right and left: Essays on dual symbolic classification*. Chicago: University of Chicago Press, 1973.

Gregory, R. L. Cognitive contours. *Nature*, 1972, **238**, 51–52.

Grindley, G. C. The formation of a simple habit in guinea pigs. *British Journal of Psychology*, 1932, **23**, 127–147.

Gross, C. G., Bender, D. B., & Rocha-Miranda, C. E. Visual receptive fields of neurons in inferotemporal cortex of the monkey. *Science*, 1969, **166**, 1303–1306.

Gross, C. G., Rocha-Miranda, C. E., & Bender, D. B. Visual properties of neurons in inferotemporal cortex of the macaque. *Journal of Neurophysiology*, 1972, **35**, 96–111.

Groves, C. P., & Humphrey, N. K. Asymmetry in gorilla skulls: Evidence of lateralized brain function? *Nature*, 1973, **244**, 53–54.

Gurdon, J. B. The importance of egg cytoplasm for the control of RNA and DNA synthesis in early amphibian development. In E. W. Hanly (Ed.), *Problems in biology: RNA in development*. Salt Lake City: University of Utah Press, 1969.

Hall, D. C. Eye movements in scanning iconic imagery. *Journal of Experimental Psychology*, 1974, **103**, 825–830.

Hall, M. M., Hall, G. C., & Lavoie, P. Ideation in patients with unilateral or bilateral midline brain lesions. *Journal of Abnormal Psychology*, 1968, **73**, 526–531.

Halle, M., & Stevens, K. N. Analysis by synthesis. In W. Wathen-Dunn & L. E. Woods (Eds.), *Proceedings of the seminar on speech compression and processing*. Vol. 2. AFCRC-TR-59-198, USAF Cambridge Research Center, 1959.

Hamilton, C. R., & Tieman, S. B. Interocular transfer of mirror image discriminations by chiasm-sectioned monkeys. *Brain Research*, 1973, **64**, 241–255.

Hamilton, C. R., Tieman, S. B., & Farrell, W. S. Cerebral dominance in monkeys? *Neuropsychologia*, 1974, **12**, 193–197.

Hamilton, C. R., Tieman, S. B., & Winter, H. L. Optic chiasm section affects discriminability of asymmetric patterns by monkeys. *Brain Research*, 1973, **49**, 427–431.

Hammer, M., & Turkewitz, G. A sensory basis for the lateral difference in the newborn infant's responses to somesthetic stimulation. *Journal of Experimental Child Psychology*, 1974, **18**, 304–312.

Harcum, E. R., & Finkel, M. E. Explanation of Mishkin and Forgay's result as a directional-reading conflict. *Canadian Journal of Psychology*, 1963, **17**, 224–234.

Harris, A. J. *How to increase reading ability*. (3rd ed.) New York: Longmans, Green & Company, 1956.

Hebb, D. O. *Organization of behavior*. New York: Wiley, 1949.

Hécaen, H., & Ajuriaguerra, J. de. *Left handedness*. New York: Grune & Stratton, 1964.

Hécaen, H., Ajuriaguerra, J. de., & Angelergues, R. Apraxia and its various aspects. In L. Halpern (Ed.), *Problems of dynamic neurology*. Jerusalem: Hebrew University, Hadassah Medical School, 1963.

Hécaen, H., & Sauguet, J. Cerebral dominance in left-handed subjects. *Cortex*, 1971, **7**, 19–48.

Heron, W. Perception as a function of retinal locus and attention. *American Journal of Psychology*, 1957, **70**, 38–48.

Hertz, R. La préeminence de la main droite: étude sur la polarité réligieuse. *Revue Philosophique*, 1909, **68**, 553–580. (Translated in Hertz, 1960)

Hertz, R. *Death and the right hand*. Aberdeen: Cohen & West, 1960.

Hewes, G. W. Lateral dominance, culture, and writing systems. *Human Biology*, 1949, **21**, 233–245.

Hewes, G. W. Primate communication and the gestural origin of language. *Current Anthropology*, 1973, **14**, 5–24.

Hill, S. D., McCullum, A. H., & Sceau, A. G. Relation of training in motor activity to development of right-left directionality in mentally retarded children: Exploratory study. *Perceptual & Motor Skills*, 1967, **24**, 363–366.

Hinde, R. A. The establishment of the parent-offspring relation in birds, with some mammalian analogies. In W. H. Thorpe & O. L. Zangwill (Eds.), *Current problems in animal behavior*. Cambridge, England: Cambridge University Press, 1961.

Hines, D., & Satz, P. Cross-modal asymmetries in perception related to asymmetry in cerebral funciton. *Neuropsychologia*, 1974, **12**, 239–247.

Holtfreter, J., & Hamburger, V. Embryogenesis: progressive differentiation. Amphibians. In B. H. Willier, P. A. Weiss, & V. Hamburger (Eds.), *Analysis of development*. New York: Hafner Publishing Co., 1971. (Facsimile of 1955 edition)

Hubel, D. H., & Wiesel, T. N. Receptive fields of cells in striate cortex of very young visually inexperienced kittens. *Journal of Neurophysiology*, 1963, **26,** 994–1002.

Hubel, D. H., & Wiesel, T. N. Receptive fields and functional architecture in two non-striate visual areas (18 and 19) of the cat. *Journal of Neurophysiology*, 1965, **28,** 229–280.

Hubel, D. H., & Wiesel, T. N. Cortical and callosal connections concerned with the vertical meridian of visual fields in the cat. *Journal of Neurophysiology*, 1967, **30,** 1561–1573.

Hubel, D. H., & Wiesel, T. N. Receptive fields and functional architecture of monkey striate cortex. *Journal of Physiology*, 1968, **195,** 215–243.

Humphrey, M. E., & Zangwill, O. L. Cessation of dreaming after brain injury. *Journal of Neurology, Neurosurgery, & Psychiatry*, 1951, **14**, 322–325.

Humphrey, N., & McManus, C. Status and the left cheek. *New Scientist*, 1973, **59**, 437–439.

Huttenlocher, J. Discrimination of figure orientation: Effects of relative position. *Journal of Comparative & Physiological Psychology*, 1967, **63**, 359–361.

Ingelmark, B. E. Über die Längenasymmetrie der Extremitäten—Eine neue röntgenologische Registriermethode. *Upsala Läkarförenings Förhandlingar,* 1947, **51,** 17–82. (Cited by von Bonin, 1952)

Ingle, D. Two visual mechanisms underlying the behavior of fish. *Psychologische Forschung,* 1967, **31,** 44–51. (In English)

Ireland, W. W. On mirror-writing and its relation to left-handedness and cerebral disease. *Brain,* 1881, **4,** 361–367.

Isaacs, J. D., Stork, J. W., Goldstein, D. B., & Wick, G. L. Effect of vorticity pollution by motor vehicles on tornadoes. *Nature,* 1975, **253,** 254–255.

Jackson, J. A survey of psychological, social and environmental differences between advanced and retarded readers. *Journal of Genetic Psychology,* 1944, **65,** 113–131.

Jackson, J. H. Clinical remarks on cases of defects of expression (by words, writing, signs, etc.) in diseases of the nervous system. *Lancet,* 1864, **2,** 604.

Jackson, J. H. On the nature of the duality of the brain. *Medical Press and Circular,* 1874, **1,** 19.

Jackson, J. H. On affections of speech from disease of the brain. *Brain,* 1878–79, **1,** 304–330.

Jacob, F., & Monod, J. Genetic regulatory mechanisms and the synthesis of proteins. *Journal of Molecular Biology,* 1961, **3,** 318–356.

Jacobs, J. *Onze rechthandigheid.* Amsterdam, 1892. (Cited by Hertz, 1960)

Jastrow, J. On the judgment of angles and positions of lines. *American Journal of Psychology,* 1893, **5,** 214–248.

Jeffrey, W. E. Variables in early discrimination learning: I. Motor responses in the training of a left-right discrimination. *Child Development,* 1958, **29,** 269–275.

Jeffrey, W. E. Discrimination of oblique lines by children. *Journal of Comparative & Physiological Psychology,* 1966, **62,** 154–156.

Julesz, B. Binocular depth perception. In W. Reichardt (Ed.), *Processing of optical data by organisms and by machines.* New York: Academic Press, 1969.

Julesz, B. *Foundations of cyclopean perception.* Chicago: University of Chicago Press, 1971.

Kerschner, J. R., & Gwan-Rong Jeng, A. Dual functional hemispheric asymmetry in visual perception: Effects of ocular dominance and postexposural processes. *Neuropsychologia,* 1972, **10,** 437–445.

Kimura, D. Cerebral dominance and the perception of verbal stimuli. *Canadian Journal of Psychology,* 1961, **15,** 166–171.

Kimura, D. Speech lateralization in young children as determined by an auditory test. *Journal of Comparative & Physiological Psychology,* 1963, **56,** 899–902.

Kimura, D. Left-right differences in the perception of melodies. *Quarterly Journal of Experimental Psychology,* 1964, **16,** 355–358.

Kimura, D. Dual functional asymmetry of the brain in visual perception. *Neuropsychologia,* 1966, **4,** 275–285.

Kimura, D. Functional asymmetry of the brain in dichotic listening. *Cortex,* 1967, **3,** 163–178.

Kimura, D. Spatial localization in left and right visual fields. *Canadian Journal of Psychology,* 1969, **23,** 445–458.

Kimura, D. Manual activity during speaking. I. Right-handers. *Neuropsychologia,* 1973, **11,** 45–50. (a)

Kimura, D. Manual activity during speaking. II. Left-handers. *Neuropsychologia,* 1973, **11,** 51–55. (b)

Kimura, D., & Archibald, Y. Motor functions of the left hemisphere. *Brain,* 1974, **97,** 337–350.

Kimura, D., & Folb, S. Neural processing of backwards-speech sounds. *Science*, 1968, **161**, 395–396.

King, F. L., & Kimura, D. Left-ear superiority in dichotic perception of vocal nonverbal sounds. *Canadian Journal of Psychology*, 1972, **26**, 111–116.

Kinsbourne, M. Sameness-difference judgments and the discrimination of obliques in the rat. *Psychonomic Science*, 1967, **7**, 183–189.

Kinsbourne, M. Discrimination of orientation by rats. *Psychonomic Science*, 1971, **22**, 50.

Kinsbourne, M. Eye and head turning indicates cerebral lateralization. *Science*, 1972, **176**, 539–541.

Knox, C., & Kimura, D. Cerebral processing of nonverbal sounds in boys and girls. *Neuropsychologia*, 1970, **8**, 227–237.

Koffka, K. *Principles of gestalt psychology*. New York: Harcourt, Brace, 1935.

Konorski, J. On the mechanism of instrumental conditioning. In *Proceedings of the 17th International Congress of Psychology*. Amsterdam: North-Holland Publishing Co., 1964.

Landauer, W. The phenotypic modification of hereditary polydactylism of fowl by selection and by insulin. *Genetics*, 1948, **33**, 133–157.

Lashley, K. S. The mechanism of vision, XV. Preliminary studies of the rat's capacity for detailed vision. *Journal of General Psychology*, 1938, **18**, 123–193.

Lawrence, D. H. Acquired distinctiveness of cues: I. Transfer between discriminations on the basis of familiarity with the stimulus. *Journal of Experimental Psychology*, 1948, **39**, 770–784.

Lee, T. D., & Yang, C. D. Question of parity conservation in weak interactions. *Physical Review*, 1956, **104**, 254–258.

Lehman, R. A. W., & Spencer, D. D. Mirror-image shape discrimination: Interocular reversal of responses in the optic chiasm sectioned monkey. *Brain Research*, 1973, **52**, 233–241.

Lenneberg, E. *Biological foundations of language*. New York: John Wiley & Sons, Inc., 1967.

Lepori, N. G. Sur la genèse des structures asymétriques chez l'embryon des oiseaux. *Monitore Zoologico Italiano*, 1969, **3**, 33–53.

Lesevre, N. Les mouvements oculaires d'exploration. *Word Blind Bulletin*, 1966, **1**. (Cited by Bannatyne, 1971).

Levy, J. Possible basis for the evolution of lateral specialization in the human brain. *Nature*, 1969, **224**, 614–615.

Levy, J. Lateral specialization of the human brain: Behavioral manifestations and possible evolutionary basis. Paper presented at the 32nd Annual Biology Colloquium on the Biology of Behavior, Corvallis, Oregon, 1971.

Levy, J., & Nagylaki, T. A model for the genetics of handedness. *Genetics*, 1972, **72**, 117–128.

Levy, J., Nebes, R. D., & Sperry, R. W. Expressive language in the surgically separated minor hemisphere. *Cortex*, 1971, **7**, 49–58.

Levy, J., Trevarthen, C., & Sperry, R. W. Perception of bilateral chimeric figures following hemispheric deconnexion. *Brain*, 1972, **95**, 61–78.

Levy-Agresti, J., & Sperry, R. W. Differential perceptual capacities in major and minor hemispheres. *Proceedings of the National Academy of Sciences*, 1968, **61**, 1151.

Liberman, A. M., Cooper, F. S., Shankweiler, D. P., & Studdert-Kennedy, M. Perception of the speech code. *Psychological Review*, 1967, **74**, 431–461.

Liberman, I. Y., Shankweiler, D., Orlando, C., Harris, K. S., & Berti, F. B. Letter confusions and reversals of sequence in the beginning reader: Implications for Orton's theory of developmental dyslexia. *Cortex,* 1971, **7**. 127–142.

Locher, P. J., & Nodine, C. F. Influence of stimulus symmetry on visual scanning patterns. *Perception & Psychophysics,* 1973, **13**, 408–412.

Luria, A. R. *Human brain and psychological processes.* New York: Harper & Row, 1966.

Luria, A. R. *Traumatic aphasia: Its syndromes, psychopathology, and treatment.* Moscow: Academy of Medical Sciences, 1969.

Luria, A. R. The functional organization of the brain. *Scientific American,* 1970, **222** (3), 66–78.

Luria, A. R. *The working brain: An introduction to neuropsychology.* London: Allen Lane, The Penguin Press, 1973.

Luria, A. R., Tsvetkova, L. S., & Futer, D. S. Aphasia in a composer. *Journal of Neurological Sciences,* 1965, **2**, 288–292.

Mach, E. *The science of mechanics.* Chicago, Illinois: Open Court Publishing House, 1893.

Mach, E. *The analysis of sensations.* Chicago, Illinois: Open Court Publishing House, 1897.

Mach, E. *Popular scientific lectures.* Chicago, Illinois: Open Court Publishing House, 1898.

Mackintosh, J., & Sutherland, N. S. Visual discrimination by the goldfish: The orientation of rectangles. *Animal Behavior,* 1963, **11**, 135–141.

MacNeilage, P. F. Speech physiology. In J. H. Gilbert (Ed.), *Speech and cortical functioning.* New York: Academic Press, 1972.

Makita, K. The rarity of reading disability in Japanese children. *American Journal of Orthopsychiatry,* 1968, **38**, 599–614.

Marcel, T., Katz, L., & Smith, M. Laterality and reading proficiency. *Neuropsychologia,* 1974, **12**, 131–139.

McFie, J., & Piercy, M. F. Intellectual impairment with localized cerebral lesions. *Brain,* 1952, **75**, 292–311.

McFie, J. & Zangwill, O. L. Visual constructive disabilities associated with lesions of the left cerebral hemisphere. *Brain,* 1960, **83**, 243–260.

Mello, N. K. Interhemispheric reversal of mirror-image oblique lines after monocular training in pigeons. *Science,* 1965, **148**, 252–254.

Mello, N. K. Concerning the interhemispheric transfer of mirror-image oblique lines after monocular training in pigeons. *Physiology & Behavior,* 1966, **1**, 293–300. (a)

Mello, N. K. Interocular generalization: A study of mirror-image reversal following monocular training in pigeons. *Journal of the Experimental Analysis of Behavior,* 1966, **9**, 11–16. (b)

Mello, N. K. Interhemispheric comparison of visual stimuli in the pigeon. *Nature,* 1967, **214**, 144–145.

Mensh, I. N., Schwartz, H. G., Matarazzo, R. G., & Matarazzo, J. D. Psychological functioning following cerebral hemispherectomy in man. *American Medical Association Archives of Neurology & Psychiatry,* 1952, **67**, 787–796.

Miles, W. R. Ocular dominance demonstrated by unconscious sighting. *Journal of Experimental Psychology,* 1929, **12**, 113–136.

Miles, W. R. Ocular dominance in human adults. *Journal of General Psychology,* 1930, **3**, 412–430.

Milisen, R., & Van Riper, C. Differential transfer of training in a rotary activity.

Journal of Experimental Psychology, 1939, **24**, 640–646.

Miller, E. Handedness and the pattern of human ability. *British Journal of Psychology*, 1971, **62**, 111–112.

Miller, L. K., & Turner, S. Development of hemified differences in word recognition. *Journal of Educational Psychology*, 1973, **65**, 172–176.

Milne, A. A. *The house at Pooh corner*. New York: E. P. Dutton & Co. Inc., 1969. P. 119.

Milner, B. Psychological defects produced by temporal lobe excision. *Research Publications of the Association for Nervous & Mental Diseases*, 1958, **36**, 244–257.

Milner, B. Interhemispheric differences in the localization of psychological processes in man. *British Medical Bulletin*, 1971, **27**, 272–277.

Milner, B., Branch, C., & Rasmussen, T. Observations on cerebral dominance. In A.V.S. de Reuck & M. O'Connor (Eds.), *Ciba symposium on disorders of language*. London: Churchill, 1964.

Milner, B., Taylor, L., & Sperry, R. W. Lateralized suppression of dichotically presented digits after commissural section in man. *Science*, 1968, **161**, 184–186.

Milner, P. M. A model for visual shape recognition. *Psychological Review*, 1974, **81**, 521–535.

Mishkin, M., & Forgays, D. G. Word recognition as a function of retinal locus. *Journal of Experimental Psychology*, 1952, **43**, 43–48.

Molfese, D. L., Freeman, R. B., Jr., & Palermo, D. S. The ontogeny of brain lateralization for speech and nonspeech sounds. *Brain & Language*, 1975, **2**, 356–368.

Money, Jean. Studies on the function of sighting dominance. *Quarterly Journal of Experimental Psychology*, 1972, **24**, 454–464.

Money, John (Ed.) *Reading disability. Progress and research needs in dyslexia*. Baltimore: Johns Hopkins Press, 1962.

Money, John, Cytogenetic and psychosexual incongruities with a note on space-form blindness. *American Journal of Psychiatry*, 1963, **119**, 820–827.

Money, John, Alexander, D., & Walker, H. T. *A standardized road-map test of direction sense*. Baltimore: Johns Hopkins Press, 1965.

Monod, J. On symmetry and function in biological systems. In A. Engstrom, & B. Strandberg (Eds.), *Symmetry and function of biological systems at the macromolecular level*. New York: Wiley, 1969.

Monroe, M. Methods for diagnosis and treatment of cases of reading disability. *Genetic Psychology Monographs*, 1928, **4**, Nos. 4 & 5.

Monroe, M. *Children who cannot read*. Chicago: University of Chicago Press, 1932.

Morgan, M. J. Embryology and inheritance of asymmetry. In S. R. Harnad, R. W. Doty, L. Goldstein, J. Jaynes, & G. Krauthamer (Eds.), *Lateralization in the nervous system*. New York: Academic Press, 1976.

Morgan, M. J., O'Donnell, J. M., & Oliver, R. F. Development of left – right asymmetry in the habenular nuclei of Rana temporaria. *Journal of Comparative Neurology*, 1973, **149**, 203–214.

Muntz, W. R. An experiment on shape discrimination and signal detection in octopus. *Quarterly Journal of Experimental Psychology*, 1970, **22**, 82–90.

Myers, R. E., & Sperry, R. W. Interhemispheric communication through the corpus callosum. Mnemonic carry-over between the hemispheres. *Archives of Neurology & Psychiatry (Chicago)*, 1958, **80**, 298–303.

Nagylaki, T., & Levy, J. "The sound of one paw clapping" isn't sound. *Behavior Genetics*, 1973, **3**, 279–292.

Needham, R. (Ed.) *Right and left: Essays on dual symbolic classification*. Chicago: University of Chicago Press, 1973.

Neisser, U. *Cognitive psychology*. New York: Appleton-Century-Crofts, 1967.

Newcombe, F., & Ratcliff, G. Handedness, speech lateralization and ability. *Neuropsychologia,* 1973, **11,** 399–407.

Newland, J. *Children's knowledge of left and right.* Unpublished master's thesis, University of Auckland, 1972.

Newman, H. H. *Multiple human births.* New York: Doubleday, Doran & Co., 1940.

Newman, H. H., Freeman, F. N., & Holzinger, K. J. *Twins, a study of heredity and environment.* Chicago: University of Chicago Press, 1937.

Nissen, H. W., & McCulloch, T. L. Equated and non-equated stimulus conditions in discrimination learning by chimpanzees: I. Comparison with unlimited response. *Journal of Comparative Psychology,* 1937, **23,** 165–189.

Noble, J. Mirror-images and the forebrain commissures of the monkey. *Nature,* 1966, **211,** 1263–1265.

Noble, J. Paradoxical interocular transfer of mirror-image discrimination in the optic chiasm sectioned monkey. *Brain Research,* 1968, **10,** 127–151.

Nottebohm, F. Ontogeny of bird song. *Science,* 1970, **167,** 950–956.

Nottebohm, F. Neural lateralization of vocal control in a passerine bird. I. Song. *Journal of Experimental Zoology,* 1971, **177,** 229–262.

Nottebohm, F. Neural lateralization of vocal control in a passerine bird. II. Subsong, calls, and a theory of vocal learning. *Journal of Experimental Zoology,* 1972, **179,** 25–50.

Ogilvie, J. C., & Taylor, M. M. Effect of orientation on the visibility of fine wires. *Journal of the Optical Society of America,* 1958, **48,** 628–629.

Oldfield, R. C. Handedness in musicians. *British Journal of Psychology,* 1969, **60,** 91–99.

Olsen, M. W., & Byerly, T. C. The orientation of the embryo in the egg of the domestic chick. *Poultry Science,* 1935, **14,** 46–53.

Olson, D. R. *Cognitive development: The child's acquisition of diagonality.* New York: Academic Press, 1970.

Orbach, J. Differential recognition of Hebrew and English words in right and left visual fields as a function of cerebral dominance and reading habits. *Neuropsychologia,* 1967, **5,** 127–134.

Orton, S. T. "Word-blindness" in school children. *Archives of Neurology & Psychiatry,* 1925, **14,** 581–615.

Orton, S. T. A physiological theory of reading disability and stuttering in children. *New England Journal of Medicine,* 1929, **199,** 1046–1052.

Orton, S. T. Special disability in reading. *Bulletin of the Neurological Institute of New York,* 1931, **1,** 159–192.

Orton, S. T. *Reading, writing and speech problems in children.* New York: W. W. Norton & Co. Ltd., 1937.

Over, R. Detection and recognition measures of shape recognition. *Nature,* 1967, **214,** 1272.

Over, R. Reaction time analysis of discrimination of direction of line by the pigeon. *Psychonomic Science,* 1969, **17,** 171–172.

Over, R., & Over, J. Detection and recognition of mirror-image obliques by young children. *Journal of Comparative and Physiological Psychology,* 1967, **64,** 467–470.   (a)

Over, R., & Over, J. Kinesthetic judgements of the direction of line by young children. *Quarterly Journal of Experimental Psychology,* 1967, **19,** 337–340.   (b)

Parriss, J. R. A technique for testing cat's discrimination of differently oriented rectangles. *Nature,* 1964, **202,** 771–773.

Pavlov, I. P. *Conditioned reflexes.* London and New York: Oxford University Press, 1927.

Pears, D. F. The incongruity of counterparts. *Mind,* 1952, **61,** 78–81.

Peele, T. L. *The neuroanatomic basis for clinical neurology.* New York: McGraw-Hill, 1961.

Peterson, G. M. Mechanisms of handedness in the rat. *Comparative Psychology Monograph,* 1934, **9,** No. 46.

Peterson, J. M., & Lansky, L. M. Left-handedness among architects: Some facts and speculation. *Perceptual & Motor Skills,* 1974, **38,** 547–550.

Petrinovitch, L., & Bolles, R. Delayed alternation: Evidence for symbolic processes in the rat. *Journal of Comparative & Physiological Psychology.* 1957, **50,** 363–365.

Piaget, J. *Judgement and reasoning in the child.* London: Routledge & Kegan Paul, 1928.

Piaget, J., & Inhelder, B. *The child's conception of space.* New York: Basic Books, 1956.

Plunkett, C. R. The interaction of genetic and environmental factors in development. *Journal of Experimental Zoology,* 1926, **46,** 181–244.

Pollen, D. A., Lee, J. R., & Taylor, J. H. How does the striate cortex begin the reconstruction of the visual world? *Science,* 1971, **173,** 74–77.

Pylyshyn, Z. W. What the mind's eye tells the mind's brain: A critique of mental imagery. *Psychological Bulletin,* 1973, **80,** 1–24.

Ramaley, F. Inheritance of left-handedness. *American Naturalist,* 1913, **47,** 730–738.

Raven, C. P. The distribution of special cytoplasmic differentiations of the egg during early cleavage in *Limnea stagnalis. Developmental Biology,* 1967, **16,** 407–437.

Restle, F. Discrimination of cues in mazes: a resolution of the "place-vs.-response" question. *Psychological Review,* 1957, **64,** 217–228.

Rife, D. C. Genetic studies of monozygotic twins. I, II, III. *Journal of Heredity,* 1933, **24,** 339–345, 407–414, 443–446.

Rife, D. C. Handedness, with special reference to twins. *Genetics,* 1940, **25,** 178–186.

Rife, D. C. Application of gene frequency analysis to the interpretation of data from twins. *Human Biology,* 1950, **22,** 136–145.

Riopelle, A. J., Rahm, U., Itoigawa, N., & Draper, W. A. Discrimination of mirror-image patterns by rhesus monkeys. *Perceptual & Motor Skills,* 1964, **19,** 383–389.

Roberts, W. W. The interpretation of some disorders of speech. *Journal of Mental Science,* 1949, **95,** 567–588.

Rock, I. *Orientation and form.* New York: Academic Press, 1973.

Rock, I., & Leaman, R. An experimental analysis of visual symmetry. *Acta Psychologica,* 1963, **21,** 171–183.

Rossi, G. F., & Rosadini, G. Experimental analysis of cerebral dominance in man. In C. H. Millikan & F. L. Darley (Eds.), *Brain mechanisms underlying speech and language.* New York: Grune & Stratton, 1967.

Rowe, S. N. Mental changes following the removal of the right cerebral hemisphere for brain tumor. *American Journal of Psychiatry,* 1937, **94,** 605–614.

Rozin, P., Poritsky, S., & Sotsky, R. American children with reading problems can easily learn to read English represented by Chinese characters. *Science,* 1971, **171,** 1264–1267.

Rubino, C. A., & Minden, H. A. An analysis of eye-movements in children with a reading disability. *Cortex,* 1973, **9,** 217–220.

Rudel, R. G., & Teuber, H.-L. Discrimination of direction of line in children. *Journal of Comparative & Physiological Psychology,* 1963, **56,** 892–898.

Russell, G. F., & Hills, J. I. Odor differences between enantiomeric isomers. *Science,* 1971, **172,** 1043–1044.

Sachs, R. G. Time reversal. *Science,* 1972, **176,** 587–597.

Saint-Exupéry, A. de. *Wind, sand and stars.* London: Heinemann, 1939. P. 139.

Salam, A. Elementary particles and space-time symmetries. *Endeavour*, 1958, **17**, 97–105.

Satz, P. Pathological left-handedness: An explanatory model. *Cortex*, 1972, **8**, 121–135.

Satz, P. Left-handedness and early brain insult: An explanation. *Neuropsychologia*, 1973, **11**, 115–117.

Satz, P., Rardin, D., & Ross, J. An evaluation of a theory of specific developmental dyslexia. *Child Development*, 1971, **42**, 2009–2021.

Schaller, G. B. *The mountain gorilla*. Chicago: University of Chicago Press, 1963.

Schneider, G. E. Two visual systems. *Science*, 1969, **163**, 895–902.

Schonell, F. J. The relation of reading disability to handedness and certain ocular factors: Part I. *British Journal of Educational Psychology*, 1940, **10**, 227–237.

Schonell, F. J. The relation of reading disability to handedness and certain ocular factors: Part 2. *British Journal of Educational Psychology*, 1941, **11**, 20–27.

Schonell, F. J. *Backwardness in the basic subjects*. London: Oliver & Boyd, 1942.

Sekuler, R. W., & Houlihan, K. Discrimination of mirror-images: Choice time analysis of human adult performance. *Quarterly Journal of Experimental Psychology*, 1968, **20**, 204–207.

Sekuler, R. W., & Rosenblith, J. F. Discrimination of direction of line and the effect of stimulus alignment. *Psychonomic Science*, 1964, **1**, 143–144.

Semmes, J., Weinstein, S., Ghent, L., & Teuber, H.-L. *Somatosensory changes after penetrating brain wounds in man*. Cambridge, Massachusetts: Harvard University Press, 1960.

Serpell, R. Discrimination of orientation by Zambian children. *Journal of Comparative & Physiological Psychology*, 1971, **75**, 312–316.

Shepard, R. N., & Metzler, J. Mental rotation of three-dimensional objects. *Science*, 1971, **171**, 701–703.

Sidman, M., & Kirk, B. Letter reversals in naming, writing, and matching to sample. *Child Development*, 1974, **45**, 616–625.

Singer, J. L., & Singer, D. G. Personality. *Annual Review of Psychology*, 1972, **23**, 375–412.

Smith, L. C. A study of laterality characteristics of retarded readers and reading achievers. *Journal of Experimental Education*, 1950, **18**, 321–329.

Smith, S. I. Angular estimation. *Journal of Applied Psychology*, 1962, **46**, 240–246.

Snow, C. P. *The two cultures and the scientific revolution*. Cambridge: Cambridge University Press, 1959.

Solzhenitsyn, A. *The Gulag archipelago*. Great Britain: Collins/Fontana, 1974. P. 475.

Spemann, H. Über eine neue Methode der embryonalen Transplantation. *Deutsche zoologische Gesellschaft, Verhandlungen*, 1906, **16**, 195–202.

Spemann, H., & Falkenberg, H. Über asymmetrische Entwicklung und Situs inversus bei Zwillingen und Doppelbildungen. *Wilhelm Roux Archiv für Entwicklungsmechanik*, 1919, **45**, 371–422.

Sperling, G. The information available in brief visual presentations. *Psychological Monographs*, 1960, **74**, (11, Whole No. 498).

Sperry, R. W. Some general aspects of interhemispheric integration. In V. B. Mountcastle (Ed.), *Interhemispheric relations and cerebral dominance*. Baltimore: Johns Hopkins Press, 1962.

Srb, A. M., Owen, R. D., & Edgar, R. S. *General genetics*. (2nd ed.) San Francisco: W. H. Freeman, 1965.

Standing, L., Conezio, J., & Haber, R. N. Perception and memory for pictures: Single-trial learning of 2500 visual stimuli. *Psychonomic Science*, 1970, **19**, 73–74.

Stern, C. Gene action. In B. H. Willier, P. A. Weiss, & V. Hamburger (Eds.), *Analysis of development.* New York: Hafner Publishing Co., 1971. (Facsimile of 1955 edition)

Stollnitz, F. Special variables, observing responses, and discrimination learning sets. *Psychological Review,* 1965, **72,** 247–261.

Studdert-Kennedy, M., & Shankweiler, D. Hemispheric specialization for speech perception. *Journal of the Acoustical Society of America,* 1970, **48,** 579–594.

Sturtevant, A. H. Inheritance of direction of coiling in *Limnea. Science,* 1923, **58,** 269.

Sussman, H. M., & MacNeilage, P. F. Hemispheric specialization for speech production and perception in stutterers. *Neuropsychologia,* 1975, **13,** 19–26.

Sutherland, N. S. Visual discrimination of orientation and shape by *Octopus. Nature,* 1957, **179,** 11–13.

Sutherland, N. S. Theories of shape discrimination in *Octopus. Nature* (London), 1960, **186,** 840–844.   (a)

Sutherland, N. S. Visual discrimination of orientation by *Octopus:* Mirror images. *British Journal of Psychology,* 1960, **51,** 9–18.   (b)

Sutherland, N. S. Visual discrimination of shape by *Octopus:* Open and closed forms. *Journal of Comparative & Physiological Psychology,* 1960, **53,** 104–112.   (c)

Sutherland, N. S. *The methods and findings of experiments on the visual discrimination of shape by animals.* Experimental Psychology Society, Monograph No. 1. Cambridge: W. Heffer, 1961.

Sutherland, N. S. Cat's ability to discriminate oblique rectangles. *Science,* 1963, **139,** 209–210.

Sutherland, N. S. Outlines of a theory of pattern recognition in animals and man. In R. M. Gilbert & N. S. Sutherland (Eds.), *Animal discrimination learning.* New York: Academic Press, 1969.

Sutherland, N. S., Carr, A. E., & Mackintosh, J. A. Visual discrimination of open and closed shapes by rats. I. Training. *Quarterly Journal of Experimental Psychology,* 1962, **14,** 129–139.

Swanson, R., & Benton, A. L. Some aspects of the genetic development of right-left discrimination. *Child Development,* 1955, **26,** 123–133.

Taylor, J. (Ed.). *Selected writings of John Hughlings Jackson.* Vol. II. London: Staples Press, 1958.

Taylor, L. W., & Gunns, C. A. Diplopodia: A lethal form of polydactyly in chickens. *Journal of Heredity,* 1947, **38,** 67–76.

Taylor, S. E. *The fundamental reading skill as related to eye movement photography and visual anomalies.* Springfield, Illinois: Charles C Thomas, 1966.

Tee, K. S., & Riesen, A. H. Visual right-left confusions in animal and man. In G. Newton & A. H. Riesen (Eds.), *Advances in psychobiology.* Vol. 2. New York: John Wiley & Sons, Inc., 1974.

Terrace, H. S. Errorless transfer of a discrimination across two continua. *Journal of the Experimental Analysis of Behavior,* 1963, **6,** 223–246.

Teuber, H.-L. Neuropsychology. In *Recent advances in diagnostic psychological testing: A critical summary.* Springfield, Illinois: Charles C Thomas, 1950.

Teuber, H.-L. Perception. In *Handbook of physiology, Section I: Neurophysiology.* Vol. 3. Washington, D. C.: American Physiological Society, 1960.

Thomas, D. R., Klipec, W., & Lyons, T. Investigations of a mirror-image transfer effect in pigeons. *Journal of the Experimental Analysis of Behavior,* 1966, **9,** 567–571.

Thompson, L. J. Language disabilities in men of eminence. *Journal of Learning Disabilities,* 1971, **4,** 39–50.

Thurber, J. *Fables for our time.* New York: Harper & Row, 1974. P. 50.

Torgerson, J. Situs inversus, asymmetry, and twinning. *American Journal of Human Genetics,* 1950, **2,** 361–370.

Trabasso, T., & Bower, G. H. *Attention in learning: Theory and research.* New York: Wiley, 1968.

Trankell, A. Aspects of genetics in psychology. *American Journal of Human Genetics,* 1955, **7,** 264–276.

Travis, L. E. *Speech pathology.* New York: Appleton-Century-Crofts, 1937.

Trevarthen, C. B. Experimental evidence for a brain-stem contribution to visual perception in man. *Brain, Behavior, & Evolution,* 1970, **3,** 338–352.

Trevarthen, C., & Sperry, R. W. Perceptual unity of the ambient visual field in human commissurotomy patients. *Brain,* 1973, **96,** 547–570.

Tsai, L. S., & Maurer, S. Right-handedness in white rats. *Science,* 1930, **72,** 436–438.

Tschirgi, R. D. Spatial perception and central nervous system asymmetry. *Arquivos de Neuropsiquiatria,* 1958, **16,** 364–366.

Turkewitz, G., Gordon, E. W., & Birch, H. G. Head-turning in the human neonate: Effect of prandial condition and lateral preference. *Journal of Comparative & Physiological Psychology,* 1965, **59,** 189–192.

Turkewitz, G., Moreau, T., Birch, H. G., & Crystal, D. Relationships between prior head position and lateral differences in responsiveness to somesthetic stimulation in the human neonate. *Journal of Experimental Child Psychology,* 1967, **5,** 548–561.

Turner, H. H. A syndrome of infantilism, congenital webbed neck and cubitus valgus. *Endocrinology,* 1938, **23,** 566–574.

Uhr, L. (Ed.) *Pattern recognition.* New York: Wiley, 1966.

Van Hof, M. W. Discrimination between striated patterns of different orientation in the rabbit. *Vision Research,* 1966, **6,** 89–94.

Van Hof, M. W. Mechanisms of orientation discrimination in the rabbit. *Experimental Neurology,* 1970, **28,** 494–500.

Vernon, M. D. *Backwardness in reading.* (2nd ed.) Cambridge: Cambridge University Press, 1960.

von Bonin, G. Anatomical asymmetries of the cerebral hemispheres. In V. B. Mountcastle (Ed.), *Hemispheric relations and cerebral dominance.* Baltimore: Johns Hopkins Press, 1962.

von Kraft, A. Situs inversus beim Alpenmolch (Triturus alpestris) nach UV-Bestrahlung von Gastrula-Keimen. *Wilhelm Roux Archiv für Entwicklungsmechanik,* 1968, **161,** 351–374.

von Woellwarth, C. Experimentelle Untersuchungen über dem Situs inversus der Eingeweide und der Habenula des Zwischenhirns bei Amphibien. *Wilhelm Roux Archiv für Entwicklungsmechanik,* 1950, **144,** 178–256.

Wall, W. D. Reading backwardness among men in the army. I *British Journal of Educational Psychology,* 1945, **15,** 28–40.

Wall, W. D. Reading backwardness among men in the army. II. *British Journal of Educational Psychology,* 1946, **16,** 133–148.

Walls, G. L. A theory of ocular dominance. *AMA Archives of Opthalmology,* 1951, **45,** 387–412.

Warren, J. M. Discrimination of mirror images by cats. *Journal of Comparative & Physiological Psychology,* 1969, **69,** 9–11.

Warrington, E. K., & Pratt, R. T. C. Language laterality in left-handers assessed by unilateral E. C. T. *Neuropsychologia,* 1973, **11,** 423–428.

Weber, E. Das Schreiben als Ursache der einseitigen Lage des Sprachzentrums. *Zentralblatt für Physiologie,* 1904, **18,** 341–347.

Webster, W. G. Functional asymmetry between the cerebral hemispheres of the cat. *Neuropsychologia,* 1972, **10,** 75–87.

Wechsler, D. *The Wechsler intelligence scale for children.* New York: The Psychological Corporation, 1949.

Wechsler, D. *The Wechsler adult intelligence scale.* New York: The Psychological Corporation, 1955.

Weiner, G., Rider, R. V., Oppel, W. C., Fisher, L. K., & Harper, P. A. Correlates of low birth weight: psychological status at six to seven years of age. *Pediatrics,* 1965, **35,** 434–444.

Weisenberg, T., & McBride, K. E. *Aphasia; A clinical and psychological study.* New York: Commonwealth Fund, 1935.

Weyl, H. *Symmetry.* Princeton, New Jersey: Princeton University Press, 1952.

White, M. J. Laterality differences in perception: a review. *Psychological Bulletin,* 1969, **72,** 387–405.

Whitteridge, D. Area 18 and the vertical meridian of the visual field. In E. G. Ettlinger (Ed.), *Functions of the corpus callosum.* (Ciba Foundation Study Group No. 20). London: Churchill, 1965.

Wickham, A. *Selected poems.* London: Chatto & Windus, 1971. P. 48.

Williams, R. J. *Discrimination of mirror images by the pigeon.* Unpublished master's thesis, University of Auckland, 1971.

Wilson, P. T., & Jones, H. E. Left-handedness in twins. *Genetics,* 1932, **17,** 560–571.

Witelson, S. F. Hemispheric specialization for linguistic and nonlinguistic tactual perception using a dichotomous stimulation technique. *Cortex,* 1974, **10,** 3–17.

Witelson, S. F., & Pallie, W. Left hemisphere specialization for language in the newborn: neuroanatomical evidence of asymmetry. *Brain,* 1973, **96,** 641–646.

Witty, P. A,., & Kopel, D. Sinistral and mixed manual–ocular dominance in reading disability. *Journal of Educational Psychology,* 1936, **27,** 119–134.

Wolfe, L. S. An experimental study of reversals in reading. *American Journal of Psychology,* 1939, **52,** 533–561.

Wolfe, L. S. Differential factors in specific reading disability. *Journal of Genetic Psychology,* 1941, **58,** 45–70.

Wolff, P. Mirror-image confusability in adults. *Journal of Experimental Psychology,* 1971, **91,** 268–272.

Wolff, W. The experimental study of forms of expression. *Character & Personality,* 1933, **2,** 168–176.

Wolpert, L. Positional information and the spatial pattern of cellular differentiation. *Journal of Theoretical Biology,* 1969, **25,** 1–47.

Woo, T. L., & Pearson, K. Dextrality and sinistrality of hand and eye. *Biometrika,* 1927, **19,** 165–199.

Wright, R. H. Odor of optical isomers. *Nature,* 1963, **198,** 782.

Young, J. Z. Why do we have two brains? In V. B. Mountcastle (Ed.), *Interhemispheric relations and cerebral dominance.* Baltimore: Johns Hopkins Press, 1962.

Zangwill, O. L. *Cerebral dominance and its relation to psychological function.* Edinburgh: Oliver & Boyd, 1960.

Zangwill, O. L., & Blakemore, C. Dyslexia: Reversal of eye-movements during reading. *Neuropsychologia,* 1972, **10,** 371–373.

Zeigler, P., & Schmerler, S. Visual discrimination of orientation by pigeons. *Animal Behavior,* 1965, **13,** 475–477.

Zurif, E. B., & Bryden, M. P. Familial handedness and left-right difference in auditory and visual perception. *Neuropsychologia,* 1969, **7,** 179–187.

Zurif, E. B., & Carson, G. Dyslexia in relation to cerebral dominance and temporal analysis. *Neuropsychologia,* 1970, **8,** 351–361.

Zwilling, E. Limb morphogenesis. In M. Abercrombie, & J. Brachet (Eds.), *Advances in Morphogenesis. Vol. 1.* New York: Academic Press, 1961.

Author Index

217

Subject Index